T0182304

BLOOMING IN THE RUINS

GUIDES TO THE GOOD LIFE
Stephen R. Grimm, series editor

Seeing Clearly: A Buddhist Guide to Life
Nicolas Bommarito

On Being and Becoming: An Existentialist Approach to Life
Jennifer Anna Gosetti-Ferencei

Growing Moral: A Confucian Guide to Life
Stephen C. Angle

Choosing Freedom: A Kantian Guide to Life
Karen Stohr

Living for Pleasure: An Epicurean Guide to Life
Emily A. Austin

Blooming in the Ruins: How Mexican Philosophy Can Guide Us toward the Good Life
Carlos Alberto Sánchez

BLOOMING IN THE RUINS

How Mexican Philosophy Can Guide Us toward the Good Life

Carlos Alberto Sánchez

OXFORD
UNIVERSITY PRESS

Oxford University Press is a department of the University of Oxford. It furthers
the University's objective of excellence in research, scholarship, and education
by publishing worldwide. Oxford is a registered trade mark of Oxford University
Press in the UK and certain other countries.

Published in the United States of America by Oxford University Press
198 Madison Avenue, New York, NY 10016, United States of America.

Library of Congress Cataloging-in-Publication Data
Names: Sánchez, Carlos Alberto, 1975– author.
Title: Blooming in the ruins : how Mexican philosophy can guide us toward
the good life / Carlos Alberto Sánchez.
Description: New York, NY : Oxford University Press, [2024] |
Series: Guides to the good life | Includes bibliographical references. |
Identifiers: LCCN 2024006474 (print) | LCCN 2024006475 (ebook) |
ISBN 9780197691007 (hardback) | ISBN 9780197691014 (epub) | ISBN 9780197691038
Subjects: LCSH: Philosophy, Mexican—History.
Classification: LCC B1016 .S26 2024 (print) | LCC B1016 (ebook) |
DDC 199/.72—dc23/eng/20240509
LC record available at https://lccn.loc.gov/2024006474
LC ebook record available at https://lccn.loc.gov/2024006475

DOI: 10.1093/oso/9780197691007.001.0001

Printed by Sheridan Books, Inc., United States of America

For my brother, Art, and my sisters, Alex, Jenny, and Patty
&
For my wife, Tricia, and my sons, Julian, Ethan, and Pascual

TABLE OF CONTENTS

Series Editor Foreword xi
Preface: How Can Mexican Philosophy Guide My Life? xiii
Acknowledgments xxv

PART I: TWO VERY SHORT INTRODUCTIONS TO MEXICAN PHILOSOPHY

1. "In the Beginning . . .": Philosophy in Mexico 3

2. Mexican Philosophy in the Twentieth Century 15

PART II: FOUR THEMES IN MEXICAN PHILOSOPHY

3. You Are *Nepantla* 27

4. You Are Your Circumstance 40

5. You Are Accidental 52

6. You Are a Singularity 65

PART III: MEXICAN PHILOSOPHY AS A GUIDE TO LIFE

7. Listening as a Form of Excavation 75

8. Be Charitable 84

9. Be Late to Parties 92

10. Don't Fear Ghosts ... or Death 102

11. Strive for Originality 111

12. There Is Hope in *Zozobra* 120

13. Engage in a Bit of *Relajo* 128

14. Are You an *Apretado* or *Apretada*? 139

15. Practice Irony, But Be Socratic about It 148

16. Set Yourself Apart 160

17. The Way of Dignified Cynicism 169

18. Don't Be a Troll 177

19. Tell Your Own Story 187

20. Love without Violence 197

21. Don't Be Too Judgy 207

22. Be Like the Rabbit 217

23. It's Okay to Be Choosy about Your Inheritance 225

24. Love What You Do 231

25. You Really Don't Have to Join a Cult 240

PART IV: *DICHOS*

26. My *Abuelo*'s Favorite *Dicho* 253

27. My *Abuela*'s Favorite *Dicho* 260

PART V: MORE ON MEXICAN PHILOSOPHY

28. Blooming in the Ruins: Mexican Philosophy as Your Guide to Life 271

NOTES 279
BIBLIOGRAPHY AND FURTHER READING 287
INDEX 297

SERIES EDITOR FOREWORD

Several ancient philosophers held that the point of studying ethics was not just to learn about ethics—as one might learn about chemistry, astronomy, or history—but to become a better human being. They also recognized that this was not easy to do. In order for thinking about ethics to make a difference in our lives, our habits and inclinations needed to be educated right alongside our minds. They therefore claimed that what mattered to living well was not just *what* we thought but *how* we thought, and not just how we thought but how we emotionally responded to the world and to other people.

The books in this series highlight some of the transformative ideas that philosophers have had about these topics—about the good life, and the practices and ways of life that help us to pursue it. They tell us what various philosophers and traditions have taken to be most important in life, and what they have taken to be less important. They offer philosophical guidance about how to approach broad questions, such as how to structure our days, how to train our attention, and how to die with dignity. They also offer guidance about how to deal with the sort of everyday questions that are often neglected by scholars, but that make up the texture of our lives, such as how to deal with relationships gone wrong, family disruptions, unexpected success, persistent anxiety, and an environment at risk.

Because the books are written by philosophers, they draw attention to the reasons and arguments that underlie these various claims—the particular visions of the world and of human nature that are at the root of these stances. The claims made in these books can therefore be contested, argued with, and found to be more or less plausible. While some answers will clearly compete with one another, other views will likely appear complementary. Thus, a Confucian might well find that a particular practice or insight of, say, Nietzsche's helps to shed light on his or her way of living in the world, and vice versa. On the whole, the idea is that these great philosophers and traditions all have something to teach us about how to be more fully human, and more fully happy.

Above all, the series is dedicated to the idea that philosophy can be more than just an academic discipline—that it can be, as it was for hundreds of years in the ancient world, a way of life. The hope is also that philosophy can enhance the ways of life we already feel pulled toward and help us to engage with them more authentically and fully.

Stephen R. Grimm
Professor of Philosophy
Fordham University

PREFACE: HOW CAN MEXICAN PHILOSOPHY GUIDE MY LIFE?

You pick up this book with some hesitation. You waver on the thought that—wait, *there's a Mexican philosophy*? You wonder: how can this "Mexican" philosophy get me on the road to a more fulfilling life? Although you may be interested in Mexican culture and history, you may not realize that Mexico has a philosophical tradition all its own, let alone an instructive one that might help and guide you.

Somewhere on the shelf beside this book, or recommended by Amazon as Products Related to This Item, are books on Confucianism and existentialism, philosophical traditions with a track record of guiding folks to clearer thinking and better living. *What is this one doing here*? If you have taken an Introduction to Philosophy course in high school or college, you will also be concerned about something else. Isn't philosophy supposed to be a disembodied discipline, free of the restrictions of place and time, and, especially, *nationality*? So why does *this* philosophy call itself "Mexican"? But even if you concede the possibility of such a thing, what can Mexican philosophy teach you that can't be learned from those well-known French, German, Indian, or ancient Greek philosophical traditions? Aren't these from places with real and established philosophies and philosophers?

There are quick and easy answers to these questions, although these are somewhat boring. There are also more knotty, complicated answers: these are more exciting.

The basic quick and easy, yet somewhat boring, answer is that, despite what you may have heard, the search for truth is not a disinterested activity: it is not disembodied. Philosophy, as the search for truth, does not provide a "view from nowhere"—it is always the product of the person, the place, the time, and even the specific circumstances in which it is conceived. This means that what philosophers in Greece have said about the "good life" and what philosophers in China have said about the same will have something to do with what was going on in either Greece or China when those philosophers were philosophizing. If this is the case, then philosophy must be a "view from somewhere." This also means that what is said about, say, "truth" in Greece will inevitably be fundamentally different than what is said about truth in China, a difference we can attribute to the ideological, geographical, historical, cultural, religious-spiritual, and socioeconomic situation of these two places.

What I'm trying to highlight is that, when philosophy calls itself "Mexican," it situates itself, it becomes a reflection of *its* place and of its time, of its people and of how these people understand and exist in "the world"—that is, in the world that surrounds them, or in their circumstance.

That's the quick and easy and boring answer to the worry over a "Mexican" philosophy. A more complicated, yet more exciting, answer is that Mexican philosophy empowers.

In my years of studying and teaching Mexican philosophy I have found the very fact of its existence empowering. It empowers in that it demonstrates that philosophy is for all, everywhere and always, and not just for or about white, Anglo, European men and their worries, fears, and curiosities. It is especially empowering to those of us who have never seen ourselves represented in the established Anglo-European intellectual tradition; empowering, that is, to those of us who, up to the moment of actually sounding it out, couldn't have imagined reading a Hispanic surname with an accent over the "a" or a double "l" in a college philosophy textbook.

I recall my sense of pride, joy, and inspiration (I am Mexican-American, and both of my parents are Mexican) when I first encountered the work of the Mexican philosopher José Vasconcelos. Coming across his name and a brief snippet of his philosophy in an anthology of Latin American writers, I was stunned by the thought that a philosopher named "José" (with an accent over the "e"!) had actually existed. This, for me, meant that the picture of philosophy to which I had been exposed over the years was actually not a complete picture. There were gaps in the story I'd been told, which was a shame, but I was thrilled by the thought that there were Mexican philosophers—and a Mexican philosophy—that could fill them. Other gaps, I thought enthusiastically, could be filled out by me if and when I gave a philosophical account of my own experience and my own thoughts. What had before this encounter with José Vasconcelos seemed abstract and impenetrable—that is, the tradition and idea of philosophy—became less so after that.

Teaching Mexican philosophy has made all of this even clearer: on hearing that *there is a Mexican Philosophy*, students are inspired to look for their own philosophical traditions. My Vietnamese, Guatemalan, Ugandan, and Filipino students have written term papers on Vietnamese, Guatemalan, Ugandan, and Filipino philosophy. The opportunity to join an ongoing conversation from your own perspective, from the standpoint of your own experience is encouraging, life-giving, and powerful to people embarking on an intellectual journey of discovery—in philosophy or any other area that calls to them. This is especially true for those who, for historical, cultural, or economic reasons, had never imagined being invited into such conversations.

But maybe you're not a student of philosophy. Maybe you have never read any philosophy before. If so, welcome! Please stick around. Even if you're not coming here out of curiosity for philosophy per se, I hope that what you find here will be helpful or meaningful in some way. What I've tried to create here is a manual for living based on my studies and readings of twentieth-century Mexican philosophy that I weave into episodes from my own life and my own experiences. These philosophical exercises will show that Mexican philosophy can help us make sense of a slew of real-world situations and, in the best of cases, that its insights can serve as sound, orienting advice applicable to important issues in contemporary life.

Mexican philosophy is full of rich resources that, I believe, can help anyone, Mexican or not. You will likely find it particularly helpful if you have had some experience with contemporary forms of marginalization, in-betweenness, insufficiency, contingency, and oppression—which is most of us. It will also help if you feel self-doubt or powerlessness when facing a world that seems out of your control—and, again, this describes many of us. It addresses these feelings by offering a way to look at existential indeterminateness and uncertainty as default modes of being human, an idea that can be comforting if only because it reminds you that you are not alone in feeling how you feel. If indeterminateness and uncertainty are default ways of existing, then we are all in the same boat. Through the lens of Mexican philosophy, you can imagine a different way to look at and tackle life's various pressures and worries, some of which are inescapable and place a huge stress on your time, your emotions, your identity, or your mortality.

Before we get to that, a quick autobiographical note. This is necessary for one important reason: if I have learned one thing from Mexican philosophy, it is that philosophy itself is not a disinterested and disembodied activity, and so the best way to tell you about it is by couching it in episodes from my own, situated life experience. My hope is that my life experience is not so dramatically different from yours and that what I've found meaningful in my twenty-ish years of studying will also be meaningful to you.

For a period, my mother, an immigrant farm worker from Michoacán, Mexico, was the second-most educated member of my family. The most educated was my father: he *finished* the third grade! My mother had barely begun her second year when she dropped out to help her family make do. So when I began the fourth grade, I was on virgin ground. The sky was the limit! There was no stopping me! My parents hoped that I would enjoy learning enough to finish high school, and maybe . . . maybe even go to college (that was a very tenuous "maybe").

As it turned out, I enjoyed learning. I even finished high school. And then I found myself in college, where I majored in advertising. So far so good. A future as an advertising executive, a chef in the kitchen of capitalism consumption, awaited me after graduation. Then, during my senior year, I took a course in Latin American Philosophy from an exiled Cuban philosopher, René Trujillo, and things took a sharp left turn. I wanted to do this instead! Because I was so close to doing so, I finished my advertising degree, but immediately headed into a master's-degree program in philosophy, and sometime later, a doctoral program on my way to a PhD. My parents were proud, of course, but they just didn't understand why I needed more schooling. They also wondered (under their breaths) about my abandoning that promising advertising career. It seemed like a waste. No one they knew had ever made money *thinking*.

I moved to New Mexico in 2001 and began working on a PhD in philosophy. Ironically, the philosophy department at the University of New *Mexico* didn't offer any courses on *Mexican* philosophy. I spent the next five years studying, writing, and thinking about German philosophy. I wrote on the German philosopher Edmund Husserl's phenomenology. From Husserl, I learned, above all, what philosophy was *ideally* supposed to be: an abstract, disembodied, science that dealt with essences in a world of ideas.

I turned in my dissertation to the appropriate administrative office on a Friday in June 2006 at about 3 p.m. Thirty minutes later I started reading a book that had been sitting on my shelf for the previous four years, Jorge Portilla's *La fenomenología del relajo*, or *The Phenomenology of* Relajo. Like my dissertation, Portilla's book dealt with "phenomenology"; unlike my dissertation, where I'd spent way too much time thinking about the abstract notion of epistemic justification (the theory of knowledge), Portilla's phenomenology treated a very concrete and specifically Mexican issue, the problem of *relajo*. *Relajo,* or the suspension of seriousness (more on this in Part III of this book), was a problem for Mexican social and cultural life that needed to be clarified and addressed philosophically. It was a mesmerizing read!

By 6 p.m., rather than celebrating my accomplishment from earlier in the day, I was angry, disappointed, and frustrated. *Where had Portilla been hiding*? Clearly, Portilla and Mexican philosophy had been *somewhere* all along—but obviously not in plain sight. They had existed in the margins of the Western tradition, in library basements collecting layers upon layers of dust. My professors had no idea that Mexican philosophy existed, and if they had, their own prejudices about what philosophy is supposed to be and who is supposed to write it would have dissuaded them from dusting off the covers and pursuing Mexican philosophy further.

But now I had found it . . . or it had found me. I pushed Husserl to the side and have dedicated myself to studying, translating, and writing about Mexican philosophy ever since. In that time, I have learned from Mexican philosophy—or rather, the various philosophers that make it up—to look for and appreciate the value (negative or positive) of my own cultural, historical, and social circumstance. I continue to use that knowledge both for creative inspiration and for personal orientation.

Meanwhile, back in those early years with Mexican philosophy, my family still didn't really know what I was up to. The year I finished my doctorate, I was presented with a national educational equity award in New York City. A publication tied to the organization giving me the award called my mother for comment. She was proud, she said; she always knew I would amount to *something*.

But she confessed that she had *no idea* what that something was. "I think he's a psychologist?" Neither my mother nor my father understood what philosophy was or what it was supposed to *do for me*. Philosophy, it turns out, is not something Mexican immigrants are clamoring to promote as either a field of study or a way of life.

Eventually, I told my parents that I was working on "Mexican Philosophy." I had to explain, first, what philosophy was thought to be, and second, what "Mexican" philosophy sought to be. My father understood: Mexico had seen its fair share of *desmadre* (that is, of chaos, violence, trauma), so maybe Mexican philosophy was an opportunity for Mexico to share what it had learned from all this. My father was on the right track.

What my father understood (even if he didn't know it) was that Mexican philosophy would speak through its historical *desmadre*—it would speak through its ruins. In fact, as we will see shortly, Mexican philosophy indeed speaks most clearly to those experiencing the aftermath of historical violence and trauma. For Mexicans and the Indigenous peoples of Mexico, the atrocity and violent destruction carried out during the Spanish conquest was the first of many traumatic events. Afterward, everyone living in Mexico had to reckon with this event, including philosophers. Later on in Mexican history, other catastrophes would come to shape Mexican identity, including the War of Independence from Spain and the Revolution of 1910.

The basic idea is that the sort of thinking that we call philosophical is filtered through the experience of historical accidents (for instance, the fortuitous "discovery" of America), catastrophes (e.g., the destruction of civilizations precipitated by the Conquest and colonization), and traumatic encounters (for instance, that between the Spanish and the Indigenous, the result of which is the Mexican person herself). And, according to one key figure in this book, Emilio Uranga (1921–1988), this is precisely what endows Mexican philosophy with a practical significance. In fact, as my father predicted, its history with *desmadre* has bestowed on Mexican philosophy certain shareable insights. Uranga puts it this way:

> We have a lesson to teach; we owe the world a lesson of a vital crisis, one that is virile, one that is brave, [one that is] radically human. . . . The image of man that will emerge here will not be original, but it will be originary, which means that in it one will be able to recognize those others that through a thousand accidents of history, of culture or society, have been framed by the catastrophic. But this "morbidity" and this "catastrophism" are only negative if one's focus is squarely on consecrating their contraries as positive.[1]

Minimally, then, what Mexican philosophy offers us as a "lesson" is the permission to look at our own lives from a place that is familiar to each one of us—from the rubble and the ruins on which we stand—and that defines each one of us and all of us together: a place that is not an objective, disinterested, no-where, but a real, vibrant *here*. It models for us a way to take stock of *who*, and *where*, and *when* one happens to be, and to build ideas or ideals out of that grounding, rather than starting with abstract ideas and trying to relate them to who, and where, and when we are. Uranga tells us that the image of humanity that should emerge from doing this will not be unique, but it will be genuine. To see the world through the lens of Mexican philosophy is, then, an opportunity to see it through the eyes of those who understand themselves as accidents of history and catastrophe. Rather than trying to "fix" ourselves, this perspective affirms our "morbidity" and "catastrophism"; it affirms our circumstance and our particularity.

❧

As we survey the landscape of Mexican philosophy, uncovering the many ways in which it can provide a helpful, illuminating guide to life, three major themes emerge. The first is that Mexican philosophy is a situated, contextualized, or circumstantial philosophy. This means that it doubles down on the controversial notion that all philosophizing, like all thinking, is always embodied and always conceived in or from a *somewhere*. Because philosophers have insisted for millennia that *real* philosophy is abstract, universal, and not tied to time and place, philosophy that takes seriously its "somewhere" is sure to ruffle more than a few feathers.

The second theme is that Mexican philosophy has by necessity a relationship with colonialism—a very intimate and defiant relationship, to be sure. This matters because what Mexican philosophy says may echo the Western tradition, respond to it, or seek to surpass it. This also means that Mexican philosophy cannot claim originality in the sense of novelty, and indeed it doesn't, as it always remains aware of its history and its context. Yet, as it struggles with its historical inheritance, it acquires a difference, becoming something other and valuable.

The final theme, which is related to the first two, is that Mexican philosophy is focused on *self-knowledge*, or what Mexican philosophers call "autognosis." Autognosis is an important theme that suggests that through or with philosophy we may be able to truly know ourselves. In this, Mexican philosophy orients us to the necessity of knowing who or what we are, where we come from, and where we're heading; it is the kind of knowledge that should help us feel more at home in a world we may otherwise not perceive as "our own."

So, please stick around. The chapters that follow will articulate other lessons and other orientations gathered from my studies and ponderings of Mexican philosophy. My hope is that they will orient you to a clearer and more fulfilling life.

ACKNOWLEDGMENTS

This book is the result of many years of thinking, reading, and talking about Mexican philosophy with students, colleagues, family, and friends. I thank first my students, especially those in my Latin American courses who, for years, have been subjected to my meandering stories and anecdotes as I have tried to connect philosophy to something real or ridiculous. Some of those stories have found their way into the pages of this book. Secondly, I thank my colleagues in the department of philosophy at San José State University who, for reasons that escape me, continue to put up with my attempts at making sense of things. I thank Rebecca Chan, Anand Vaidya, Janet Stemwedel, Jordan Liz, Etienne Brown, Noah Friedman-Biglin, and Rianna Beltzer. Third, I thank my colleagues *not* at SJSU, without whom thinking of Mexican philosophy would be a very lonely endeavor: Robert Sanchez, Manuel Vargas, Clinton Tolley, Guillermo Hurtado, Carlos Pereda, Aurelia Valero, Sergio Gallegos, Francisco Gallegos, and Amy Oliver, who are tirelessly at work making the study of this tradition acceptable to an international academic audience. I thank also Stephen Grimm for inviting me to write this book, and Lucy Randall at OUP, a most brilliant editor who helped shape what's inside. Then there's my family, who generously allowed me the time to write: my wife, Tricia, and my sons Julian, Ethan, and Pascual, for their unending love. Finally, I thank my parents, Patricio and Guillermina Sánchez for their struggle . . . and for surviving in spite of it all.

PART I

TWO VERY SHORT INTRODUCTIONS TO MEXICAN PHILOSOPHY

1 | "IN THE BEGINNING . . ."

PHILOSOPHY IN MEXICO

The former monastery of Tiripetío, eighty miles southeast of my father's hometown of Acuitzeramo, Michoacán, has the distinction of being the place where, almost 500 years ago, philosophy was professed in the Americas for the very first time. Taught in a course intended for future priests, monks, and members of the political and social elite, it was led by the Augustinian friar Alonso de la Veracruz in 1540 (nineteen years after the Conquest of Mexico) and covered a range of topics, including logic, metaphysics, and various other themes found in the philosophy of Aristotle.[1] Thus, one could claim that Tiripetío (also the first home of advanced studies in Mexico and the Americas) is the birthplace of, what today we call, "American philosophy."

"This must be how Greeks feel whenever they bring up the thing about Socrates," quipped my farmworker father when I brought this up, referring to the countless times his Greek *mayordomo* had bragged about Greece being the birthplace of Western culture while never forgetting to mention that a guy named Socrates invented "philosophy." While my father didn't know exactly what philosophy was or why I (or his Greek boss) would be excited about it, I could see, once I told him, that he was proud of having been born and raised so close to the site of Veracruz's historical achievement.

Today, Tiripetío is mostly known for its monastery, built in 1537, and not for its being the birthplace of American philosophy . . . or, if you prefer, for philosophy *in* the Americas. This is because, in Mexico, philosophy never strayed too far from the monasteries and the universities. There, it was part of a curriculum centered on evangelization and the administration of the colony. Thus, philosophy remained hidden, cloistered with monks and made available only to a few of Mexico's social and political elite.

And so, for 400 of the last 500 years, philosophy and the teaching of philosophy in Mexico did not change much from the time Veracruz taught his first course. Philosophy remained European philosophy that just happened to find itself in Mexico. This is unsurprising, especially when we consider how Western philosophy has been traditionally understood: as universal and ahistorical, capable of fitting in anywhere, regardless of cultural, historical, or social differences. According to this understanding, philosophy is immune to change. Or so that tradition insists.

But why only 400 out of 500 years?

The particular struggles of the Mexican people, Mexico's geographies, its histories, its political and social situations, and its cultures—neither European nor Indigenous, but both and neither and in between—from the start exerted a certain pressure on the "universalist" pretensions of European thought. This all came to a head at the beginning of the twentieth century when Mexican thinkers began to recognize that philosophy as traditionally understood would have to change, that it would have to adapt to the terrains, the cultures, and the histories of America if it was to serve any special function. It is then that *philosophy in Mexico* begins to become conscious of itself as *Mexican philosophy, filosofía mexicana*—no longer just Western philosophy that happens to find itself in Mexico, but a philosophy that is distinctively Mexican. We can imagine this process as the blooming of a flower that, while native to European gardens, blooms now in an altogether different soil and, because of this, blooms differently and, some would say, imperfectly.

That one day we would be talking about a "Mexican" philosophy was inevitable, since philosophy as traditionally understood— namely, as an abstract and universal sort of thinking—will always fail to address problems specific to the different cultures that make up our human community. This would be like treating different illnesses with the same medicine. Moreover, because of its tendency toward abstractness and universality, philosophy as traditionally understood appears uninterested (because it is supposedly a "disinterested" activity) about *who* it is addressing or *why*. In Mexican history, European philosophy assumed, as did the conquerors and colonizers themselves, that Mexico was just like any other place, and that Mexican problems were not much different from those that philosophers had encountered before in Europe—as if, for example, Mexican illnesses were just like European illnesses. But of course this could not be further from the truth! For Mexican philosophers, it eventually became clear that the so-called universal truths of European philosophy do not speak to or about *realities* like Mexico, and that in fact, and against 2,500 years of philosophical dogma, truth and meaning are influenced by history, experience, and geography. Circumstance, it turns out, really matters.

At the beginning of the twentieth century, the affirmation that there was, in fact, a "Mexican way of thinking" was liberating. First, it liberated philosophically minded thinkers from the need to think like Europeans; second, it freed them to propose that a Mexican philosophy was possible and necessary. Once they began working this out, it was clear that Mexican philosophy was on to something; that thinking from the Mexican cultural, historical, and existential experience revealed truths and offered ways of seeing that supposedly disinterested or universal philosophical methods or theories just could not.

Veracruz's philosophy course marks a key moment in the history not simply of *philosophy in Mexico* but of *Mexican philosophy*. Although the course itself can be seen as no more than a footnote to the agenda of colonization, it nonetheless puts us right at the time and place where Mexican philosophy got its start, while also showing us that philosophy has been part of Mexican culture since the start.

You may wonder in what sense a philosophy course would benefit the colonizing agenda. To put it simply, when done in the right way, philosophy clarifies and justifies. Offering a philosophy course at that specific time in Mexican history would not merely teach students how to disentangle good from bad thinking, nor was it to offer students a "guide to life" in any contemporary sense of the word. Teaching a philosophy course nineteen years after the Conquest would help clarify and justify the religious and political aims of the conquerors. Veracruz's students needed to learn logic, hermeneutics, and moral philosophy, for at least two very important reasons: one, in order to better read, understand, and more clearly communicate the Gospel (the evangelizing mission); and two, in order to intellectually justify the treatment of the conquered to themselves, to Europe, and to history (the colonizing mission).

Consider this example. In his arguments in favor of the Spanish conquest, colonization, and the forced conversion and continual subjugation of Indigenous people, the theologian and lawyer Juan Ginés de Sepúlveda (1490–1573) deployed Aristotle's philosophy in order to argue that Indigenous people could be mistreated because they were "natural slaves," in accordance with Aristotle's definition in his *Politics*. In this case, philosophy was certainly in the service of the colonizing mission. Now, Veracruz didn't share Sepúlveda's opinion, nor did he teach that Indigenous people were natural slaves. Nevertheless, he did believe philosophy to be an instrument in the service of *a* mission, which, for him, was a mission of civilizing and converting.[2]

Again, my reason for emphasizing this starting point is to show that philosophy in the Americas is as old as Mexico itself. Stories like Veracruz's also show that philosophy has not always been the disinterested, detached activity that Monty Python makes it out to be in the popular episode in which famous philosophers attempt to play soccer but can't seem to move the ball toward the goal. Philosophy has, in fact, often served the interests of the state, of religion, and even of those oppressed by states and religions. This doesn't make philosophy necessarily pragmatic, but it does show that it oftentimes finds itself in the service of a certain "mission."

Now, the fact that in the Americas philosophy was first taught in a monastery also means that philosophy has not always been for everybody. Inaccessible to folks who, because of their social, racial, or economic status, were poorly educated, illiterate, or simply lacked the time to pursue such things, philosophy in Mexico remained the privilege of the very few for over 400 years. Although my grandfather was born and died within 100 miles of philosophy's American birthplace, he had no idea *what* it was or *that* it was. What's interesting about this is that my grandfather was familiar with the word "philosophy," as were my grandmother, my father, and my mother, but what they understood by the term was that it referred to a kind of daydreaming—a form of escapism from the worries and demands of everyday life. As they saw it, for someone working from sunup to sundown just to put food on the table, there was simply no time or reason to escape in this way, dreaming about ideas.

I'm not sure where this common understanding of philosophy as a sort of daydreaming comes from. But if I had to guess, I would say that it came from the colonial elite themselves (the politicos, the Church, the rich), who, while privately valuing big-idea-type thinking as both a luxury and a means to maintain social control, publicly presented such activity negatively as unfruitful and unhelpful, something for selfish daydreamers or insensitive troublemakers. And they did so because a good chunk of colonial indoctrination was geared toward encouraging work and discouraging idleness; in this context, "philosopher" was introduced into everyday speech as a derogatory term. Thinking didn't feed you, work did! I recall helping my grandfather during the planting season. He'd often catch me daydreaming when I was supposed to be sticking corn kernels into the dirt, get frustrated, throw a stone or a stick at me, and yell "Stop philosophizing and get to work!"

Meanwhile, as my grandfather and generations of Mexicans avoided the pitfalls of daydreaming, philosophy shaped the country. First, as with Veracruz, philosophical thinking confronted New World realities and helped justify, via readings of ancient Greek texts, the conquest and colonization, the humanity of Indigenous peoples, and the political actions of the state. Later, after the Wars of Independence from Spain in the early nineteenth century and the periods of Reform that followed, Gabino Barreda (1818–1881) taught philosophy in the service of the dictatorship. This was an important moment that spanned the *Porfiriato*, the rule of Porfirio Díaz (1876–1880 and 1884–1911). Barreda professed that the future of Mexico ultimately depended on educational reforms that emphasized science and technology over and against theology and theoretical philosophy. A Mexican interpretation of French positivism, Barreda's philosophy justified efforts by the dictatorship to shape the future of the country along scientific lines. The basic idea was that cultural attachments to the past, as well as a stubborn dependence on Catholicism and folk superstitions, had gotten in the way of progress. Only by getting rid of these attachments could Mexico evolve out of its past and into the more prosperous future. This could only be achieved if society was managed by scientific-minded people along scientific ways of thinking.

Eventually, the positivist social reforms backfired: Mexicans soon caught on to this new scientific or technological indoctrination and grew tired of being told how and what to think. And so, at the beginning of the twentieth century, an intellectual revolution began to take shape, though the common people took little notice. It was a revolution against the dictatorship and against positivism. The emerging revolutionary "anti-positivist" philosophers rejected positivism, with its "universalist" pretensions, as out of touch with the needs of the Mexican people. They called instead for a reexamination of the mysteries of human life, insisting that not everything was quantifiable, measurable, or empirical.

One of the best known of these anti-positivists was José Vasconcelos (1882–1959), whose name, you will recall, first led me to take notice of the gaps in the philosophical story I had previously been told. Vasconcelos called for an appreciation of the unknowability and unpredictability of all things, especially of scientific knowledge. The scientific or technological obsession of the times was oppressive and restrictive, closing off the world of possibilities. Freedom depended, says Vasconcelos, on ridding oneself of those restrictions and being open to what is not measurable or quantifiable, but nonetheless real or possible. Positivism would have to be overcome and in doing so, Vasconcelos continues, "it seems that we are relieving ourselves of a weight on our consciousness and that life has broadened. The renovating longing that fills us has begun to discharge its indeterminate potency in unconfined spaces, where everything seems possible."[3]

That "weight" would be cast away in an intellectual *and* a popular revolution. Philosophers would be the first to see its promise: that with a revolution, a "renovation" would occur, one "where everything is possible." Unbeknown to most folks, including my grandfather, who, having been born in 1901, was not yet ten years old by the time the Revolution broke out, it was a longing for renovation that sparked the conflict. Again, philosophy was right there in the thick of things.

It is as a reaction to positivism that a philosophical tradition that had been here since 1540 becomes "Mexican philosophy." It is now that we see it as a philosophy about the Mexican circumstance, understood as a totality that includes what can be seen, like the history and culture of Mexico, but also what remains hidden, like the Mexican spirit. Anti-positivists like Vasconcelos or Antonio Caso (1883–1946) will show that philosophy does not need to be restricted by what is seen and measurable. Caso, for instance, wonders about love and faith and how these can be verified without being quantified. "Faith," he says, "is the confirmation that—alongside the world ruled by the natural law of life—there is a world ruled by the supernatural law of love."[4]

We can say, then, that Mexican philosophy blooms during the period immediately before and immediately after the Revolution of 1910. It is nourished and characterized by a spirit of resistance, resilience, and self-discovery. In the years after 1920, after the end of the war, after the assassination of its revolutionary heroes, and after the creation of its Constitution (1917), philosophical thinking arrives at a new mission: to be an instrument of self-understanding. Philosophy, that is, helps make sense of what being Mexican means, now, after 400 years of having been *told* what being Mexican means. It is after the Revolution that Mexican philosophy becomes a way of thinking about and from a history of traumas: the Conquest, colonization, independence, and Revolution. Together, these form a crucial aspect of its circumstance, and thinking from and about its circumstance will be Mexican philosophy's defining characteristic.

While it's still the case that, in Mexico, philosophy, as an academic interest, is reserved for those who have the time or money necessary for its pursuit—this, almost 500 years after that first course was taught—it's also true that more people are aware of its existence, and in 2019 it was even included as a social right in Article 3 of the Mexican Constitution. Philosophy, say its advocates, should play a role in the formation of the Mexican citizen!

Mexican philosophy has also grown in popularity in the United States. It is seen by some as part of a more global effort to decolonize philosophy (to make philosophy less European), and by others as a tradition that forces philosophy to be more inclusive and representative of the human community. In either case, quick Google or Amazon searches will yield enough material to take a deep dive into its history, its figures, and its concepts. And this book can itself serve as a starting point, a way to familiarize yourself, very concisely, with its basic themes and ideas, keeping in mind that the history of philosophy in Mexico, and Mexican philosophy, is much richer and more diverse than I will make it out to be here. I, of course, encourage you to pursue the subject more seriously, especially if you, like me, find the very notion that there *is* a Mexican philosophy empowering.

That I've twice mentioned that Mexican philosophy is empowering may frustrate some folks. It will frustrate you if you believe that philosophy is about knowledge, wisdom, and logic and that it matters little how it makes you feel. But, as someone for whom the discovery of Mexican philosophy was quite literally life-changing, let me say it for a third time: Mexican philosophy is empowering. This is especially true if you're Mexican or Mexican-American. It is empowering to know that there is a philosophical tradition that belongs to you, one grounded on your heritage or that of your parents or grandparents, one that emerges in spite of European colonization. And even if you're not Mexican, it can be empowering because *now you know* that there is a philosophical tradition born from a concern with its own circumstance, one that cares about being a "view from somewhere," and representing a way to do philosophy that you, too, Mexican or not, can adopt. In this last sense, philosophy belongs to us all, always. And that's empowering *and* liberating.

There's a bigger lesson in all of this, of course. The picture that we are given about what's available to us is never complete. Hidden in the corners of a photograph may be a detail, something we've always missed even if we've looked at the photo our entire lives. The same is true with philosophy. The picture we've been given seems incomplete. And it seems incomplete because it is overly focused, or zoomed in on Europe and its figures and traditions. But if we look closer, we see details accidentally captured by the photo, in the margins, pointing to a larger scene. That's usually where we find what's truly meaningful: in the margins of the picture, captured accidentally in the photograph. As we look closer, that accidental capture becomes the focus and the margin becomes interesting.

This theme, of being accidental to a larger picture, runs through the work of Mexican philosophers. As we saw with the anti-positivists, like Caso and Vasconcelos, and as we see in our photograph metaphor, Mexican philosophy recognizes that the picture of the world offered by Western thinking is not complete or is overly focused. That is the colonial picture of things, one which can also be thought as a fabrication, a myth, an imperfect and very accidental conception grounded on its own situated, "Western" perspective. Mexican philosophy urges us to return to this picture and reconsider its incompleteness; it asks us to focus on the margins, on the circumstances, and on the accidentality of our lives. This is an empowering idea.

2 | MEXICAN PHILOSOPHY IN THE TWENTIETH CENTURY

Philosophy can be broadly defined as the impartial pursuit of truths that are foundational, universal, and timeless. Philosophical truths will be general and not particular. Plato (one of the founders of the Western philosophical tradition) says in his dialogue *Gorgias*, philosophy "should not be pushed too much into details." This means that, according to Plato, the task of the philosopher is to disinterestedly, or impartially, contemplate the big picture.

Mexican philosophy does not shy away from big-picture thinking. But it suspects that such thinking tends to leave things out. So it traffics also, and with more intensity, in detail-oriented thinking. Detail-oriented thinking can be generally characterized as a more engaged, or biased, pursuit of concrete, particular, and circumstantial truths. We have, for instance, Jorge Portilla's (1919–1963) meditations on the concept of *relajo,* a nihilistic attitude that he believes characterizes modern Mexicans; María Elena Bermúdez's (1916–1988) philosophical critique of the machismo of Mexican men; Luis Villoro's (1922–2014) reflections on the objectification of the Indigenous peoples of Mexico; Leopoldo Zea's (1912–2004) analysis of Mexican positivism; and Rosario Castellanos's (1924–1974) defense of Mexican women's right to education. In these and other ways, and in defiance of Plato's admonition, Mexican philosophy pushes itself into the details as it addresses problems grounded on the realities of the concrete, social world.

The notion of "pushing itself into the details" is another way of saying that philosophical reflection will not stick solely to abstract and universal issues. Zea says that, in the twentieth century, philosophy in Mexico "descends from the world of ideal entities and toward the world of concrete entities such as Mexico, itself a symbol of the men and women that live and die in its cities and in its mountains."[1] This "descent" from the realm of abstraction to the realm of concreteness is not something peculiar to Mexico, of course—it can be seen in Germany with Karl Marx's economic and political philosophy and in the United States with John Dewey's pragmatism. But this descent seems to be a necessary one for Mexicans who, in the twentieth century, demanded that philosophy be less alienating and more responsive to their own crises, one of which had to do with the urgency of coming to terms with their own national and cultural identity (*Are we Spanish? Indigenous? Both? Neither?*). Ultimately, the "descent" that Zea mentions makes possible the emergence of a philosophy that is concretely and intimately Mexican.

In the hands of the living and the dying, philosophy is given a specific task, one demanded by its place and circumstance. It now takes seriously the Mexican historical experience of conquest, colonization, and *mestizaje* (the mixing of races)—or, what is the same, it recognizes the value of Mexican history, circumstance, and identity. Its texts reflect and articulate the wisdom and knowledge of philosophers who think, meditate, and live that history, that circumstance, and that identity. It is in this sense that "Mexico" serves as a point of departure, and the picture that Mexican philosophy worries about is the picture that living the Mexican experience reveals.

Now, Mexican philosophy, understood in this way, is genuinely Mexican in the sense that it grows out of a difference that cannot be translated by or interpreted through other experiences or concepts meant to make sense of those other experiences. This is not to say that Mexican philosophy has invented an entirely new conceptual vocabulary to talk about reality; it has not. Rather, it has adopted and adapted Western as well as Indigenous ideas, transforming them into tools of resistance, inner resources for withstanding historical and existential upheaval, and ways to understand the modern world. Ultimately, such adoptions and adaptations lend Mexican philosophy its unique character.

Zea also reminds us that even Plato was bounded to his own, Greek world. Once we realize this, it becomes clear that Plato's philosophy cannot possibly be as universal as we've been led to believe. We in the West are simply used to perceiving the Greek (like the Roman and the European) perspective as a neutral, universal default perspective that is relevant and useful for us today and always. But it's worth questioning this. Philosophers, when they philosophize from Greece or France or Germany, cannot but see the world through their own, situated, experience. This means that philosophy, when done by Europeans, is European philosophy. And it also means that this philosophy is not foundational, or universal, or timeless, or placeless, but rooted in a particular experience. Zea puts it this way:

> [W]e have a series of problems that are only given in our circumstance . . . that can only be resolved by us. The positing of such problems will not diminish the philosophical character of our philosophy, because philosophy tries to resolve problems posed to one in one's existence. The problems posed . . . will have to be specific to circumstance where one lives.[2]

For Zea, philosophy is a toolkit for solving problems unique to our own lived experience or circumstance. In this sense, philosophy is pragmatic, helping us navigate existential predicaments that arise in particular circumstances. Now, predicaments, or crises, or problems will naturally be different from one circumstance to another; Mexicans will worry about issues different from those that worry Europeans or US citizens. Indeed, as Zea says, "Our situation is not that of the European bourgeoisie. Our philosophy, if it is to be responsible, does not make the same commitments that contemporary European philosophy does."[3] Nor should it.

A noteworthy example of what Zea is talking about is Emilio Uranga's refusal to accept the European notion of "humanity." He does this because the European notion of "humanity" is loaded with prejudices it has accumulated throughout the millennia. One of these prejudices is the notion that to be human is to be "substantial," or to have an essence. The problem is that the essence of what it means to be human is almost inevitably going to be defined along political, religious, and ultimately racist lines. Thus, in this case, to refuse the European notion of humanity as substantial is to refuse racist and derogatory interpretations of Mexicans themselves. "Any interpretation of humans as substantial creatures seems to us inhuman," proclaims Uranga.[4]

Uranga's rejection is grounded on a more philosophically motivated suspicion regarding the status of essences or "universals." Although "human" has been offered as applicable to all, as a universal, it is in fact an exclusive category that can be instrumentalized against those that cannot meet the Eurocentric requirement of what does and what does not fit under the "human" umbrella. The paradox is that the same civilization that invaded Mexico and treated the people it found there as less than human then insists in its philosophy that the category "human" is available to all, Mexican or European. Of course, this is merely rhetorical, as history has shown that Mexicans (Indigenous and others) have been treated as a species apart—a far inferior one—by conquerors and colonizers.

We can now more clearly make out what "Mexican" in Mexican philosophy refers to: it indicates not only a grounding in national and historical origins but also a focus on the particular historical experience of Mexicans. With this, it affirms a different orientation and set of commitments that show that Mexican philosophy is not simply an echo of Western philosophy. The commitments of European philosophy are to universality, whether that is the universality of "truth" or "humanity." The commitments of Mexican philosophy, on the other hand, are to the particularity of its own situation, which is the situation of Mexicans seeking to take responsibility for their own life or the life of their communities. It is in this that Mexican philosophy makes itself available to us all: it serves to clarify a path and to guide anyone seeking to take such responsibility and make such commitments.

None of this is to say that philosophy, as traditionally understood, should no longer be thought of as universal and abstract. Sure, we can think of it that way. But it is universal and abstract only in a universal and abstract way. Philosophy becomes a *useful* way to spend one's time only when it grapples with questions immediately related to a concrete, real existence or circumstantial need.

The story of how Mexican philosophy came about in the twentieth century is tied to a certain version of Mexican history itself. It is a version that can be told as follows:

After the fall of the Aztec empire (1521), life under Spanish colonial rule amounted to subjugation under the threat of death. The conquest of the Aztec capital, Tenochtitlán, in August of 1521 was especially deadly, with an estimated 100,000 Indigenous people killed during the siege. In the years that followed, over eight million Indigenous people were wiped out by either European diseases, to which they were not immune, or the brutality of the colonizers. The survivors were eventually integrated into an unfamiliar political and religious situation and subjugated to the needs and wants of Spanish colonial ambition. But even in conditions of subjugation and marginalization, remnants of Indigenous culture survived. These remnants slowly found their way into the everyday life of the conquerors and colonizers. In the decades that followed, what remained of Indigenous culture mixed with the culture of the invaders, and in this mixing of cultures a new kind of human identity was created: the mestizo, not Indigenous and not European, but an impure hybrid of the two—what we now call a Mexican.

Mexicans would spend the next four centuries seeking recognition and approval from Europe (all the while avoiding a confrontation with their Indigenous heritage). But Europe would not take them into account or take them seriously, and would use them only as a means to its own ends. Europeans would consider the Mexicans *impure*, a mere accident of history and inferior due to this impurity and accidentality. Mexicans would internalize this sense of inferiority and sink into marginality, where they would remain until the early nineteenth century, at which point they would emerge in violent outbursts of self-affirmation, demanding independence and freedom.

The mestizo sought independence in a war that began in 1810, and achieved it by 1821 (this is the Mexican War of Independence). Now free of political ties to Spain, mestizos endeavored to create a new social and cultural situation better suited to their needs. This proved difficult. For inspiration they turned to France—a country which at this time was between its major revolutions and was redefining the structure of power and society for a new age. France, however, took advantage, invaded Mexico in 1861, and conquered it. Only six years later, during a period of social and political reform, would they be forced to withdraw.

By 1877, a strongman, a dictator, promised to lead Mexicans into the future. His name was Porfirio Díaz (1830–1915). Díaz likewise turned to France, and in an effort to open up the country to industry and a more technological tomorrow, his ministers imported the philosophy of positivism, a social philosophy developed by Auguste Comte (1798–1857) that insists that only a scientific approach to social problems can bring about order and progress. This offended the mestizos, who refused to forget their superstitions, their poetry, their art, and their traditions so as to make room for order and progress. Along with the subjugated Indigenous peoples, the mestizos eventually staged a revolution. The Mexican Revolution began in 1910 and ended in 1920. No one is sure who won. Afterward, the mestizos realized that the Revolution, while inevitable, revealed something about themselves: that for four centuries they hadn't known who they themselves were. This revelation was a cause for profound meditation, as the mestizos now sought to affirm themselves in spite of their history, in spite of their accidentality, in spite of their impurity— to assert their difference, a difference that is not European but all their own. They have done this with philosophy.

Mexican philosophy comes of age in the twentieth century, in the period between 1920 and 1960. It is guided by variations of one simple question: *What does it mean to be Mexican*? That is, if Mexicans are neither fully Indigenous nor fully Spanish but both at once, if they are accidental products of history, and if the Mexican character is unlike the character of those in other parts of the world, *who* or *what* are the Mexicans? The ultimate goal of asking this question and its variations *philosophically* is to arrive at a place of self-confidence and self-love—in other words, to overcome the sense of inferiority that has plagued them historically and move confidently into the future. Uranga asserts the reason this way: "We have arrived at that historical and cultural age in which we demand to live in accordance with our own being, and from that demand arises the imperative to clarify the morphology and the dynamics of that being."[5]

During this period of self-examination (roughly 1920–1960), the Mexican government also sought to reintegrate a disintegrated country through a sort of popular nationalism that promotes the virtues of the Revolution and its heroes. The philosophical search for what it means to be Mexican (for *lo mexicano*, or Mexicanness) tracks this effort, but has a very different purpose. While both the philosopher and the nationalist seek a commonality that can unite many experiences under a common national identity—that is, as "Mexican"—for the philosopher the search is, above all else, about finding the *meaning* of Mexican existence itself.

The preceding paragraphs have provided a (very brief) framework for how Mexican philosophy comes into its own in the twentieth century. What is clear is that Mexican philosophy is tied to Mexican history in very intimate ways. The colonial, Eurocentric idea of philosophy insists that, to be properly philosophical, philosophy ought not have anything to do with history, and insists that philosophy's truths should transcend whatever can be victimized by time. Mexican philosophy, by grounding itself in history in this way, violates this principle. It wouldn't surprise us, then, if the very idea of a "Mexican" philosophy offends more than a few historians, philosophers, and academics.

That the concept may offend philosophy purists should not be taken as a serious concern, as purity is an unattainable ideal, the pursuit of which usually does more harm than good. I personally don't find the concept concerning, because I believe that calling philosophy "Mexican" or "Honduran" or "French" or "American"

can be both empowering *and* transformative. Believing that your own ethno-cultural, historical, or existential experience has philosophical value can infuse your life with a new purpose: namely, to discover that value. As a result, you may now see the world, yourself, and your experience as saturated with meaning in a way that you were unable to do before coming to this realization. In fact, this is an explicit motivation in Emilio Uranga's philosophy. He believed that finding the value of one's unique experience could be transformative, writing that "More than a straightforward and rigorous meditation on the being of the Mexican, what brings us to this kind of [philosophical] study is the project of bringing about moral, social, and religious transformations in our being."[6] This is another way to say that philosophy shouldn't be so detached and impartial, abstract or universal, that it fails to impact your community, your relationships, or you personally.

My hope is that you too will be compelled to bring about moral, social, and other transformations in your own being as you read this book. My approach in what follows involves distilling lessons that, through various readings of Uranga, Caso, Villoro, Portilla, Frost, and others, your life can guide you in a way that is both entertaining and instructive.

PART II

FOUR THEMES IN MEXICAN PHILOSOPHY

3 | YOU ARE *NEPANTLA*

The year is 1987. My fever is 102° and shows no signs of breaking. My mother cuts thin potato slices and puts them on my forehead like Sticky Notes. The thin slices absorb the fever. The fever cooks them slightly, boils them a bit, and they break apart into tiny hash-brown flakes as she peels them off my face. After a few rounds of this, I get back to a tolerable 99°. She brings in a glass of water and a cup of hot rue tea with lemon leaves. It tastes like gasoline. I feel like I've been run over by a tractor.

The fever returns that night. We're out of potatoes. The cold shower she pushes me into doesn't work. She wakes my father and we drive to the hospital. He's scared, not for my health but for the possibility that immigration may be called in and get them both. *What would happen to my sister and me?*

They hook me up to an IV and explain to my parents that I will be okay. It's just a flu; it's been going around. I just need rest and liquids.

The doctor asks how long I've had the fever. "It's been a few days," my mother tells him. "But it was worse a couple of nights ago."

"Why didn't you bring him in then?" he asks in cracked but intelligible Spanish. There's a concerned look on his big, round face.

He's already sizing up my immigrant mom, judging her parenting. We can all see it. My father is nervous.

"Did you give him anything?" he asks, taking notes on a yellow pad.

"I just put potato slices on his forehead to get the fever down."

"Why?!" he barks, slamming down his pen on the notepad. He's annoyed. "*Señora*, in America, if a child is sick, you bring him to the doctor. You don't cure him at home with potato slices!" He turns to the nurse, who's been standing there the whole time. "These people!" His white face is red with anti-immigrant emotion.

As the doctor storms out, my mother turns to the nurse. "This is how we've always done it. My grandmother did it. No one has died from the potatoes. Besides, he was drinking *suero*." (*Suero* refers to pediatric electrolytes, or Pedialyte.)

"We know that you know what you're doing, *señora*. The doctor just doesn't really understand," says the nurse.

What the doctor didn't understand was that my mother had not yet become fully assimilated to the American way of doing things. She still had a foot in the old ways while trying to find her footing in the new. My mother was neither *here* nor *there* but somewhere *in between*, in the middle of two possible *ways of doing things*. My mother was *nepantla*.

The exasperation felt by the doctor over my mother's *nepantla* was first recorded by Spanish priests almost five hundred years earlier, during the early days of American colonization. An interesting account of an instance of *nepantla* in the colonial era was left by a Catholic priest in sixteenth-century Mexico. The following is a fictionalized version of that event; certain names, places, dialogues, and emotional outburst have been made up, by me, so as to keep you reading.

Sometime in the mid-1500s, a Spanish-born Dominican friar, Diego Durán (1537–1588), is sent by the church to a small Mexican village in the state of Morelos. He settles into his role, doing God's work on weekends and strolling the dusty streets during the week, his hands behind his back, waving and smiling at the townsfolk. He admires the progress of the evangelizing mission. There's an innocent smugness to him.

The friar is a quick learner. He's gotten to know the ins and outs of the town and its people by sitting in on the conversations of the elders in the churchyard. In doing so, he's learned Nahuatl and won the trust of the people. It took time, but most now come to Mass. He takes their confessions. Most attend Mass and confession only because he's there; otherwise they wouldn't. He believes he's winning them over for Christ! But he also knows that, secretly, they still practice their ancient rituals. He despises this about them but can't stop it, so he says nothing. He prays that they will eventually come around.

On one particular Monday, he notices one of the Indigenous men, whom he calls Matteo, working a bit harder, with more urgency. It looks like he's trying to earn extra money. Matteo goes from here to there without rest throughout the week. The friar admires Matteo's tenacity, his work ethic, his perseverance. On Saturday, Matteo begs for money outside the church, more proof that he will not stop until he's achieved his goal—whatever that may be. The friar is impressed. Perhaps, he thinks, the church will benefit financially from the man's efforts come Sunday.

Matteo goes on like this for weeks. Surely, the friar thinks, he must have a small fortune by now!

A few weekends later, on a Saturday afternoon, the friar walks out of the sanctuary into a commotion. There's music in the square. People laugh and drink. Some dance. There's food aplenty. This is a *fiesta*! But what are they celebrating? And who? The friar is confused. Today is not a saint's day. He asks a woman stirring a clay pot over a fire as to the reason for the celebration. What she tells him is deeply upsetting. Matteo, whom the friar has witnessed working tirelessly for weeks and begging for money on the weekend is having a party. It appears he's getting married. He has invited the entire town to join him. All the food and drink is on him—his treat!

What an absolute waste! the friar thinks, and angrily storms into the crowd, intent on finding Matteo and giving him a good talking-to. He finds Matteo taking a drink from a large *cántaro* of *pulque*.

"Welcome to my fiesta, *padre*!" says Matteo joyfully.

"What are you doing!? I saw you toiling away for weeks, begging for money, working yourself to exhaustion, and all for *this*?! You don't need *this*! Have you gone mad? There's so much more that you could have done with your money! Did you at least give alms?"

"Listen, *padre*, this is what we've always done. Before you came here, before your people came here, we celebrated with one another in this way. We are a community. My marriage is not just about me—it's about us, together! This is our tradition."

"Oh, I know of your traditions. Most are demonic! And careless, purposeless celebrations like this just remind people of those other satanic traditions you held at those monstrous pyramids. You should be giving to the needy and confessing your sins, preparing for Christ's return!"

Matteo listens attentively to the friar. And after allowing him to finish complaining, he says (according to Durán, who would come to record this in the mid-1570s), "Don't be alarmed, *padre*, but we are still *nepantla*."[1]

Now, what Matteo was trying to tell the "alarmed" priest was that the process of assimilation into which he was being forced by the colonizing project was still in progress, and that, at that moment in time, Matteo and his Indigenous community were *in between two cultures*: on the one hand, the Spanish, Catholic culture represented by the church and the friar himself, and on the other, Matteo's Indigenous culture, represented by rituals and community. In saying he was *nepantla*, Matteo was trying to tell Durán that he was no longer living as he once lived, but not yet living as the Spanish wanted him to live.

To this, the friar expresses anger and exasperation. Much work, he thinks, is still to be done to rid these people of their demons. Durán later writes:

> Incited by the devil . . . these miserable Indians remain perplexed and neutral regarding matters of faith . . . they believe in God and at the same time still adore their idols and appeal to their superstitions and ancient rituals, mixing one with the other.[2]

As I read Durán's words, I think of the round-faced doctor that scolded my mother those many years ago.

You should know that I've taken some liberties with Durán's account. There's no way for me to know, for instance, that Durán walked with his hands behind his back or that the Indigenous man's name was Matteo. But in a passage from his *History of the Indies of New Spain* of 1581, Durán records the exchange in which he learns that the Indigenous people can't yet be what he wants them to be because, as he's told, "we are still *nepantla*."

The importance of Durán's account of *nepantla* is that it has motivated twentieth-century Mexican philosophers to think about their own existential condition, and continues to encourage us today to think about ours. Of particular interest is Durán's own analysis of what he believed the Indigenous man meant by *nepantla*:

> And while I understood what he meant to say with that vocabulary and that metaphor, which means to be in the middle, I turned and insisted that he tell me what middle it was in which they were. He told me that, since they were not very well rooted in faith, that I shouldn't be alarmed since they were still neutral in the sense that they neither depended on one law or another, or better put, that they believed in God and at the same time relied on their ancient customs and demonic rites [*costumbres antiguas y ritos del demonio*], and this is what he meant with that abominable excuse that they still remained in the middle and were neutral.[3]

We can imagine the townsfolk in my fictionalized account, as they celebrate the wedding, feeling the same way: all are in a state of transition from the old to the new, in transit toward an unknown "yet," suspended "in the middle" of a monumental cultural shift, moving always farther from what is known and familiar toward what is strange and uncertain.

Based on what Durán tells us, we can interpret *nepantla* in the following way: Nepantla *is the state of being caught in between different worlds—the world that is "home" and an unfamiliar or alien world*. We can even imagine it as a sort of traveling from one place to another, where *nepantla* is that space between the two where you find yourself as if suspended in between the demands of home and those expectations that the destination may put on you. Your commitments to both are suspended as you travel, while you are on the way. In this state, you are in-between, uncommitted, and "neutral." To be neutral is to live as without a "horse in the race," divested of commitments to either the past or the future. This is why, if you are *nepantla*, you act as if what matters is the present and not necessarily what is expected of you. You are free to treat a fever with potatoes or Pedialyte or both. You feel uprooted, yes, but also free.

In Durán's retelling, the Indigenous Matteo, in declaring his neutrality, his being in-between, or his middle-hood, is also declaring himself free from an obligation to the Church, and thus free to pursue what remains of his traditions. In saying that "we are still *nepantla*," he is voicing the belief that they are *still (todavía) on the way*. This is a condition, moreover, which the Indigenous people know all too well—a sentiment reflected in the Indigenous man's attempt to reassure the "alarmed" priest.

Mexican philosophy recovers and reappropriates the concept of *nepantla* and applies it to modern Mexicans, who likewise exist "in the middle of" different histories (European and pre-Hispanic histories), cultures (Spanish and Indigenous cultures), religions (Catholicism and Indigenous spiritual practices), and geographical spaces (the United States and the rest of Latin America). We can say that the transition begun by the Indigenous man in Durán's chronicle has never been and will never be completed, whether by the Indigenous peoples themselves, by the modern Mexican people, or by Mexican-Americans (and indeed most other Latinx people in the United States), who remain always *on the way*, always *in between* cultures, histories, languages, and nations.

One philosopher who recovered this concept is Elsa Cecilia Frost (1928–2005). Frost recounts Durán's story and takes it a step further, proposing that *nepantla* makes sense of not just the in-betweenness of the Indigenous people but also the in-betweenness of the colonizers. Matteo was not the only one "in between" a Spanish future and an Indigenous past; in a similar way, so was Durán. The friar, says Frost, was between his Spanish past and his Mexican future. As Frost sees it, the early Spanish colonists began to experience a transition similar to what was being experienced by the Indigenous peoples—a transition to an unknown and uncertain cultural future. By the time the Spanish friars and soldiers realized what was happening to them, the process of *nepantla*—of being in-between—was well underway.

Recalling Durán's account, Frost imagines the Indigenous Matteo as secretly recognizing that he was not the only one who was *nepantla*. As Frost says, "the indigenous man knew that he was in a better situation than Durán, who did not even know that *the Spanish were also* nepantla."[4] She continues, "The colony was inhabited by Indians who no longer thought of themselves as such and Spaniards who slowly ceased being so. Both different from their parents and, at the same time, creators of a new way of living that in the last instance is what we call culture."

A straightforward historical example of how the Spanish became *nepantla* is related to food. When they first arrived, the Spanish refused to eat Indigenous foods. As time went on, they grudgingly came around to eating them so long as they could add European spices. There came a time, however, when what they were eating was neither Indigenous nor Spanish but something in between, a hybrid food that borrowed from both. This mixing of cuisines would go on for some time; indeed, the process continues to this day, in Mexico and globally. Today, Mexican food (the hybrid) is in a constant state of transition, always changing, always on the way to becoming new or other.

A more complicated example is Roman Catholicism. While the goal of the earliest Spanish missionaries may have been to rapidly convert their new subjects to an orthodox version of Christianity, it was not easy to convince a population with a rich and ancient spiritual tradition to change allegiances. Catholicism itself had to change to meet this challenge or risk failing in its evangelizing mission. The most striking example of this change was the sudden inclusion into the Catholic faith of the Virgin of Guadalupe in 1531, ten years after Cortés conquered the Aztec capital. A cursory review of Aztec cosmology shows that the Virgin of Guadalupe bears a striking resemblance to the native goddess of earth and corn, Tonantzin (Nahuatl for "our mother"). In fact, the purported place of her apparition is the same place venerated by the Aztecs as the home of that same goddess, the Hill of Tepeyac. Whether or not the Virgin was introduced intentionally by the Catholic church as a strategy to lure Indigenous peoples hesitant to convert to Catholicism is beside the point. The fact is that it had that effect. Thus, when my mother, a Catholic, asks God to intervene on her behalf, she implores Guadalupe and not, as the Pope would prefer, Jesus. And so, Catholicism *in Mexico* most definitely changed, proving that it, too, was in a state of *nepantla*, in between cultures and traditions, uncommitted to one specific tradition or orthodoxy. In fact, in Mexico Catholicism is still changing and adapting to meet the needs of the circumstance. In recent times, for instance, Mexican Catholicism has adopted some very strange "saints," such as Jesús Malverde, the patron saint of narcotraffickers, and La Santa Muerte, the patron saint of death and the downtrodden.

A less complicated way to understand what Frost is saying is by thinking about culture itself. A culture that borrows from other cultures can become a third thing, a *nepantla* culture. This is a transitional culture, a culture that is not static but dynamic, always in a state of change and always on the way to becoming something else. In our day, Mexican-American, Asian-American, Irish-American, Italian-American, and Filipino-American cultures are *nepantla* cultures: cultures in between cultures, appearing always as if in transition from one tradition to another, but never fully one or the other. Mexican-American culture is conscious of itself as transitional, as always in the process of becoming "American" while never quite getting there. To be Mexican-American is to exist in an indeterminate zone between a Mexican historical inheritance and the promise of the "American way of life." As a Mexican-American, I watch myself always moving further and further away from that inheritance (linguistically, in the practice of cultural customs, in the naming of children, and so on) yet never getting close to the

"American" ideal. My experience is one of movement, transition, adaptation, and more transition.

Ultimately, what Frost adds to an understanding of *nepantla* is reach. *Nepantla* is experienced not only by those who are caught in the middle of things (of times, of countries, of laws, of history), but also by those who have to deal with them. Although my mom is *nepantla*, having her toes firmly planted in both a herbalist past and a pharmaceutical present while not truly occupying either, so perhaps is her doctor, for whom speaking Spanish has become a necessity. I've always wondered if he went home right after his encounter with my mother and considered whether, in fact, a potato could suck out fevers.

Father Durán seems to have understood *nepantla* as just another excuse available to the Indigenous people to *not* do what was required of them, and this annoyed him. As far as he was concerned, saying "I am *nepantla*" was a stalling tactic, a way to delay assimilation for one more day. He wasn't wrong. At least for the Indigenous peoples, being "in-between" meant that they could practice rituals belonging to their old ways while already living in their new colonial condition. Moreover, being "neutral" with respect to any one way of living gave them time to figure out how to exist in this "new" world, one constructed atop the ruins of the "old."

Ultimately, Durán believed that *nepantla* was a strategy of resistance, but not in a good way. Rather, to him it was a symptom of a greater evil, one keeping the Indigenous people at a distance from their own salvation (in Christ). Angrily, he calls them "miserable" and "perplexed" (*perplejos*), which is to say confused, perhaps thickheaded. But, he says, in their thickheadedness they are also "*sutil y mañoso*," or "subtle and conniving."[5] Avoiding their responsibilities by claiming to still be *on the way*, in-between, or *nepantla* is proof of their conniving subtlety.

But there are two ways of understanding the charge that someone is *sutil y mañoso*. We can translate the term *mañoso* either negatively or positively. Negatively, it can be translated as "conniving," which insinuates that the person is deceitful or sneaky. One is advised to keep an eye on them, as what they do is always self-serving and suspect—they are not to be trusted. More positively, we can translate it as "cunning," which suggests that the person is crafty and wily and has developed certain *habits* (*mañas*) useful in achieving certain ends in unorthodox or unfamiliar ways—you can count on these *mañosos* to get things done!

Durán understands *nepantla* as a *maña* in the negative sense of "ploy" or "deceit." This negative identification continues in modern-day Mexico, in Mexican-American and Latinx life in the United States, and in many other populations in our own time for whom *nepantla* is a way of existence. Our *maña*, cunning, or craftiness is often misidentified as deviousness, making it easier to marginalize or disparage us (much as Durán depreciated the Indigenous people). This negative reading is inscribed in an ideology of domination, but one that we need not accept. We may instead read *maña* in a positive sense as "cleverness," and thus as a strategy of self-preservation and resistance available to those existing in between worlds or cultures, or indeed between past and future catastrophes. The imperative for us, and also for you, is this: *Let us be* mañosos!

To be *nepantla* is simply to be in the middle of a process, whatever that process may be. Understood in this simple way, we can say that most human beings are *nepantla*. We find ourselves constantly in between ways of life, in between traditions, in between dramatic paradigm shifts. The looming threat of environmental catastrophe reminds us that we as a species currently sit somewhere between a livable and a toxic world. We are all always on the way to more technology, less breathable air, and greater social divisions.

To recognize that we are (*still*) *nepantla* is thus to recognize that we are on the way to a completely unknowable future. This is frightening. But it also means that we don't have to commit to any one way of life or set way of relating to people, things, or ideologies. Depending on the circumstance, we should all be *mañosos*, or cunning. We must navigate this life aware that we are always in the process of transition and therefore free to change our minds about those things that will have the greatest effect on our persons—aware, that is, that we are not stuck on this or that commitment, but instead free to allow ourselves the simple luxury of becoming who we may become.

4 | YOU ARE YOUR CIRCUMSTANCE

The history of philosophy is filled with pithy one-liners: "One cannot step into the same river twice" (Heraclitus), "The only true wisdom consists in knowing that you know nothing" (Socrates), "I think, therefore I am" (Descartes), "Whatever cannot be said must be passed over in silence" (Wittgenstein), and "Man is born free, but everywhere he is in chains" (Rousseau), to cite but a few.

Of course, these phrases are remembered not only because they're terse and crisp; they represent, in fact, profound insights into the secrets of the human condition. Philosophers cite them constantly and dedicate books to unpacking what they mean. But they have also inspired or provided insight for many a nonphilosopher, even those unfamiliar with who said them or why. Socrates' insight, for instance, pops ups regularly in popular culture to remind us that those among us who claim to know everything aren't really wise, while Heraclitus's observation can still fill us with dread at the thought that, yes, he's right, everything is constantly changing.

An insight that inspired a generation of Mexican thinkers comes from the Spanish philosopher José Ortega y Gasset (1883–1955). In his *Meditations on Quixote*, written in 1914, Ortega set down the following: "I am myself and my circumstance, and if I don't save it, I don't save myself."[1] Standing in contrast to the more general insights proposed by Socrates and Rousseau and the abstract truism of Descartes's famous "Cogito ergo sum," Ortega's words are an injunction to return to one's immediate, lived situation so as to find out who one really is. While it is as universal as many other world-famous philosophical maxims, its message is actually a denial of universality—a reminder that what has the most impact on a person's life is his or her particular environment. It tells us that what is truly meaningful about one's life is not something intangible but rather something concrete: namely, the place where one stands, the everyday details of one's situation, those things that create one's identity in context. In a brief, illuminating phrase, it describes the nature of one's identity (which is a marriage of *self* and *circumstance*) and also what one needs to do on its behalf—namely, "save it," or preserve it by understanding it, advocating for it, or loving it.

Centuries after Mexico's conquest and colonization, and in the decades after its Revolution, Mexican philosophers were hungry to forge a new identity for themselves, while also preserving the identity that linked them to Mexico's past. For them, Ortega's maxim, which we can also think of as a guiding principle, served as fertile soil out of which an entire philosophical orientation would grow and thrive. Drawing inspiration from Ortega's powerful words, a concern for one's identity and one's circumstance would become the hallmark of Mexican philosophy in the twentieth century.

I cannot overstate the impact of Ortega's seemingly obvious observation that the circumstance in which one finds oneself matters a great deal. The key to understanding its impact lies in how we think of "circumstance." Ortega tells us that the word is Latin in origin, a mash-up of *circum* and *stantia*, and refers to things that *stand around*. So the mountains, the streets, the forests, the sky, the earth . . . these are all "circumstance." But "circumstance" is also language, existing knowledge, culture, tradition, history, prejudice, authority, and so on. So circumstance is *everything* around us—the totality of our habitat, our home, and our world.

Referring to this key principle in his work, I designate Ortega's philosophy as a "circumstantialism." Even before it found its way to Mexico, this idea had already paid dividends for a generation of Spanish philosophers who sought a way to justify their own Spanish way of philosophizing, their own Spanishness. It provided a way to account for the influence that place—the very specific place that one happens to occupy in the world—has on the construction of consciousness and identity.

During the 1930s, a number of Spanish philosophers fleeing Spain's Civil War sought refuge in Mexico. Among these was a former student of Ortega, José Gaos (1900–1969). Teaching at the National University of Mexico, Gaos professed that one's circumstance can do more than shape one's identity—it can also ground a unique and authentic philosophy or worldview. This was, indeed, something that Mexican philosophers had sought since gaining independence more than a century earlier. (The irony here is, of course, that having gained independence from Spain in the early part of the nineteenth century, they would now look to Spain to gain philosophical independence, and that the core of

that philosophy would be a stress on the importance of one's specific situation—a place-specific philosophy imported from former
colonizing power to former colony!)

Because a disembodied, abstract, "view from nowhere" approach to philosophizing was unlikely to gain traction among a
people with historically and socially pressing concerns, Ortega's
circumstantialism (as introduced to Mexico by Gaos) was welcomed as a breath of fresh air. Mexican philosophers in general,
but especially those who gathered around Gaos, adopted and
adapted the principle of circumstance and allowed themselves to
believe that philosophy could be earthly, historical, and responsive to their needs. We see this adoption and adaptation time
and again and in different ways in the early works of Mexican
philosophers like Samuel Ramos (1897–1959), Jorge Portilla
(1919–1963), Rosario Castellanos (1925–1974), and Emilio
Uranga, and more recently in the twenty-first-century writings
of Guillermo Hurtado (b. 1962) and Mario Teodoro Ramírez
(b. 1958).

Leopoldo Zea's (1912–2004) interpretation of it, however,
stands out. Early on, in 1945, he reads circumstantialism in the
following way:

> The truth of each individual or generation is nothing more
> than the expression of a determinate conception of the world
> and of life. This means that philosophical truths, as attempted
> solutions to the problems of life, are circumstantial, each one
> dependent on the individual that expresses them, and thus
> in turn, on a determinate society, a determinate historical
> epoch, or, in one word, on a circumstance.[2]

What Zea is saying here is that what a particular group of people designate as "truth" will be true because it answers a particular question or addresses a particular worry arising out of, or attached to, the circumstance belonging to that particular group. This doesn't mean that "truth" will necessarily be different for that group of people than for another group of people, since two groups of people can share the same truth, but only that *the truths they value* will allow them to make sense of their own reality or corner of the world. So circumstantialism is not a sort of relativism in which what is "true" *here* is incompatible with what is true *there*. If what is true in *that* circumstance solves worries for this circumstance, then that truth can also be true in *this* circumstance. The important thing, according to Zea, is that what is true for us is that which is a "solution" that solves a problem in the circumstance in which we live.

In the same essay, Zea points out that not only truth but *all philosophy* is entrenched in a circumstance. Historically, philosophers have avoided thinking that it is. But Socrates spoke from and through his cultural and social situation, as did Heraclitus and Rousseau, even if they masked their circumstance in various ways. Greek philosophy, French philosophy, and German philosophy are all, in their own way, respectively Greek, French, and German. But the circumstantial nature of those philosophies has never been an issue, and Zea rightly points out that their claim to universality has always gone unquestioned. It has always been dogmatically assumed that what they say is true for all and true without question, even to those outside their circumstance.

The nondogmatic view about this states that we are all embedded in and intersected by our circumstance. Mexican philosophers like Zea and his contemporaries built a philosophical tradition on that principle, affirming the circumstantialism of their thinking. The very "truth" of each "individual or generation," says Zea, "is nothing more than the expression" of the circumstance. For this reason, Zea concludes, it makes sense to talk about a "Mexican" philosophy, as this will be nothing more than the expression of everything that makes up the Mexican circumstance.

To conceive of oneself as endowed with the ability, capacity, and opportunity to speak philosophically from one's unique place in the world is a challenge to the historical restrictions that deemed philosophy as strictly a Western practice, rooted in Greece and intimately wedded to the historical unfolding of European history. Again, this is an empowering and liberatory idea, as it allows us to insert other experiences and other histories into the narrative. Another way to say this is that the move to characterize philosophy as circumstantial can be seen as a way to affirm the right of non-European peoples to philosophy, even if it had its roots in the words of a European philosopher. This is a right to a view of philosophy as liberated of the Western demand for abstract, impersonal, and alienating universality.

The fact is that for centuries Latin American philosophers were subjected to a type of philosophical colonialism that reflected the political and economic colonialism of the times. Since the conquest and the colonization, there had not been an original or authentic Mexican philosophy in the New World. Imported philosophical systems, systems that did not reflect either the Mexican circumstance or its crises, had been brought to the Americas to solve problems that they were not equipped to solve. Philosophers had adopted these foreign systems without question, and the result was that Mexican philosophers had spent the better part of 500 years merely thinking through the ideals and conceptual registers of their European ancestors. But Ortega's circumstantialist principle allowed Zea to propose the notion that an original, authentic, Mexican philosophy is possible only when it is rooted in Mexican history, cultures, traditions, languages, and traumas.

There is, of course, an elephant in the room. The elephant is this: Isn't circumstantialism, which comes from Ortega, a Spaniard, another type of philosophical colonialism? The answer is no, not if what is adopted and adapted is just this principle. Circumstantialism has been adopted in the New World without adopting other (social, political, or philosophical) commitments to which Ortega's philosophy may have been committed, and it has been adapted to reflect the particularities of Mexican history and culture. What we have, then, is a philosophical principle filled out by the Mexican experience that also reflects the way in which it can serve to give voice to the voiceless, or, in the present case, to justify a people's right to philosophy.

Ultimately, Mexican philosophy teaches us to be circumstantialists without resorting to a shortsighted relativism or a conceited nationalism. This circumstantialism will not be relativistic or conceited because, while it will be anchored to the ground beneath our feet, it will always lend itself to other times, other peoples, and other circumstances seeking a voice or a justification for philosophy. As it lends itself to us, now.

☙❧

Ortega's circumstantialist "principle" is often condensed to the phrase, "I am myself plus my circumstance." But we can't forget that there's more to it; the oft-repeated part is only a fragment. The rest says: "and if I cannot save it, I cannot save myself."[3]

Let us unpack this. For starters, the principle is formulated like an equation, in which the "I am" is the sum total of a "self" and the self's "circumstance" (myself + circumstance = I am). This suggests that the "myself" is something other than the "I am." That is, if the "myself" is not yet an "I am," and the "I am" is the capacity to think, love, fight, work, and so on, then the "myself" is something like the bare fact of my existing. Secondly, if the "myself" is the bare fact of existing—simple vital energy—and it only becomes an "I am" after the addition of the "circumstance," then the important stuff that makes the "I am" is added by the "circumstance." This means, moreover, that the circumstance contributes the content for the bare existence of the "myself." And thirdly, the second part of the principle says that if the circumstance cannot be "saved," then the "myself" cannot be saved. This simply points back to the essential connection between myself and the circumstance that produce the "I am." We can summarize it this way: I must save my circumstance if I am to save my bare existence and be a proper moral person.

But what does it mean to "save" the circumstance? The charge here is not to change the circumstance but to "save" it. Notice that you can "save" a certain something without changing it. If a toddler is struggling in the pool and about to drown, I can jump in and save her. I take her out and, once on dry ground, she will probably go back to running around the pool. I didn't change her, and she can continue as she was. Or we can think about "saving" in another sense: namely, that of safeguarding something. You safeguard a prized possession by protecting it from thieves, from the elements, or from a fire. To safeguard your circumstance is to protect it in this way, to prevent its annihilation or its ruin. Or, finally, you can save something by restoring it, reviving it, or reenergizing it. The sixteenth-century mansion was saved when new owners restored its crumbling façade, applied new paint, retrofitted the foundations, and so on. Now people can book it on Airbnb. In all three cases, to save something is to act on its behalf. So the principle tells us to act on behalf of *our* circumstance. The benefit of doing so, it tells us, is that doing this will also benefit us.

But while we are taking apart the layers of meaning of this important phrase, we can't miss a crucial implication. If we think of the air we breathe, the planet's temperature, the thickness or thinness of the ozone layer, and so on, as part of *our* circumstance, it becomes clear that allowing its ruin will bring about our own. According to circumstantialism, we *are* the air we breathe and the ozone layer; without them, there is no "I am" or "self." So in order to save myself I must save them.

Now, what is the point of all this? The more general point is that the circumstance matters and to ignore it in our philosophical accounts—and in how we think about our lives—is to sacrifice what is most essential to our very existence. The more specific point is that caring for your circumstance involves listening to it, thinking about it, and speaking on its behalf. I could spend the entire day lost at work, debugging complex systems, waitressing, teaching English to immigrant children, and so on, while not once paying any mind to my surroundings, to my circumstance. This being "lost at work" means that I've *lost track of* both myself and my circumstance. The worst part is that, in losing myself, I forget to take care of my mental and physical health, and forget to enjoy life or other people; and in losing my circumstance, I forget to advocate for my friends and family, to fight for justice, or to care for the environment. Only in listening, thinking, and speaking for my circumstance do I find myself, as my people and my environment are intimately tied to one another.

Therefore, the instruction is simple: make sure not to lose track of your specific place in the world. More generally, make sure that your thoughts and actions respond to the demands of the circumstance, to what this circumstance says when you listen to it.

Someone may object: My circumstance is fine—it's my thinking that's got me all tied up in knots! Well, again, one's thinking and one's circumstance are intertwined in such a way that they are reflections of one another. In order to change one's thinking, one must change one's circumstance, and in order to change one's circumstance, one must change one's thinking. Neither takes priority over the other.

This simple idea may seem obvious. But it is not. What will always be obvious is the priority of the ego, the self, the "I am"—the importance of *the thinking thing*. Mexican philosophers sought to invert this and prioritize the circumstance, while deprioritizing the self by highlighting its dependence, its finitude, and—as we will be discussing more later on—its accidentality.

Philosophers, most notably René Descartes, have suggested that human thinking can be pure, certain, and infallible when it is grounded only on itself. This is a rejection of the influence of history, geography, and the world, and a prioritizing of the mind as the source of all knowledge. Descartes's famous statement "I think, therefore I am" captures this view. Against Descartes, Ortega argues for the inconceivability of the sort of disengaged reason that ignores the significance of history, culture, and geography in any account of human existence. Against the pure, ahistorical, and detached *Cogito ergo sum*, Ortega proposes that thinking and circumstance—that is, those things that make up the world that is particular to each one of us—are inseparable from one another, and that one cannot exist without the other.

Ortega proposes that the circumstance is the launching pad for our most ambitious aspirations. He writes: "My natural exit toward the universe is through the mountain passes of Guadarrama or the plain of Ontígola. This sector of my circumstantial reality forms the other half of my person; only through it can I integrate myself and be fully myself."[4] That is, my thinking, my philosophy, my understanding of the cosmos and my place in it, are filtered through that space that I occupy and that informs and "forms the other half of my person." The circumstantialist principle thus asks us to be aware of where we stand, to take inventory and stock of our surroundings, to know *who* we are based on *where* we are, and—once we know this—to recalibrate our relationships to our community, the environment, and truth in a way that reflects the needs of and opportunities afforded by the circumstance.

With this, Zea (echoing Ortega) affirms the notion of a subject immersed in and completed by his or her particular circumstance, one that includes, among other things, his or her specific geographical space and history, but also the air, the whales off Monterey Bay, and the Arctic ice caps. The circumstance, then, can be small (my particular community) or big (the planet), depending on how I allow myself to understand it. For instance, when I think of my own circumstance, it comprises the farmworker community in California, Mexican-American culture, the history of my parents' immigrant struggles, the history of philosophy, my moral and political values, the ozone layer, the Pacific Ocean, and the people that I care for and love. I will interpret the world through my circumstance, and what I say will be meaningful and impactful because of that.

5 | YOU ARE ACCIDENTAL

In one of Vicente Fernández's (1940–2021) most enduring and emblematic ballads, "El hijo del pueblo" (Son of the People), the legendary Mexican crooner celebrates his Mexicanness by proclaiming a deeply held cultural belief: he sings that he, like all Mexicans, is "a descendant of Cuauhtémoc and a Mexican by fortune" (*Mexicano por fortuna*).

This is a melancholic song overall, but this line, one of its most recognized, is saturated with history and trauma. Over the years, it has become an anthem for Mexicans wherever in the world they find themselves. As it comes on—on the car radio, at a party, over the supermarket speakers, at a bar—witness men, women, and children sing its somber verses as if it were a most intimate prayer. People drink to it, cry to it, and commune with one another as they lean into the phrase "Mexicano por fortuna . . . ."

In this line, the protagonist reaffirms an Indigenous descendancy from the last Aztec emperor, who on being captured and tortured by the Spanish, was later hanged by Hernán Cortés , the Spanish conquistador responsible for the brutal destruction of México-Tenochtitlán in 1521. The murder of Cuauhtémoc at the hands of Cortés signals the fall of the Aztec empire and the rise of Spanish colonial rule. Hernán Cortés' brutal treatment

of Cuauhtémoc prefigures the subjugation and dehumaniza-
tion of the rest of the Indigenous population at the hands of the
conquerors—especially of Indigenous women, who were raped or
killed in alarming numbers. The brutality of these events, particularly the sexual exploitation of Indigenous women, would bring
about the modern Mexican.

In the song, the phrase "Mexican by fortune" has a double significance. On the one hand, it means that Mexicans are a product
of luck and might not have appeared in history had things been
different. If only Cuauhtémoc had put up more resistance, his
hundred-thousand-man army would have easily defeated Cortés
and his rugged band of hundreds. As a result, the sexual violence
that produced the modern Mexican would not have occurred.
In this sense, being Mexican by fortune is just being a product of
the worst sort of luck! On the other hand, it also means that despite the violence that produced them, Mexicans are a product of
good fortune. In this reappropriation of the Mexican origin story,
Mexicans express pride in having survived and persevered in spite
of their origins and in spite of how they've been treated. They
reappropriate this act of luck and the suffering and the subjugation attached to it for the sake of pride *and* unity. "This is why I'm
so proud," continues Fernández, "of being from the most humble
barrio," because here, in his barrio, which is part of his circumstance, everyone is fortunate in the same way. "Fortune," then,
doesn't point to Cuauhtémoc's miscalculation or the violence
that followed, or to "the worst of luck," but to a profound sense of
belonging. And so, when I listen to "El hijo del pueblo," the phrase
"Mexicano por fortuna" immediately transports me mentally into

a community of my compatriots, where we are "fortunate" to be Mexican together.

Fernández's notion of "fortune" is reflected in Emilio Uranga's "philosophy of accidentality."

∽∾

Accidentality is the central concept in Uranga's philosophy. In his *Analysis of Mexican Being* (*Análisis del ser del mexicano*), he writes: "the being of the human being as accidental is the most important affirmation that we make."[1] Uranga insists upon accidentality as what defines the "being" of the Mexican, or *how Mexicans exist*. But accidentality also defines any being—any existence—that is temporal and concrete. "The concrete," he says, "is the accidental,"[2] and vice versa.

What does it mean to be accidental? It means that your existence is not necessary. Or, that you did not have to exist. Yet here you are. It means that you are a product, or a bi-product, of luck, chance, fortune, or maybe grace. It also means that your being here is not guaranteed, that the ground you stand on is, Uranga says, "unstable quicksand" that may swallow you up at any moment.[3] In short, to be accidental is to exist precariously.

Accidentality is familiar to you, but in a somewhat superficial way. You know that what you own—your car, house, phone, espresso machine—are accidental in the sense that you didn't have to own them or in the sense that they may be taken away (by a thief, a fire, bank repossession). You may also believe that where you are in life is a result of chance encounters, serendipitous decisions, or accidents the consequences of which could've gone a completely different way. In my case, there is a possible world where my parents never met, never made it to the United States, a world in which I was never born, and never wrote these words. Yet here I am, purely by accident.

A more philosophical way to understand accidentality is to think of it in relation to what philosophers call "substance." A substance is radically independent of anything else, it is self-sufficient, and it is that on which other things depend or that which makes other things possible. For Uranga, essences and ideals are substances. Thus, the European ideal of humanity is a kind of substance whereby to be accidental is to be an accident of that ideal. The implication of this is that if certain people are accidental to the ideal, then they are *less than* human, or inhuman.

But ideals are only aspirational, they are not real. In other words what is real is not substance, but accidents. This, however, has not stopped some groups of people from representing themselves as substantial, as embodying an ideal (e.g., the ideal of humanity) or being the reason as to why other peoples exist. This was the case with the Spanish during the period of colonization. Misrepresenting themselves as embodying the ideal of humanity led Mexicans, and other non-European peoples, to believe that they were *less-than* human, as inferior and inhuman. The truth is, however, that all of us are accidental, particularly in the sense that none of us is fully self-sufficient (not one of us is a fully formed substance lacking nothing); but also, in the sense that as finite, mortal creatures, we owe *what* we are and *that* we are to randomness and good fortune. In other words, none of us is substance and all of us is insufficient, accidental, and dependent on life, the planet, the universe, and each other.

It is important to keep in mind that accidentality is not a psychological attitude; it is not something one merely thinks about oneself. It is something one is. This is why thinking about accidentality is of utmost importance, because we have to rid ourselves of the illusion that some people are necessary, sufficient, and *not* accidental. According to Uranga, most people exist in this illusion.

But what makes this a Mexican idea and not just an observation about the human condition as a whole (since, after all, we are all accidental)? The answer is simple, though it will perhaps be a bit unsatisfying. This is a Mexican idea, Uranga says, because Mexicans exist in a certain "proximity to the accident," which means that Mexicans, more than most, are aware of their accidental condition. His reasoning is that peoples whose identities are born of violence, or what he calls "catastrophe," and whose history or circumstance is defined by constant peril, will think of themselves or their being as accidental or precarious or a result of fortune. People who don't see themselves born from catastrophe will perhaps say to themselves that their lives are accidental but not really mean it; it is likely to be a mental exercise, in which "accidentality" is just an intellectual idea. These people will not make accidentality a theme of their everyday thinking, assuming that their lives are somehow necessary, destined, or, as Uranga says, "substantial." But Mexicans, who are reminded of their accidentality by their history, by their music, and by their circumstance, will live as though they are, in fact, accidental, and consider necessity and substantiality as fanciful notions reserved for those who have nothing to worry about and nothing to risk. We can see here a reason for the title of this book: Mexican philosophy emerges from a thinking about a concrete reality shaped by a history of catastrophe: Mexican phi-losophy blooms in ruins.

Well, okay, you might say. But isn't it equally true that anything that anyone does—even the fact that anyone exists in the first place—is a historical accident? The fact that your parents met one another and had you, the fact that you chose the path for life that you did, perhaps based on a sequence of events that could have gone another way—can't we trace all of this back ad infinitum? Simply, yes. Welcome to accidentality. It didn't have to be the case that *any of us* existed, but we did and we do. Seemingly by chance. Existence itself, it turns out, is an accident. All of it.

This is not complicated. But the point that Uranga wants to get across is that it is one thing to recognize this fact, but quite another to *accept* it and make it part of the way we live our lives. In fact, Uranga tells us, firmly grasping life's accidentality is a healthy way to live. He wants us to recognize and accept our accidentality and *become accidental*. This means shedding all illusion to neces-sity, perfection, and the self-sufficiency that belongs to things not affected by chance or circumstance.

Recognizing and accepting your accidental condition requires conscious effort. It is not automatic: it is a *project*. Uranga calls this the *project of accidentalizing yourself*. It requires you to keep your accidentality always at the foreground of your thinking, so that you may become more aligned with the reality of your true human condition. And you must take on this project if you're tired of living inauthentically, or under the exhausting illusion that you are radically self-sufficient, morally perfect, or invincible, that is, constantly avoiding the thought of your own death. The real difficulty with taking on the project of accidentalization, however, is that it will clash with what you ordinarily believe about yourself—namely, that you are on this earth *for a reason*, that everything in your life points to its being somehow destined to be here. But, again, you must actively work at getting rid of these illusions, because the truth is that none of us can be certain about ourselves in this way: we are all accidental.

When we embrace our accidentality, we can more easily navigate a world we know to be in a constant state of becoming and transformation. We may even become comfortable with disaster, with trauma, with our own imperfections. The project of having to be accidental involves not slipping into the delusion of our own necessity and our own permanence by understanding that we are products of chance and circumstance. If we take on the project of accidentalizing ourselves, we will try to recall that our very life may be the result of an accidental encounter between two people, that we didn't have to be born—and that any one of these days could be our last day. In accidentalizing ourselves we return to our accidental origins. But perhaps this is too heavy a thought. In that case, a lighter version of this project of accidentalization will involve remembering that *all that we have*—our possessions, our careers, and our families—is revocable, that it could all be taken away at a moment's notice. A wrong turn at an intersection, a casual glance at a menacing stranger, leaving the house ten minutes early—any of these could result in the loss of all that we have or all that we are.

The lesson is this: the project of having to be accidental, or accidentalizing oneself, involves not forgetting our accidentality, in whatever degree of sophistication we can recall it. I try to keep always in mind that the person I am today is a result of many different accidents, traumas, or happenings that I was lucky to survive or live through. However, at the same time, the project also involves keeping in mind that, although I may think of myself as a *result* or *product* of those accidental encounters, and thus delude myself into thinking that the process of becoming who I am is somehow complete (because that's how we think of a "product" or a "result"), the reality is that accidents can happen at any time, accidents that have the power to change me again, and again, and again.

Early Mexican colonial history could be seen as a time when Spaniards in particular and Europeans in general minimized their own accidentality by asserting the superiority of both their race and their worldview. Key to their confidence was the belief that the conquest and the colonization were God-ordained and that their success with both proved it. Believing that one is carrying out a divine mission is a conceit that goes hand in hand with a belief in one's goodness, perfection, and necessity. Those not sharing this mission, but rather being subjugated by it—which in America included Indigenous people, African slaves, and hybrid Mexican mestizos—were treated as inferior and disposable, even though saving the souls of these peoples was ostensibly meant to be of utmost importance to their Christian conquerors.

It was easy, then, for the Spanish to think of themselves as defined not by accident or finitude but by substance—by permanence, objectivity, righteousness, and necessity—while considering those they conquered as accidental, as not meeting the ideal of humanity, and thus as not truly human. Of course, non-Spaniards (especially the Indigenous peoples of Mexico, African slaves, and mixed race mestizos) eventually internalized this disdain, reading their human accidentality as inferiority. And this played into the colonizing mission, because colonialism prefers subjects with inferiority complexes—subjects who believe themselves to be unworthy or undeserving of good things or good treatment. Oppressive systems demand subjects who recognize themselves as subservient and inferior, and who believe, at the same time, in the superiority of their opposites. Colonialism needs its subjects to exist vulnerably, as perpetually threatened by erasure or extermination.

However, those who recognize their accidentality don't have to accept the worldview that puts them at the bottom of the power totem pole. They don't have to accept their subjugation. Knowing that their sense of inferiority is an illusion, one that hides a more *human* contingency, can become a source of power, which can set people on the path to challenging the way things are. This is all part of what it means to take up the project of accidentalization, and why it was such an important idea for Mexicans in particular.

So Uranga proposes that one "choose accidentality" so as to be true to oneself. For Mexicans, choosing accidentality means choosing, as he puts it, "the negation of Spanishness which presents itself as 'substantial.'"[4] For the rest of us, choosing accidentality means choosing the negation of anything that presents itself as perfect, self-sufficient, and necessary. Nothing *has to* be the way that it is. Ideas, cultures, politics—all are up for radical rethinking and change once you realize the accidentality at their core.

In an abstract sense, there are reasons to believe that *who I am* and *what I am* have been determined by fate or necessity. After all, in spite of all obstacles and challenges, *here I am*! A led to B, and B led to C, and A, B, and C were necessary moments that made D inevitable. Or I could believe that God, in His infinite mercy, grace, and goodness has determined my life in such a way that who I am and what I am is exactly as He intended it. So, yes, reasons are available to me to believe that such things as my identity, my profession, and my future have been and will continue to be just as they were always bound to be. But there are also reasons to believe that who I am and what I am have been a matter of accident or fortune. That I have not been determined by necessity or divine fate, but by randomness and chance. That as a product of randomness and chance, or accident, my entire existence, my identity, my profession, and even my race and the culture could have been otherwise.

The problem with thinking that our very existence is accidental is that we must also consider the possibility that there's no point to our lives. There is no predetermination to my existence, I am not here *for a reason*, so why even continue—what's the point? There are two possible reactions to this question when it comes up: either we retreat back to the illusion and re-substantialize ourselves, or we rush toward the likelihood of our accidentality, dedicating our lives to making *something* of the accident. To substantialize ourselves is to forget our accidentality and comfortably sink back into the idea of our own necessity, to the idea that says, "I was always meant to be here." To rush toward the idea, to take on the project of having to be accidental, is to remain uncomfortable, vigilant, and always ready for change—to exist in the idea that says, "I'm not sure what's next."

But, so long as everything is going well—with job, family, politics, sports teams—we don't have to worry about our accidentality. When all is well, we feel substantial, independent, necessary. There is no room or time in our productive, important lives for questioning how fragile each aspect of our lives really is—how it all could have been entirely different. However, with the loss of a job, a divorce, bankruptcy, or a missed opportunity, a consciousness of accidentality returns in full force, usually in the form of the "what ifs": *What if I'd only had a different attitude at work? Then I'd still have my job. What if I had been more attentive to my partner? Then they wouldn't have had an affair, and I wouldn't be asking for a divorce. What if I had majored in Computer Science? . . . What if I'd invested in Google back in 2001? . . .* And so on.

The what-ifs are a superficial way to recognize our accidentality. But it is when the what-ifs begin to circulate in our minds that we begin to feel the uncomfortableness of our true condition. We begin to realize, if only in passing, that nothing about life is necessary. A more profound realization would be to admit that, for years, we've ignored that which makes us genuinely human: namely, that who and what we are is a result of randomness and fortune (good or bad). And maybe that's not the worst thing. If anything, it will keep us on our toes for whatever comes next.

~⚬~

No one is surprised when the sons or daughters of a famous actor become actors themselves. My guess is that they aren't surprised either; it is as if they are *meant* to follow in some existing footsteps. Similarly, no one wonders when the son or daughter of intellectuals becomes an intellectual. I know of a number of philosophers, for instance, whose parents were philosophers. These folks are usually very sure of their career choice and confident of what they know. They've known they wanted to be philosophers since they were children; it is as if they were *meant* to be philosophers, and their whole life is aimed at living up to that expectation—perhaps surpassing it.

My parents were immigrant farmworkers from Mexico. I learned to read and write English when I was seventeen. I went to an underperforming high school and a state college. My grades were not that great. Now that I am a philosophy professor, I am often confronted with the question: Why did I choose academia, and why philosophy? The insinuation here is that, as a Mexican-American, as the son of immigrant parents, as a first-generation college student, and so on, this course of study *should not have been an option*. My answer is usually given in the form of an account that begins, *"Well, it just so happened that"* this and that happened. . . .

I suspect that sons and daughters of philosophy professors don't get asked this question. Why? Because they fit the mold. They are destined. They are chosen. In their determination, they are somehow substantial.

I am accidental. That I am a philosophy professor is an accident. And I know this. More significantly, it is important that I know this, if for no other reason than that knowing this keeps me vigilant. In my own life, I have adopted an attitude of accidentality.

Vigilance is the practice of this attitude. I am vigilant not to conform too confidently to my role, not to take it for granted. If I feel twinges of entitlement, privilege, or elitism, I seek to catch and correct them quickly.

To adopt an attitude of accidentality is to commit to care for my circumstance, for those that I love, for my health, for my work, since I know that everything stands on an unstable foundation that could crumble at any moment. To be vigilant is not to be fearful or paranoid about losing it all, though. Rather, to be vigilant is to care for and love what I have now, with the knowledge that accidentality is the natural condition of things. It is to believe that *it is my fortune* to be who and what I am.

6 | YOU ARE A SINGULARITY

My mother's *mole* is the absolute best. I'm not exaggerating when I say this; it just has the perfect blend of spices, tomatillos, red chilis, pork fat, and flour. She's been making it the same way for decades, and she says it's a recipe passed down from her mother, who got it from her mother, and so on. She makes it for me whenever I visit, and I dread eating *mole* anywhere else. Other *moles* just aren't as good.

Puebla, Mexico, is known the world over for its *mole*. I had to try their version when I visited some years ago, and I hated it. It was sweet. It tasted like chocolate. I asked the cook why it tasted so chocolaty, and he said, "because it has chocolate in it." *Chocolate*?! Why? I asked, and he responded authoritatively, "Because that's how you make *mole*!" I asked around, and, sure enough, *that's how you make mole*!

So what was my mother making my entire life? Why was she calling it *mole* if it wasn't *mole*? I asked her. She said, "There's a lot of ways to make it"—regional ways, that is—"and this is how *I* make it. You want it or not?" Of course I wanted it.

Since then, I've had many discussions with foodies of all stripes and most assure me that what my mom makes is *probably* mole. More likely, however, what she's making is some type of chili concoction or her own brand of Mexican spicy curry. But if it is *mole,* the question becomes whether there is an "essence" to *mole* against which my mother's *mole* comes up short.

It turns out that there are so many different kinds of *mole* that it would be hard to pin down this "essence." Regardless, does that "essence" really matter to my mother? I don't think so. The idea that, should such an essence or standard exist, my mother's *mole* then stops being *mole* seems crazy to me. But if I insist on calling it *mole,* is the idea then that it is simply falling short of some established universal standard?

I think that what my mother calls *mole* really is *mole,* just different, reflective of where she learned it, who taught her to make it, and her own tastes. That it fails to meet a certain standard doesn't bother her, or me; whether it may bother *mole* purists is another question. But then, we have to imagine that the essence used by *mole* purists is also reflective of some environment, some tradition, and some tastes, in which case talking about essences just becomes ridiculous and accomplishes nothing.

A number of Mexican philosophers think about essences in a similar way; just as there is no one fixed thing that is *mole* but only a lot of different variations, by region and even by family, the essence of a thing or a concept is likewise not fixed. As with my mother's *mole,* ideas, practices, achievements, and even philosophy are thought to be connected, in an intimate, personal way, to environment, to tradition, and to *history* (though perhaps not to tastes). Essences are historical. This is connected to the idea that, for

Mexican philosophers, what is real is what is accidental, circumstantial, rooted in time and place. This is counter to what the history of Western philosophy insists on: namely, that what is real are substances, ideas, and universals. For instance, the essence of what it means to be human: If a kind of existence does not resemble that essence, then according to many in the Western tradition it is not human or is less than human. Based on what we remember of Mexican history and the way that for hundreds of years Mexican people were treated as less than human, it's no surprise that Mexican philosophers are suspicious of such essentializations—and of essences in general.

The Mexican Leopoldo Zea addressed the belief, common amongst Mexicans themselves, that a Mexican philosophy will always simply be a "bad copy" of European philosophy. This belief is grounded on the presumption of the authenticity of European philosophy, the presumption that it is the *ideal* or *essence* of all philosophy, and that any deviation from it, any difference between it and a foreign set of beliefs reveals that the latter is either non-philosophy or a forgery. Zea gives us the following insight:

> [W]e have to go to the history of our philosophy from another point of view. That other point of view must [look at] our incapacity to make nothing else but bad copies of the European models.... However, simply being a bad copy does not make [our philosophy] necessarily bad, but merely distinct.... To recognize that we cannot realize the same systems as those found in European philosophy is not to recognize that we are inferior to the authors of that philosophy; it is only to recognize that we are different.[1]

Here, Zea considers a principal bias against a uniquely "Mexican" philosophy: namely, that as *philosophy* it is merely a "bad copy" of European philosophy. His response is worth repeating: "being a bad copy does not make [our philosophy] necessarily bad, but merely distinct."

There is an implicit bias at work in the Western conception of philosophy: namely, that philosophy that originates in the "First World" represents the "essence" of philosophy and everything else is just a copy, even a bad copy that can't measure up. To overcome this bias, we must adopt "another point of view," says Zea, one in which Mexican philosophy, just like my mother's *mole*, is not a "bad copy" of the essence but rather simply different or *other*.

Again, the way we conceive of wrongness or bad "copies" is always relative to the authority of the essence or the ideal. But this authority is always bound up with existing power relations relative to a culture or tradition; thus, what is thought of as the "essence" of something such as philosophy or humanity will depend on who it is who has the power to make such determinations—for instance, Europeans during the period of colonization. Recognizing that the essence is relative in this way, we can then say, with Zea, that simply because we are doing something in a different way does not mean that we are doing it wrong or badly. In being a copy or instantiation of some purported essence or standard, our way is not bad but "merely distinct"—simply a different way to do things. The example of my mother's *mole* illustrates the value of this idea, but there are other, more existentially relevant cases in which thinking this way could be helpful.

I myself have often felt like a bad copy, and *out of place*. This usually happens when I find myself in situations where I question my belonging—in moments when I feel my difference. Feeling like a bad copy is not an easy feeling to work through, especially when it's followed by the thought that I don't belong where I am because I'm a fake, an impostor who will soon be unmasked. During my first committee meeting as a faculty member at my university, I was suddenly struck by the thought that I had no business being a faculty member at all. As my colleagues engaged in a discussion about course requirements, calendars, and student learning objectives, I could only focus on the fact that I was the only person of color in the room. The others spoke to each other with a certain authority, or privilege, that was both intimidating and impressive. I didn't say a word, as I was frozen in fear—the fear of being found out, the fear of being discovered as a charlatan, a bad copy of what a professor is supposed to be like or what a professor is supposed to say. I was questioning myself, my credentials, my knowledge. I left that meeting without having contributed once to the discussion.

That semester, I read Zea's essay for the first time. I found comfort in the distinction he makes between something being a bad copy and being merely distinct. I told myself that was not a bad copy of what a professor was supposed to sound like or look like, but merely a variation on an old theme. I wasn't an impostor; I was just *not like them*. And while my contributions would be distinct, they would still be meaningful. I made sure to leave my mark on every committee meeting after that.

Or consider a more dramatic example. My cousin Felix went to prison when he was sixteen years old for a gang-related crime. The state decided to make an example out of him, and so they sentenced him to twenty-five years. He served the first nine at juvenile detention centers, the rest in state penitentiaries. He was released at the age of forty-one. Upon his release, the judge advised him to be a "model citizen" or risk getting sent back to the penitentiary. Felix had no idea how to be a "model citizen," nor had he any idea of the minimum requirements to achieve that status. He struggled to fit in, and he felt uncomfortable being in public. He watched television and social media trying to figure out how to be "normal." It was a struggle just to leave his house, since everywhere he felt like a fraud, a bad copy falling short of the model. We spoke one summer night and he confessed that he could never be a model citizen and should just be put back in prison, "where I belong." I asked him what it meant to be a model citizen and he could only think of one characteristic of such a person: "he's not a criminal." For the next few months, we spoke often about "model citizens" and how they did not exist. I reminded him that what the judge meant when he instructed him to be one was only that he should live a life within the bounds of the law. I told him that no one outside the prison walls is a model citizen, and that what's great about being "free" is that we all get a chance at being who we are capable of being.

In the years since, Felix has gotten more comfortable with being his unique brand of human. He's funny, hardworking, introspective, and filled with a certain sort of wisdom—a wisdom earned in solitary confinement and nights without hope. Today, he still struggles against the social stigma of being an "ex-con," a status imposed on him by others. But he perseveres in the knowledge that, just like "model citizen," "ex-con" is only a social construct passed on as an essence that he does not have to fit, and that the only way to truly enjoy his freedom is to be himself, flaws and all.

If we constantly compare ourselves to an essence or ideal, we are sure to come up short. The problem arises when we perceive this coming-up-short as an inadequacy, an powerlessness to meet a certain standard, a certain essence. This leads to thinking of ourselves as impostors when we are around others whom we falsely credit with having met the standard, or *being* the standard. Both Felix and I had to realize that we'd confused essences for reality and needed to change our thinking before the list of our perceived inadequacies and shortcoming became too long to manage, before we again succumbed to the lie that we were impostors and not merely distinct.

The struggles of Mexican philosophers to decide whether there is, in fact, a "Mexican philosophy" teaches us that *there's no right way to be like the ideal*. The ideal is usually a myth and unreachable. We are distinct, and that's what is true about us. Each one of us should live according to our difference, accepting it and valuing it, or risk always feeling that we don't fit the mold, like impostors.

Returning to my mother's *mole*.

Making *mole* is a process that begins early in the morning. To see my mother making it, you would think there's no process at all. Her measurements and her portions all seem improvised. It is as if she's playing loosely with the paradigm, the ideal, the essence, the substance of *mole*—or as if she's blind to it. What comes out, though, is a delicious and exciting culinary achievement! (At least for me . . . her son.)

A friend of mine—a philosopher who thinks philosophically about bread and other culinary matters—urges me to think of *mole* as a verb rather than a noun[2]—in other words, as an activity rather than an end product. This means that my mother's *mole* can radically differ from the ideal and still be *mole*, since it is the act of making it that matters. We can think of life in the same way—that it's the act of living it that matters, not whether we live it according to a certain essential conception of life. For my cousin Felix, what matters is that he live according to who he truly is rather than to the ideal of an anonymous "model citizen" that none of us can ever be.

In either case, life or *mole*, what matters most is the intention to create, to engage with the process, even if the flavor profile of the final product may turn out to be radically unfamiliar. I think this goes to the heart of the matter: *there truly is no* right *way to do philosophy*, mole, *or life.* We just do it, hoping that what comes out is recognizable as an accomplishment.

PART III

MEXICAN PHILOSOPHY AS A GUIDE TO LIFE

7 | LISTENING AS A FORM OF EXCAVATION

I worked as a dishwasher at a roadside diner during my last three years of high school, and eventually saved enough money to buy a (very) used 1979 Oldsmobile Cutlass Supreme. I loved that car. I knew everything about it; I knew what made it tick. I could tell if something was "off" just by putting my foot on the gas pedal or my hands on the steering wheel. I recognized every vibration and every sound. I knew what belonged and what didn't. Listening to its sounds as I turned the ignition switch, I could tell when something was loose and needed tightening, when something was stuck that needed oiling, or when something was sparking that shouldn't. Because I didn't enjoy getting stranded on the highway (which happened more than once), I'd run frequent checks before leaving my house. If nothing was vibrating or smoking, I would just listen. Listening usually provided much more information than looking, and knowing there were no audible problems would give me the confidence to drive away without worry.

That was many years ago. These days, I don't think about my car. I don't listen to it or feel it. It just goes, managed by mysterious technological spirits I can't even begin to comprehend. In fact, I no longer diagnose things by listening to them or feeling them, although I sense that I should. Wisdom tells us that it is wise to listen—to listen to ourselves and to each other. If I listened to my body as I listened to my car, I would be in much better shape. Doctors recommend that we "know" our bodies and do no more than what that intuitive knowledge tells us that we (or our bodies) can handle. Some people religiously heed that advice: they "listen to" their bodies, educate themselves about their bodies, set boundaries on their activities, and do what it takes to keep their bodies running efficiently. But most of us ignore this advice, going through life oblivious to the state of our machinery except during physical exams, when the doctor listens on our behalf and implores us to get some exercise and to cut the bread, rice, and alcohol from our diets. These recommendations are meant to be good for us, to help us, to restore us, to save us. And they are based on carefully listening to what's happening inside of us.

Attentive listening is a tool that Emilio Uranga wanted his contemporaries to cultivate, but for a more profound reason, namely, for the sake and well-being of Mexican culture. Uranga surmised that in order to more precisely diagnose the cultural spirit one first had to perceive it. But a cultural spirit is not something that can be easily grasped—it does not give itself to perception as other things do. To grasp the cultural spirit (what Mexican philosophers called "*lo mexicano*") one had to attentively *listen to its being*, to that which lent it its essence and its meaning. He called this sort of attentive, and profound, listening "ontological auscultation."

Before embarking on a rigorous pursuit of philosophy under the critical eye of the exiled Spanish philosopher José Gaos in the early 1940s, Uranga studied medicine. Not surprisingly, then, auscultation becomes a central idea in his philosophy. "Auscultation" is a medical term that refers to the act of carefully listening, usually with a stethoscope, to the internal processes of the human body, listening for those noises or vibrations that indicate whether it is healthy or diseased. We can then think of philosophy as auscultation, imagining it as a sort of attentive listening for those noises and vibrations that may tell us if something is wrong with us, with our culture, or with our world.

For many years I struggled with something I call "post-immigrant fear."[1] As the child of undocumented immigrant parents, I grew up looking over my shoulder for *la migra*—immigration enforcement. Although I am a US citizen and supposedly not subject to the kind of deportation order that would return my parents to Michoacán, from a young age their fear of deportation became *my* fear. I carried this fear with me into adulthood. It became especially acute when I started going to conferences as a fully documented philosopher, with a credential (my doctorate) that showed that I was what I said I was. I would tell myself that it was just a matter of time before someone would question my status, ask for my papers, and, finding them unsatisfactory, have me deported out of conferences and the profession. This fear was real. It filled my life with a profound anxiety (*zozobra*) treatable only with drugs, alcohol, and many other aids to self-forgetting.

Overcoming this fear required confronting it. But doing so meant listening to my trauma, which meant spelling it out for myself and, eventually, to others. This was not easy. Facing what's underneath our fears, supporting them and feeding them, can be just as scary as the immediate cause of the fear itself. In talking about my fear I was able to listen to it, to pay attention to what I was saying to myself, and thus to see it for what it was. It was the fear that *I did not belong*, that *I was not enough*. But why did I think this? Was I the only person who thought this about themselves? That couldn't be the case. It soon became clear to me that my fear was not a flaw of my own psychology but something more fundamental and common, something that connected me to others. Perhaps I was not alone.

Uranga's auscultatory analysis of the Mexican cultural spirit confirmed my own findings. He writes:

> [Our character] has been revealed to us as permanently fatalistic, in a dangerous communication with limit situations, and from this unending dialogue with the physiological and foundational aspects of human being there has emerged a *mode of being* on which we find an original layer that has been informed by everything, that absorbs everything.[2]

As he listens to the Mexican spirit, Uranga hears its music, its poetry, its politics, and these speak on behalf of a people who are "permanently fatalistic"—that is, conscious of their own human limitations and aware of their accidentality. But this fatalism is rooted in, what he calls, "an original layer," a ground-level of human existence shaped by experiences, past traumas, and habituations; it is a ground that has been "informed by everything." This "original layer" is the ontological layer and it can only be gasped with profound and attentive listening—ontological auscultation—which is a listening that can grasp what is otherwise ungraspable: the basis of who and what we are.

This is why for Mexican philosophers auscultation is a way to get to the bottom of things—this is why it is an excavation. Moreover, like the information given to us by our physicians, what philosophical auscultation reveals can go a long way toward revealing our inner world to ourselves. This "knowing ourselves" Mexican philosophers call *autognosis*.

The term *autognosis*—from the Greek *auto*, "self," and *gnosis*, "knowledge"—means "self-knowledge" or "knowledge of one's self." The result of *listening to yourself* is autognosis, which is knowledge of both *who* you are and *that* you are. In other words, by means of auscultation you can come to know the rhythm of your heart, and because there *is* rhythm, know that you are something rather than nothing. In Mexican philosophy, autognosis is tied to an "imperative"—that is, to a philosophical command. Abelardo Villegas (1934–2001)—a student of Gaos, Uranga, and Zea—explains it this way: "The *imperative* to know Mexico is urged in our philosophy . . . the imperative to know ourselves implies a knowing what we are, and that we exist. Mexican thought in this century displays a task of self-knowledge."[3]

This imperative is central to Mexican philosophy. It is what Mexican philosophy commands its philosophers, but it applies also to you. It involves two different moments of knowledge: the first, that you come to know "what" you are, and the second, that you come to know "that" you are. Together they form the sort of knowledge that will allow you to assert yourself in the world, to say that you belong, that you are *somebody* and that you are worthy of recognition. But autognosis is impossible without auscultation.

Uranga proposes auscultation for the sake of autognosis. This approach can be expected to yield information that is useless for advertisers and the Mexican Tourism Board but that can tell Mexicans quite a bit about the meaning of their existence. Through auscultation and autognosis, they can cut through the static and the distortions making up the stereotypical image that Mexicans have of themselves and that non-Mexicans have of Mexicans.

The value of this strategy is that anyone can employ it, not just Mexicans or people thinking about Mexicans. Imagine driving to work in the morning and seeing a billboard that suddenly and unexpectedly insults you, telling you that if you don't vote for this particular presidential candidate, then you're "un-American." You spend the day obsessing over your Americanness and cursing the candidate who authorized this blasphemy! You begin to resent coworkers who you *know* will vote for that candidate, and you imagine that they huddle in the break room talking about your un-Americanness.

What philosophy as auscultation suggests is a moment of meditation and listening so as to get past the surface feelings of anger and resentment. Going past the billboard, the message, the imagined gossip, you find the ground of your personality, of your identity, something that tells you that that's not at all who you are. You are not a political identity but a *person*, struggling, like most people, with your accidentality and your many existential projects. But you realize, too, that your feelings of offense and resentment triggered by the billboard are perhaps misplaced and certainly unnecessary. Here you come in contact, perhaps for the first time, with that which makes you different, that which distinguishes you from the demographic targeted by the billboard or the political messages that you have found offensive. And this difference is that you are capable of touching the ground of your own being. Auscultation for the sake of autognosis can be practical in this way.

The idea is that listening to yourself through patient meditation will do for you what it has done for many philosophical Mexicans. Doing as they have done will amplify that individual and unique difference that makes you who you are, that distinctiveness that has been quieted by others so as to define and control you. Uranga imagines this as a process of ripping off masks, and tells us that the moment for doing so is now:

> The moment of crisis has arrived, the instant of discomfort, in which we feel that the style of being with which we have become accustomed is not appropriate and authentic, and the violent gesture with which we have tried to rid ourselves of it has made us see that, by detaching ourselves from the spurious, we likewise rid ourselves of a mask. [O]ur autognosis articulates . . . the imperative of unmasking, of radically refuting the "impostor" within us . . . after this, [whatever remains] is no longer exclusively a Mexican returned to his truth, but is more accurately a person—simply a human being.[4]

We can generalize Uranga's call for self-confrontation. The moment has arrived for me and you to reject the image of ourselves that has been imposed upon us—to reject the "impostor within," that copy of ourselves that gets offended by billboards or by people who have no idea that such resentment exists. Just as denying the fabricated image of a Mexican humanity will require an "instant of discomfort," so will denying what we have for so long thought about ourselves. After all, this means refusing to accept those things about us that have previously defined our identity. But it will be painful also because it means shining a spotlight on the trauma that created that identity—my post-immigrant fear, for example—in order to see what has made us who we are. This principle of psychology is also a principle of Mexican philosophy, one tied to the command, the imperative, to know oneself, for the sake of living in accordance with one's own truth and not someone else's.

What useful lessons can *you* draw from the philosophical attempt to find the true meaning of what it means to be Mexican? First, the lesson about ausculation: you must learn to *listen* to your inner self, learn to diagnose yourself by being attentive to what "sounds right" and what doesn't. Then there's the lesson about autognosis: by listening, you can come to *know* yourself. But the payoff of knowing yourself will be, at the very least, the knowledge that you are no more and no less accidental than anyone else, and that whoever you are, you are singularly and authentically. So what you learn once you undergo your own auscultative excavation will be a truth or truths previously hidden beneath layers of trauma, interiorized objectifications, and socially imposed self-conceptions. It is on that truth or those truths—what Uranga called the "original layer"— that you must build. What you build will be nothing short of a new future. This future world will necessarily reflect your own spiritual and material circumstance, but also your own genuine personality and your unique ambitions.

Ultimately, what you build will be informed and influenced by trauma, suffering, and pain, yes, but also by the recognition and affirmation of your own uniqueness, your value, and your individual personality, a personality that is never perfect, never ideal or substantial, but imperfect and always accidental—a true humanity.

8 | BE CHARITABLE

The Jardines de Humaya cemetery on the outskirts of Culiacán, in the western Mexican state of Sinaloa, is the final resting place of Mexico's most notorious narco-traffickers. Surrounded by immense white walls, this cemetery is not for the common dead; it is reserved for drug lords who, before dying, designed and financed the construction of their lavish grave sites in the tradition of the Mayan Snake Kings!

Built with profits from the massive international drug-trafficking trade, it is a cemetery of excess and extremes. It is a necropolis, a true *city of the dead*, with avenues, Wi-Fi and cable access, functional plumbing, playgrounds, state-of-the-art security systems, and, of course, tombs. The tombs are *actual* houses, whose style depends, I suppose, on the preferences of the narcos who ordered their construction. A house in the baroque style sits elegantly next to a colorful two-story modernist-style building, while behind it stands a postmodern three-story tower with see-through windowpanes, reaching for the sky. I've seen such streets and houses before in the more luxurious areas of San Francisco or the Hollywood Hills. What makes these different, however, is that no one actually *lives* in Jardines de Humaya.

This *neighborhood of the dead* is home to some of the most no-torious gangsters in recent Mexican memory. Here, narcos built for themselves final resting places that reflect their status, wealth and power. In the extravagance of their burial chambers, they have sought to mimic the extravagance of their lives. These tombs are monuments to a life lived in luxury or its pursuit, ultimately sym-bolizing and reflecting what they believed to be their true *worth*.

Jardines de Humaya and the narco lifestyle are exaggerations of the notion that one's worth is measured by the toys one has when one dies. Such exaggerations represent an ideal for contemporary capitalist society, whose motto could be: *Tell me what you have, and I'll tell you who you are*!

Antonio Caso (1883–1946) would attribute the unnecessary ex-travagance of Jardines de Humaya to individuals who see life in purely economic terms. These individuals represent a manner of existing that Caso calls, "existence as economy."

According to Caso, humans, like other animals, require a spe-cific amount of energy to fulfill their basic survival and reproduc-tive needs. But, sometimes, they have more energy than required, or they don't use up the energy nature has allocated for these pursuits—they thus carry excess energy. A distinguishing feature of our humanity is that we are capable of reinvesting that surplus. "Existence as economy" refers to a manner of existing where we spend that excess energy on *ourselves*, which we do when we live opulently, or build lavish monuments to our own memory.

A less damning characterization of "existence as economy" is the idea that to live life *economically* is to *make the most of* our energy, our money, or any of our advantages in a way that mirrors a capitalist economic process working as it should. According to this economic model, our life—which Caso defines as "the energy of egoism"—is an opportunity to do *more for ourselves* than what will keep us alive or propagate the species. "Life is always bound to interest," says Caso, referring to the way in which what we do is always tied to personal goals or ambitions. Caso continues: "To nourish, to grow, to reproduce, to play, to make tools, to die, all of this is pure economy, the pure effect of egoism, the formless imperialistic thrust."[1] In other words, economic life is essentially selfish.

There's a simple formula that captures the concept of existence as economy: "*Life = Minimum effort with maximum gain.*"[2] In a life lived as "economy," a *good* life is one resulting from getting the most out of doing less—from "profiting" the most. The formula itself reflects an investment strategy designed to generate profits or "surplus." But such a life is the height of egoism. Caso says that to live in this way is to live in accordance with the "vile economic interest of wild ferocious beasts." This beastly existence ultimately requires the domination of others, who will be forced to spend *their* life energy for the sake of *my* gain. A consequence of this is that, in using others only as means, I narrow my world. Alienation from others and selfishness are default modes of our "existence as economy."

One can see how success in America is measured according to Caso's economic formula. Those at the top—the wealthiest, the ones with the excess—are those who have figured out how to get the most out of their own energy investment while doing the least or using the energy of others. There are also those who don't need to spend any of their energy simply because of their lot in life—the ones who have what we would call "generational wealth" or some other inherited privilege. Most narcos, investment bankers, Silicon Valley venture capitalists, and corporate overlords live according to Caso's economy formula. Young people, influenced by messages they absorb from their families, their schools, and social media, often choose courses of study or lay out their career paths with the goal of reaching a place in life where they can exert the least energy for the largest gain. I'm never surprised to see my brightest students lured onto these paths. But to live this way is surely to miss something.

There are other ways to live, according to Caso: as "disinterest" and as "charity."

To live life as "disinterest" is to give up on life as economy, to abandon the obsession with profit or excess. To live life as "disinterest" is to live "aesthetically," which means being aware and in awe of the world without wanting to dominate it, control it, or profit from it. Living in this way "appears as a shocking waste" to others. Caso uses the example of the artist to illustrate this idea. The artist ideally lives to contemplate the world, capture it in images or music or words, and take nothing from it. The artist's life is not bound to interest, so her activities consist in dedicating herself to her art in a non-totalizing, non-egotistical way which is respectful of others, of life, and of the world. The artist invests her surplus energy in her art and is not interested in generating excess or dominating others in the process. Because artists use their excess energy on their artistic pursuits, they will more than likely suffer from a lack of economic security.

The third way to live is the one that interests us here. This is what Caso calls "existence as charity." To live life charitably is to live so as to *donate* or *gift* one's excess energy to others. While the capitalist spends his surplus energy or time or money on himself, and the artist spends it on his art, the charitable or "good man," Caso says, "sacrifices egoism to come to the aid of his neighbor, to prevent his pain, and such a sacrifice is free."[3] Donating, or gifting, one's energy stock, including one's money, time, and body, is the essence of living charitably.

Charity is an investment in others. The excess or surplus of vital energy goes into the development of something other than my own ego, my own comfort, or my own interests. Because this goes against my natural inclination—that is, against everything that I am as a biological, rational, and cultural animal—this is a sacrifice! When, on Saturday mornings, I offer my time at a shelter for the unhoused or those struggling to make do, I am donating my excess energy. If there is no excess energy to give but I still get up and go, I am utilizing energy I need to survive. This is a sacrifice.

To live charitably is to live sacrificially. Caso calls this "the good" and puts it into a formula: *Sacrifice = Maximum Effort with Minimum Gain*. "The good," says Caso, referring to "charity" and "sacrifice," "has its roots in the profundities of spiritual existence."[4] In other words, the enthusiasm for charitable living is not found or motivated by the ego or the self. The enthusiasm for charity comes from outside the self, motivated by a non-self, a non-I, who may be a friend, a stranger, a humanitarian cause, or, even, God. In this way, living charitably resembles living a mystical life. The formula describes "the good" as doing the most while getting the least. St. Francis of Assisi, Martin Luther King Jr., Mother Teresa, Mohandas Gandhi, Cesar Chavez, and Malala Yousafzai have lived this way. They are individuals who, by all appearances, put their maximum effort into the cause of others while seemingly getting minimal returns. I say "seemingly," however, because "minimal returns" refers to a surplus or to profit or some gain in line with economic life. These individuals get less of *that*, but what they *do* get, they get in abundance: inspiration, love, a deeper and broader sense of humanity, connection, compassion, and so on. Such historical examples of charitable personalities represent an ideal that may seem unreachable. However, being charitable in this way is not impossible.

When I think of charitable people, I think of one of my graduate-school professors—let's call him "Dr. B." He's left a mark on my memory as one of the most generous people I've ever met. Whenever I think of Dr. B, what comes first to mind is that he always carried two wallets. I learned of this one very cold morning as we walked back from a café across campus. A man wrapped in a thick, heavy blanket sat outside the Student Union. He appeared cold, hungry, and tired. He would reach out of the blanket with a cup asking pedestrians for change. As we passed the man, Dr. B, promptly and without interrupting our conversation, gave the man his own coffee, then reached into his left back pocket, took out his wallet, and proceeded to give him twenty dollars. "Get yourself something to eat," he told the man in a soft, caring whisper. We continued on our way as Dr. B picked up our conversation where we had left it. I was impressed, so I interrupted him and asked him about the twenty dollars—I hadn't given the man anything, and if

I'd had twenty dollars to give him I probably wouldn't have done it. He said, "Oh, that was his money, it wasn't my money." I didn't understand, and I told him so. "Well, you see," he said, pulling out a wallet from the back pocket on his right side, "this is for me and my lunch. I can get what I need with what I have here." Then pulling out a wallet from his left back pocket, "And this one is for whoever needs it. I want to make sure I don't spend *this*—hence the two wallets!" He must have sensed my confusion, or my guilt, or my ignorance, because he stopped walking, turned to me, and said: "Being greedy is very lonely. Selfishness is very lonely. When you're generous, the world gets much bigger. I'd rather live in a bigger rather than a smaller world, wouldn't you?"

Referring back to Caso's discussion of charity, Dr. B's actions exemplify the view that what one "gains" if one lives in accordance with "the good" cannot be measured. While Dr. B's sacrifice is not the sacrifice of a Martin Luther King Jr., it is nonetheless a sacrifice. He could reinvest his surplus on himself, but he chooses not to; rather, he gives without expectation or self-interest. According to Caso, Dr. B is exemplifying what charity as an action is supposed to look like. There is no exchange demanded or expected between the giver and the receiver. Caso even goes so far as to say that to act in such a way is to be "perfect." For Caso, perfection is not an ideal, something to strive for but never reach. Perfection is possible, and it is simply being charitable and sacrificial in what one *does*. In reaching for that second wallet when another's need requires it, Dr. B exhibits a certain kind of non-ideal "perfection." Caso writes: "Be perfect, that is to say: be active, charitable."[5]

❧

So why live this way? If you are not self-sacrificing by nature, perhaps cut from different cloth than people like the Mother Teresas and the Dr. Bs of the world, why go out of your way to adopt these practices? What is to be gained by living like this? What's in it for you? It's just as Dr. B explained it to me: in contemporary culture, only a life of charity will overcome the seemingly unavoidable feeling of alienation that comes with having more and more. In sacrificing your excess, or in giving of what you have, you also give of yourself and, in so doing, join yourself to another need and another life. Another way to say this is that in giving of yourself you empty out your ego and become less self-obsessed, less self-interested, and less lonely.

Of course, it is difficult not to live in accordance with selfish interests. But it is possible, and doing so is freeing. By freeing oneself from the bonds of ego and the world, and returning the surplus to others, one is adding to the world and freeing others to do the same. It can thus be said that charity is the ultimate act of self-love. There's a terror in being trapped in your own ego desires, in constantly bending to the demands of selfishness. Getting out of yourself by surrendering your ego frees you from that terror. If there is a perfect way to live, this is it!

What we learn from Caso is that a good life is lived in acts of charity, that living charitably and sacrificially can free us from our compulsion to accumulate and make us more responsible and more caring people. So heed Caso's imploration, a plea that certainly transcends his time and place: "Charity is action. Go and commit acts of charity."[6] You don't have to leave your house to do this. If, as they say, charity begins at home, then start there. Simple enough.

9 | BE LATE TO PARTIES

My wife's Filipino family swears that being late to parties is an essential feature of Filipino life. So much so, that if the party is planned for two in the afternoon the invitation will indicate that the party starts at one in order for it to start *on time*. Now, I had experienced this before, not just with Filipinos but with Mexicans. Growing up, the regular start time for a Saturday evening *carne asada* was "one to four, somewhere around there." This usually meant that folks would start showing up at five or six. I recall an uncle's funeral, the announcement for which stated that the burial would be at three. Everyone, including the dead uncle (in his casket, of course), showed up at five. But this was just the way it was. No one ever seriously complained.

Some will object that these are just hasty generalizations about certain groups of people. And I'm sure that there are Filipinos and Mexicans who show up when they're told. But the ones I've known really are unconcerned with being on time, so let's just call it a pattern that I've recognized with those I've known. What the pattern reveals is that those folks who consistently show up late are not showing up late on purpose; that is, being on time or being late does not seem to be the goal of Filipino or Mexican party-goers. It's simply that lateness, for them, does not seem to be the anxiety-inducing issue that it is for most people. If you ask my father-in-law, he would tell you that the notions of a punctual arrival or a punctual departure are mere suggestions.

But why is this problematic? Because this phenomenon seems to undermine a cultural value prevalent in the United States and in many industrialized countries around the world. It is a cultural value tied to work schedules and the monetary worth of time. So we are encouraged to be on time, to be *punctual*. Socially, however, we are asked to be punctual not for the sake of work or money but rather in order to be polite, respectful, professional, dependable. In short, to be punctual is to be virtuous. In contrast, being late identifies us with some of society's worst vices: rudeness, laziness, unprofessionalism, undependability, and, even, anti-sociality.

Because social messaging tells us to avoid those vices, a person can become obsessed with punctuality. But unlike other obsessions, this one is not frowned upon. From an early age, school bells have ingrained in us the idea that we must be careful with our time, thereby reinforcing the notion that being punctual is a condition for being successful. Blame capitalism, colonialism, religion, or any human ideology that relies on the surgical division of time for the accomplishment of its rituals.

It's no wonder, then, that punctuality can become a part of one's identity. One can become the person who is known by others as *always on time,* which they also translate as dependable and even trustworthy. Especially because of this relation with dependability, some set punctuality as a goal in their personal development: they yearn to be known and recognized as someone who never shows up late, who always arrives on the dot, who considers tardiness an unnatural, uncivilized vice. They want to be known and remembered as people who not only strive to be punctual but who are actually punctual *all the time*—to every appointment, on all occasions, yesterday, today, and tomorrow. They want to embody the very essence of punctuality.

But the question becomes: can one ever really *be on time*? The answer to this question is related to how we understand values.

Jorge Portilla's theory of value proposes that values are the filters through which we see the world. That is, we see, understand, and appreciate the world *through* values, or through the way in which a thing in the world presents itself to us as valuable or meaningful. Values *belong to* the world but are not *of* the world. They are created by human beings and left there, in the world, so that others can make sense of earthly life. Because human beings create them, the emphasis placed on some values will vary from culture to culture. The value of punctuality has a different weight for the British than it has for the Mexican. Being punctual will be more valued in cultures that also value economic existence and less valued in cultures that value artistic production or charity (see previous chapter).

When we say that value is created by human beings, we mean that value has been added to society by history, society, or culture. Because values don't belong to the thing itself, out there in the world, independently of human activity, it is possible not to value something even if told (by history, society, or culture) that the thing is valuable. However, to value the thing is to respect its value, to respect what others have said about it, to respect history, culture, and society. Portilla says that when we respect the value of the thing, we will respect, accept, and obey what that value demands of us when we encounter it.

That chair in the corner has value: it is worth what you paid for it, so it has monetary value, but it also has use value, in that you can use it to sit, and value as meaning, in that you can make sense of what it is as an object given the value placed on it by others. The latter was given to it by society some time ago and is connected to its use or function. What Portilla means when he talks about *respecting* the demands of value is that, when I sit on the chair, I respect its use and meaning value, since I'm doing what one is supposed to do with a chair. I am doing what the chair *demands* of me when I encounter it: it demands I sit on it, and I if do, then I'm respecting its value. Alternatively, I can put the chair on top of the kitchen sink and use it to dry my socks. In this case, I am not doing what the chair demands, which means that I am not respecting its value.

In short, a value carries with it a set of demands: these are imposed on things by people, by history, by the circumstance, and so on. The value of an idea, for instance, will find me doing something in an effort to fulfill its demands. Portilla writes:

> There is not a single act in the life of human beings that does not owe its first warning signs to the demand of value. We all run dizzyingly after ourselves, directed always by those indications that foreshadow and allude to the fullness of our own being. Value attracts us like a whirlwind in the center of which our own self appears, illuminated by value's aura. All of our acts are ordered toward the realization of some value.[1]

As I make my way through life, attending to those demands becomes a duty, and fulfilling them an accomplishment. Values, in this sense, guide my very existence. I want to be the person who fulfills them, and I eventually tie the fulfilling of values to my identity.

As a somewhat different illustration of what Portilla means by the "demands of value," take the value of education. In the immigrant Mexican community, as in most immigrant communities, education is a *supreme value*. My parents would say things like "we came to this country so that you could have an education" and "I don't care what you do, so long as you get an education." The goal for them was to make sure that I responded to the demands of this value regardless of any and all challenges. This meant going to school consistently, getting good grades, taking my classes seriously, and, very importantly, not complaining about doing so. I vividly remember the night a mother skunk crept into our kitchen through a broken floorboard in our dilapidated trailer. My father heard it, snuck up on it, and hit it over the head with a shovel to scare it away. Nothing happened to the mother skunk, but before it ran off with its litter of baby skunks close behind, it sprayed the entire living room. I was sleeping on the living-room couch, so it sprayed me too. I can still feel the spray on my face, dripping down my neck, burning my eyes—it feels like gasoline on my bare skin and tastes like diesel fuel mixed with rotten eggs but much, much, worse. My mother quickly rushed me to the shower, where she dumped some tomato juice on my head, hosed me down, dried me, and after all that, told me to go to sleep because I had to go to school in the morning. Yes, she sent me to school smelling worse than the skunk that sprayed me!

I was in the third grade. Not surprisingly, I was sent back home on the school bus, windows open all the way, with a note from the teachers asking my mother why she had sent me to school *in my condition*. My mother's answer was consistent with her values and with how much she valued my education. She looked at me, looked at the note, and in her angriest Spanish said, "So you don't learn if you stink? *Están locas!*"

The value placed on education in our community demanded sacrifice and effort. In sending me to school smelling like sulfur and death, my mother was just doing as the communal value demanded. Portilla says that a value "appears then as a norm of my self-constitution, as the perpetually elusive and evanescent indication of what my being ought to be."[2] My mother attended to the value placed on education by our community and used it as a norm that would guide her to become the person she wanted to be—a mother who cared for her son's future.

Living up to the demands of value is a lifelong project, and most of us will very often come up short. Here we get at what Portilla's theory of value has to do with punctuality. Punctuality is a value. In our postindustrial, hyper-capitalist era, punctuality might almost be *the* value. If, as they say, "time is money," then *being on time* is a foundational economic principle. We want to always be on time for the sake of money. But, again, the idea of wanting to be on time hides a more profound desire to achieve some sort of coincidence with the value of punctuality. So we work on bringing about this coincidence by doing what the value demands—namely, *we avoid being late.*

I said that more often than not, one fails at fulfilling the demands of value. Continuing with the example of punctuality, no matter how many times I am on time, no matter how often I've obeyed the demands of the value of punctuality, I still cannot define myself as "being punctual" since I may always be late to my next appointment. That goes to show that the coincidence I desire between myself and values is always under threat of falling apart *in the future*. I cannot simply and always "be punctual" because the next day the rotation of the earth may affect the synchronization between my phone and an orbiting satellite and I might arrive a bit late.

What qualifies my fulfillment of a value, whether punctuality or education or generosity, is always a fact of the past. In the case of punctuality, I will say that "I *arrived* on time," "I *was* on time for work," "I *showed up* on time for the event," but there is no way to tell if next Tuesday I will arrive on time, or if I will arrive at all. Portilla likes the example of punctuality because it more clearly illustrates how we can fail at fulfilling it.

> Getting dressed hurriedly in the morning, drinking a cup of coffee in a rush, walking down the street in long strides and perhaps running, distressed, after a bus that barely stops to let me get on—[these] are nothing but the external signs of my determined (intentional) pointing toward the constitution of my own "punctual being." If after all of this, I finally do arrive on time to the office at the hour stipulated by a set of rules and breathe a sigh of relief, then, am I punctual yet? It is evident that this is not the case. It is simply that today I got to work on time. Value has escaped me once again.[3]

This paragraph, written in the 1950s, could easily describe our current state of robotic hurriedness. It is the need to fulfill this value that we can blame for road rage, work-related injuries, and other time-related stresses. We want to achieve what Portilla calls "punctual being"—we want to be punctual at whatever cost. However, arriving on time once or a million times does not make me punctual in the sense that my very being, the way that I exist in the world, is itself punctual. There is more to life than being punctual—or generous, or trustworthy. Besides, tomorrow or the next day I may fail at being punctual, generous, or trustworthy.

It is said, for instance, that in eighteenth-century Königsberg, Prussia, townsfolk would set their watches by the impeccable routines of the philosopher Immanuel Kant. Day after day he would take his evening walk at the same exact time, so people knew what time it was when he passed by. But was he at one with punctuality? Had he achieved a "punctual being"? A day came in 1804 when he no longer passed by, when he was no longer punctual. Death made this so. Hence, the answer is no, he was not at one with punctuality. Ultimately, Kant was just a person with a good track record of having kept a strict routine. What this means is that a value, like punctuality, or generosity, or politeness, is only a guide for my actions, something that helps me make sense of and act on the world in which I live.

Portilla says that one truly becomes punctual, or one completely fulfills the demands of the value of punctuality, only in retrospect. This is when all of my "on times" are collected into a memory of me, and the final verdict by those who knew me becomes "He was punctual." As with other values, this means that one completely fulfills the demands of punctuality only in death; one is finally truly punctual only as a corpse. Portilla says:

My punctuality is but the ideal unity of all my actions geared toward it, and it will only acquire body and solidity when, after my death—that is to say, once every possibility of my being late has been canceled—some generous soul points out the magnificent fact that I was never late anywhere.[4]

And so, after all my successful attempts at getting to my office on time or showing up to events right on the dot, I can fool myself into thinking that I've achieved a perfect marriage between a *value* and *my being*, but this will not be a true marriage. Only death guarantees that I will never be late again—dying right on time might be my last punctual arrival, and after this there will be no more appointments. It is then that I will have arrived at that permanent state of punctuality where ideal and reality finally meet. Just ask Kant.

Now, I suspect that being perfectly punctual seems possible to us because of how it feels when we *fail* to be on time. If the goal is to be on time, *not* being on time feels disappointing. But more than disappointing, it may even feel like a personal failure. Lateness when we wanted to be on time can briefly ruin our mood, disturb our sense of integrity, and seems to blemish our very identity. That we can feel this way convinces us that being absolutely punctual might be a possible goal. The same goes for other values. Meeting the demands of the value of generosity will always be difficult, and not being perfectly generous may distress us unnecessarily. The best thing to do, as with punctuality, is to remember that these values are human inventions meant only as guides, and not fulfilling them is always an option.

The lesson is simple: remember that, in order to be happy, have a peaceful life, or achieve inner tranquility, you need not obey every demand that values place on you. These demands are usually mere suggestions or social constructs, like the value of punctuality. Allow yourself the freedom to disobey when possible. It's not a big deal.

So, while alive, be late to parties. You gain nothing by trying to be on time, but you may gain something by being late: more time to get lost in the world, more time to enjoy the journey before getting to the destination, more time to be alone with yourself. Your capitalist, colonized habits may violently react to this strategy, but that final appointment with death is always just around the corner, so why hurry?

10 | DON'T FEAR GHOSTS ... OR DEATH

When my mother was still a child, her father, Ignacio, would spend weeks in the mountains of Michoacán looking after a small herd of cattle. It would take him three to four days to drive the cows to a small plot of land miles from his home. He did this alone, trekking through mud and over rocky slopes on rustic paths until arriving at some grassy hillside overlooking a clearing, surrounded by dense forest, where he'd settle into a tiny shack he had constructed for these occasions.

Thunderstorms were frequent. On one of these stormy nights, a week or so into one of his stays, as lightning lit up the hillsides and water drummed fiercely on his wooden roof, he saw a man walking up the path he himself had taken days before. Even when the man's face was lit up by the lightning, he could barely make it out.

"Ignacio!" the man yelled.

"Pedro?!" replied my grandfather. It felt good to see a familiar face—or any face at all.

"I'm wet, Ignacio! Can I come in and warm up?"

"Claro que sí!" yelled my grandfather. He put more wood on the fire and poured hot water into a tin cup, stirred in instant coffee and some mezcal for a kick, and placed it in Pedro's wet, shivering hands. "What are you doing up here, Pedro? And in the rain?"

"I'm heading up north," said his friend. "I have urgent business up there, and this is the fastest way." My grandfather thought for a second. Taking this route north didn't make much sense. And in the middle of the night? And in the rain? He wanted to ask his questions, but he didn't. His friend's face told him he was tired. So he offered Pedro one of his wool blankets and told him to lie down in a corner and rest.

"Ignacio," Pedro began as he settled into a cozy spot near the fire, "can I ask you a favor?"

"Anything, Pedro."

"Before I left, I was supposed to deliver a liter of milk to Cleotilde— you know, the widow who lives by the church—and I never did. I hate to leave without doing that. Can you do that for me when you get back? It's been bothering me, and I would like to keep that promise." My grandfather thought it a strange request. But a liter of milk was not a big deal and it wasn't an inconvenience, so he agreed. "I will do that, Pedro. Now rest, and I'll see you in the morning."

My grandfather woke up early, before the sun rose, and finding his shack empty, figured that Pedro had already left. He *had* said he had urgent business. My grandfather stayed in the shack for a few more days and then journeyed home.

On returning, the first thing he did was milk a cow. Filling up a liter bottle, he took it to the widow Cleotilde. He knocked on the door. "Hello, Cleotilde. I'm here because I ran into Pedro three nights ago in the mountains and he asked me to bring you this liter of milk that he promised but hadn't delivered. So here you go!" Cleotilde's face lost its color. She hurriedly made the sign of the cross. "But Ignacio," she said, concern in her voice, "Pedro died five days ago. We buried him the day before yesterday."

"Well," said my grandfather in a matter-of-fact way, "then this makes sense. Maybe now he'll rest in peace."

Years later, when my grandfather told me and my cousins this story, I asked, "Did it scare you to think that you spent the night with a ghost?" I was about ten years old.

"Not one bit," he replied. "I'm scared of the living, not the dead. The dead usually don't want anything from us. And when they do, it's important. Besides, we often spend our nights with ghosts. Some of them we don't know, or remember, or care about. I was blessed to have shared a fire and a mezcal with one that I actually liked. You don't get that chance too often." He laughed and continued doing what he was doing. I stayed up that night with a blanket over my face.

I tell this story to my students when talking about death in Mexican philosophy. I tell it because it illustrates the view that, according to certain Mexican philosophers, death is not to be feared, but embraced.

The Mexican idea of death contrasts with the European or Western idea. Western philosophers never tire of suggesting that the very thought of our eventual demise should serve some purpose. From Socrates to Seneca to Freud to Heidegger, Western philosophy is obsessed with recommending that, in order to live a good and authentic life, one must first come to the hard realization that each one of us will, *inevitably*, die. Heidegger says that we are always "being-toward-death." So, we are advised to *live in the now*, since death is always just up ahead, ready to strip us of everything we are and everything we have. We are told to enjoy the moment, to be better people, because we get closer to death with each minute that goes by. Death *is* our future, and there's no future after that.

This future-pointing attitude toward death is neatly described by Sigmund Freud when he says that "the goal of all life is death." Likewise, in his famous *The Denial of Death*, Ernest Becker writes that death is a "mainspring of human activity." Becker is clear that the fear of my future death *inspires* me to live in a way that "avoids" it or "denies" its inevitability. In order to forget what lies ahead, I will keep myself busy and productive.

In this way, the idea of a future death forces us to live in the tomorrow—to live in the anticipation of our demise. This informs our plans and expectations. The insurance industry and Western religion both bank on it. An insurance policy comforts our fears regarding those hardships that our death could occasion in others, giving us control over a future without us. The same is true of our belief in resurrection, the coming Messiah, everlasting life, and so on: by making death secondary to what comes after, such notions mean to assuage our fears over its radical unknowability.

On this view, the last moment of our own specific lifetime is set as the limit for all we can possibly achieve *in this world*. And so the goal of this life should be to live the most fulfilling life possible before we reach that limit. If we keep the fact of our inevitable end clearly in our mind's eye, the thinking goes, then it is possible to fill our daily calendars with meaningful activities. If we stay mindful of life's finitude, we won't waste our time doing things we hate. In this way, death bestows meaning on our life.

In the context of the Western idea of death, ghosts should not exist. I'm not saying that they don't, or that people don't believe they do, only that they *should not* exist. If death is the end of all life and of all possibility of living, the existence of a ghost is a logical and existential impossibility.

Now, the Mexican conception of death says that we coexist with death, and thus that we coexist with ghosts. In simple terms, this means that we live with the death of our loved ones, with the death of our neighbors and *their* loved ones, and so on; those deaths are a presence that keeps us company in the present. This coexisting with death means that death is not in the future, waiting to "take me out"; it is *now*, communing with me in this room in which I write, watching me, and sometimes allowing itself to be seen, like Pedro's ghost. Mexican philosophers say that death is a mirror of life, by which they mean two things: one, that our own individual deaths will reflect back a life well or badly lived; and two, that death reflects the present back to itself, as a mirror reflects what is facing it. In both cases, what this means is that death has no future.

The distinction between the Western and Mexican conception of death is made by Octavio Paz (1914–1998) in his *The Labyrinth of Solitude* (1951). There, the Mexican poet, philosopher, and Nobel Prize winner says that the Western, or non-Mexican, conception "points forward," while the Mexican conception "points backward." To say that the Mexican attitude points backward is to say that death is not an event that is yet to happen, but rather that death has already happened and is now here, as a coexistence, like the ghost of an old friend. People in the West tend to overlook the deaths that have already happened and instead dwell on the idea of death as an expectation, while people in Mexico (and other parts of Latin America), given the ubiquity of premature death in their history and in their present, are unable to forget the loss of their forebears and friends. (A crude example: Since 2007, Mexico has averaged over 30,000 deaths per year due to cartel violence. For much of the population, this has led to a literal "living with death" that is also a constant reminder that death is always already here.)

I recall my very first Día de los Muertos. My mother, aunts, and cousins took a trip to Villa Mendoza, the town where my mother was born, and to the small cemetery on the town's outskirts where her mother, my grandmother, is buried. My mother spread a blanket over the small grave mound and placed some marigolds on top of a simple cement cross. We all sat on the blanket eating *pan dulce* and drinking Pepsi from glass bottles. My aunt placed half of a *concha* at the foot of the cross, along with half a glass of cola. After a short prayer, the aunts and my mother talked about their mother. They recalled her sense of humor, her short temper, and those times that she chased them around the yard with various solid objects for doing what they were not supposed to be doing. They recalled their love for her and her love for them. She was a good woman and a good mother. They told her they missed her and asked her to look after us. Toward the end, they had a few laughs at her expense. After an hour or so, we all said goodbye to *abuelita* and went home. I remember wondering if she was actually dead, whether she liked Pepsi or *conchas,* and when she would have a chance to eat them.

This relationship with the dead is really a relationship with death itself. Paz says that the Mexican is "familiar with death, jokes

about it, caresses it, sleeps with it, celebrates it."[1] This familiarity
was evident at that first Día de los Muertos at my grandmother's
grave. As we celebrated her, those of us who never actually met her
in life also learned that her life *meant* something: she was a good
mother, she had a sense of humor, she believed in discipline, she
loved *pan dulce*. The celebration was reflective of her life. It is for
this reason that Paz says, "Death is a mirror that reflects the ... ges-
ticulations of the living."[2]

A living with death, whether this is taken literally (as with the
scourge of cartel killings) or not, means that death is not a *yet to
happen*. Like the act of living itself, Emilio Uranga says that "the
Mexican does not leave death for 'tomorrow.' "[3] Death is a matter
of today, of now; that is, we are not "beings-toward-death" but
rather "beings-with-death," coexisting with it in an intimate and
familiar way, reciprocally sharing in meaning and significance.
This means that Mexican philosophers, unlike Freud and Ernest
Becker, do not think of death as the source of a meaningful life,
but rather think of life as giving meaning to death. If death mirrors life, we must live so that our lives are meaningful. Paz expresses this when he says, "If our deaths lack meaning, our lives
also lacked it." Clearly, if at my funeral it becomes obvious that
my death lacks meaning, then that just means that I have lived a
meaningless life.

The point is not to separate life and death as if they were radically different things. "Life and death are inseparable," says Paz,
"and when the former lacks meaning, the latter becomes equally
meaningless." In other words, if there is an exchange of meaning,
as Becker and Freud insist, it does not flow from death to life but
from life to death: life bestows meaning on death. So live well.

Another point is this: do not live motivated by the fear that someday you will die, but live as if death has already happened and there is no death to look forward to, only life and more life. Of course you will die—that is a fact—but don't allow that fact to dictate the way you live in the now. This would be to allow death to rob you of your most precious possession: time. If you live without fear of death, there's nothing it can take. As Paz puts it, "death neither gives nor receives: it consumes itself and is self-gratifying."[4] In Emilio Uranga's words, "death, in happening, will not deprive [us] of anything,"[5] because it "neither gives nor takes because there's nothing to take and there's nothing to give"[6]

There is a famous line from Paz's *The Labyrinth of Solitude* that says: "Tell me how you die and I will tell you who you are."[7] Paz's declaration, a variation of "Tell me who your friends are, and I will tell you who you are," highlights the idea of death as a mirror. The friends with whom I surround myself will tell others about me. Likewise, the way of my death—the way my life comes to an end— will inform others about the kind of person I was. The person who accepts that any moment could be his last and decides to live so that his death will be a reflection of his life is using that life as the criterion for meaning, not his death. The question should not be, *How will I die?* but rather, *How am I living?* This is a question that both respects the presence of death and prioritizes the value of life over it.

So the Mexican conception of death does not regard death as a target that will correct one's aim. It insists, rather, that we are always in communion with both the living and the dead and we carry this sense of coexistence wherever we go. Of course we will die, *eventually*. But this fear is not motivating. What is motivating is the desire to live fully now, while knowing that death is already here, mirroring what I do.

In retrospect, my grandfather's brief encounter with Pedro's ghost, and his attitude about it once he found out that this was in fact a ghost he had seen, shows a comfortable acceptance, a peaceful ease, with death itself. He was not particularly shocked, and he wasn't afraid. In fact, he felt enriched by the experience. It felt good to have communed with his friend, however briefly. And let's not forget about the milk. If death is a mirror of life, then the fact that my grandfather was not surprised that Pedro wanted to fulfill his promise to Cleotilde after death reveals how Pedro was in life: someone worthy of respect and admiration until death and beyond.

11 | STRIVE FOR ORIGINALITY

I struggle with anxiety whenever someone asks me what I do for a living. Eight out of ten times I say "I'm a teacher," which I immediately change to "professor" when the person asking follows up with "What grade?" Saying I am a professor, however, requires elaborating what it is that I profess. "I teach ethics at the business school," I say, which I technically do—I sometimes teach Professional and Business Ethics, which is mostly populated by students from the school of business, so I am not really lying. This usually does the trick, as most people find it hilarious that a course called "Business Ethics" exists in the first place. I spend a few minutes explaining how the oxymoron makes sense, then we move on.

In these moments of discomfort and unease, what I am always trying *not* to say is that I am a philosophy professor—or, God forbid, a "philosopher." I avoid saying this because the revelation is always followed by a delayed, inquisitive, somewhat surprised response—normally something like *How do you teach philosophy?* or *What do you philosophize about*? I say "normally" because, in my case, there's always something additional that my inquisitors want to know: that is, how *a guy like me*—who they can clearly see is Mexican or Latinx, obviously non-Anglo, admittedly the son of immigrant farmworkers and from an underprivileged socioeconomic background—ended up in philosophy. More urgently, they are curious about what *a guy like me* philosophizes *about*—which can be another way of asking if I am capable of philosophizing in the first place.

Questions seeking to get at the "aboutness" of my philosophizing, or versions of it, are the ones that always get me. So I've tried my best to dodge them. I dodge them not because I don't know what to say but because I fear that my answers will not be philosophical enough, that they will expose my incapacity to think philosophically. Responsible for this lack of confidence is my impostor syndrome, which tends to flare up when the need to justify myself arises. In these moments, I expect my imminent unmasking, the revelation that there's nothing philosophical about me or what I have to say. To my anxious ears, it always seems as though two other questions lay disguised in "What do you philosophize about?": the one about my capacity to do so, and a weightier question about whether I have anything *original* to say. The question about originality, in my mind, gets to the heart of the matter, to the unspoken question: *Are you really a philosopher?*

When I am unable to dodge the questions, I rack my brain for something that sounds both brilliant and definitive. But what I end up saying is never brilliant or definitive. I say that I think about the relationship between circumstance, history, and identity, say some things about Mexican philosophy and the influence of the Spanish exiles, and then change the subject to something that will take the spotlight off of me. Sometimes this works; most times it doesn't. This is because what my interrogator really wants is for me to say something not only brilliant and definitive but also profound, something that will make her say "Hmmmmmmmmm" with an index finger to her temple. In short, she wants me to say something she has never heard before, something philosophical *and* original.

It has taken me a long time to get comfortable with the anxiety that comes with saying that I'm a philosophy professor. What's helped has been the recognition of a simple truth. And the simple truth is this: that I do not have anything original to say, if by original you mean novel and never-before-uttered or thought. That's because everything I can or will say has already been said before by people more competent and more profound than I will ever be. This does not mean that I can't be original in another sense— namely, in the sense that I can say something that *originates in my experience*, my trauma, my struggles, and my victories. I can be original in the sense that I am the unique origin of my ideas. Recognizing this simple truth gives me the confidence to talk about philosophy as a *making sense of my experience*, but it has also helped me deal with that impostor syndrome that can otherwise fill me with angst and self-doubt .

Originality becomes a real worry for Mexican philosophers be- cause they suspect that, in light of their colonial history and other imperialist incursions into their country and culture, they will not be taken seriously if they don't say something original. At the same time, they are aware that having an original idea is almost im- possible, given that everything worth saying has probably already been said. All of this calls into question the very possibility of phi- losophizing, and specifically makes it hard to imagine an original Mexican philosophy, or an original *anything*.

Like many shy teenagers, I at one point yearned to be a poet. I would spend hours upon hours thinking about words, sentences, and ways to put them together so that they would say something that, in my mind, had never been said before. I had notebooks filled with poems, some of which rhymed and some of which didn't: love poems, poems about nature or death or birds, and so on. So as to encourage me, one of my teachers handed me an anthology of nineteenth-century poetry. By the time I finished reading a section on Lord Byron, I realized how much I had over-estimated my own abilities. His themes, his style, his technique convinced me that he was the greatest poet who had ever lived and that there was no way that I could compare. He had said every-thing I wanted to say, but much, much better. I was dazed by his genius and convinced that nothing original could roll out of my pen or my head. So, in defeat, I stopped writing poetry; I wouldn't write another poem for many years.

The idea that one does not have anything original to contribute to a project or a tradition or a field can keep one from even trying to do so. This led Leopoldo Zea to make the distinction I intro-duce above: *originality as novelty* versus *originality as origin*. He suggests that because everything that is worth saying has already been said, we should intend, in philosophy as in life, to be original in the sense of origin rather than in the sense of novelty (trying to say or do something that has never been said or done before). Speaking of an original Mexican philosophy, he writes: "One must attempt to do purely and simply philosophy, because what is [our own] will arise by itself."[1] If the goal is to have an original idea, for instance, the trick is to simply express the idea from our own circumstance, from our own experience, and by doing so what is original in the idea will come through in the process of expressing it. Who we are will always stamp or color the things we do or the thoughts we express. Talking about death from a Mexican perspective, for instance, will reveal a difference that belongs only to that perspective. It will be a Mexican idea of death, which, while it may not be novel (others may have had it before or have it now), will be original because it is grounded on a particular origin.

Let's consider a different example. Let's think about the musical genre known in Mexico as the *corrido*. The *corrido* is a type of traditional folk song or ballad popular in many parts of Mexico and the United States. In the early part of the twentieth century, *corridos* told tales of revolutionary heroes—usually tragic tales of bravery, sacrifice, and betrayal. The genre changed dramatically in the second half of the century, when ballads began to tell well-known stories not about national heroes but about narcotraffickers and their criminal activities. Nowadays, the best-known corridos are *narcocorridos*, which tell stories about very specific personages who have achieved notoriety in the narcotrafficking world, otherwise known as *narco-culture*; the people they sing about are typically not well known outside of this context. Today's *corrido* lyrics can be disturbing, usually portraying decapitations, assassinations, or revenge plots associated with the criminals who the song is about. Throughout the years, however, the style and form of the *corrido* has not changed. You recognize a *corrido* or *narcocorrido* when you hear it because the music sounds the same from one *corrido* to another. The question becomes, then, can someone, today, write an original *corrido*? The answer is yes. Because novelty is not something that the audience expects from a *corrido*, since it would be stylistically unrecognizable. Listeners expect a familiar-sounding ballad that originates in a specific, situated, experience, one that draws on the life of the person whose story you are telling—a ballad that has very identifiable origins. Now, it will help if the author is familiar with what they're signing about, since the *corrido* will tell us about a specific world, and about how people in that world think about existence, death, love, and so on. Ultimately, a *corrido*'s originality will rest in the specificity of the story, as well, of course, on the voice that sings it.

In a general sense, then, the fact is that worrying about originality (again, in the sense of novelty) will only hold you back. An obsession over uniqueness can paralyze you. You may freeze, become afraid to engage the world confidently—or worse, afraid to think with your own voice and from your own experience, as happened with me and Lord Byron. It is easy for us to sabotage ourselves with worries over imitation, over producing "bad copies" of something previously said or created; dismayed by such thoughts, we may resolve to cease any attempts at creative expression. This is the essence of the impostor syndrome that plagues me when I'm asked about what I philosophize about. Zea believed that an impostor syndrome likewise plagues many Mexican thinkers, who worry that they are mere imitators, nothing but inferior versions of their Western counterparts.

In calling for a distinction between these two senses of originality, the implication is that you should not worry about imitation or about being an impostor. It helps to remember that who you are or what you express will always reflect your very own experience, and even if you say or think something that has already been said or thought, your individual experience will always serve as a filter, lending what you say or think its own difference. More importantly, recognizing that, like everyone else, we were born into a civilization already in progress, we can see that almost none of us is likely to have an original (novel) thought. So, none of us is an impostor, and all of us belong—literally—to an origin from which we communicate with the universe and with each other.

Leopoldo Zea recounts an episode when a critic accused him of "charlatanism" because Zea insisted that philosophy should be understood not as an impersonal, disinterested activity dealing with themes laid out by the history of Western philosophy, but rather as a reflection of its own peculiar circumstance. According to Zea, the critic's complaint was that "to speak of themes which are not found in the [Western] philosophy books, in the texts of the great teachers" was to be "engaged in the ridiculous." The critic argued that to treat of themes such as Mexican life and its worries was "to reduce [*rebajar*] philosophy . . . to an instrument of *ends alien to the eternal.*" In other words, Zea was ignoring the fact that philosophy, when considered in its essence, is only concerned with eternal questions. The critic then lobs one last accusation at Zea, telling him "You are putting *huaraches* on Aristotle."[2]

For the unfamiliar, *huaraches* are simple sandals made of leather and yarn popular among Mexico's poorest communities. We can assume, I'm sure, that the critic thinks that to wear *huaraches* is to lack sophistication, refinement, or style. So what the critic is really saying is that to put *huaraches* on Aristotle is to demean not only Aristotle but philosophy itself. The critic obviously does not see Zea's Mexican project as original in any meaningful sense.

I disagree. We have to think that putting *huaraches* on Aristotle is original not only in the sense of novelty, since no one had done this before, but also in the sense of origin, as Aristotle is forced to do the work that Zea's circumstance requires. This is to force Aristotle to walk in common footwear and as a common man with common people in the real world.

To put *huaraches* on Aristotle is to allow philosophy to speak from and on behalf of the circumstance, from that place in the universe that forms us, informs us, and determines our perspective on things and the world. If what we say is allowed to carry with it the whole of our experience, if it is filtered by our circumstance, then what is original, in the sense of place, will emerge from it organically. It is then that our contribution, whatever that may be, will announce a uniqueness and singularity that we can honestly call "original." "Our solutions," Zea insists, "will bear the mark of our circumstances."[3]

The pressure to be original in the sense of novelty can be suffocating, which is why so many people fake it. Because it is a sign of prestige to create the first, the new, the never-before-seen, some will just ignore the fact that they, like everyone else, were thrown into an already-created world where the best we can hope to do is improve on what has already been done. Even if we know that novelty is impossible (or at least extremely difficult), that everything is based on something previously created, we might rather obscure the origin of a particular idea and claim originality than admit that what we've created or invented is influenced by the entirety of our experience.

One last example: My son is a musician. He spends hours listening to music and hours creating it. Although only sixteen, he already understands that originality in the sense of novelty is neither possible nor desirable. It is not possible since every musician must work with the same basic musical elements; and it is not desirable since, after all, he has his heroes and wants to assimilate his sound as much as possible to theirs. But my son also wants to create *his own* music. My advice to him echoes Zea's insight: just create music, and what is truly yours will emerge on its own! And this goes for everything else as well. As a chef, your goal should be to create those dishes that you want to create, inspired by your own experience, tastes, and passions, and whatever is original about your cooking, what will distinguish you, will emerge on its own. Even if you use recipes downloaded from the internet, your dishes will bear the mark of who you are. The same applies if you're a philosopher, a fashion designer, or a poet.

12 | THERE IS HOPE IN ZOZOBRA

Every Labor Day weekend since 1926, New Mexicans have gathered at a local park in the state's capital, Santa Fe, to celebrate the "Burning of Zozobra."

Inspired by an annual tradition of the Yaqui Indians of northern Mexico, where an effigy of Judas, the betrayer of Jesus, is blown up with all manner of fireworks, the Burning of Zozobra likewise centers on an effigy—this one of Zozobra, a monstrous, twenty-foot-high, puppet-like figure made of paper and wood. Unlike Judas, with his religious-historical significance, Zozobra represents all the anxiety, fear, and negativity endured by the community the preceding year. Still, both the blowing up of Judas and the burning of Zozobra symbolize power and control over that which appears as otherwise unavoidable (Judas' betrayal of Jesus over two-thousand years ago) or uncontrollable (our human fragility).

The Zozobra monster is named after the psychological-existential condition known as "zozobra." The term is of Spanish origin with Latin roots. You can hear it in its pronunciation: "zozobra" sounds somewhat like "sub-supra," a coupling of the Latin *sub* and *supra*, "under" and "over," and can refer literally to the floundering of someone drowning who thrashes wildly above and below the water's surface in a desperate struggle against the pull of the ocean's floor.

This feeling of drowning can also overtake us in our everyday lives. It comes in the form of anxiety, despair, uncertainty, restlessness, and fear. An emotionally stifling feeling, it may come upon us gradually or suddenly, but when it does, it can feel like it will tear us apart.

Before continuing, a word of clarification: it is easy to conflate the emotional suffocation of zozobra with what we typically know as "anxiety." But they are not the same. To feel anxious is to feel nervous, worried, or fearful about some future event. It is typically somewhat shallow by comparison, and this is evident in the way we deal with it: meditation, exercise, deep breaths, sedatives—any of these will help us cope with anxiety. Zozobra is much more complex. It involves not only the emotions associated with anxiety, but also others we don't normally associate with it, together with an acute awareness of its inevitability and our own finitude. Thus, gripped by zozobra we *feel* anxious, restless, uncomfortable, discontented, threatened, indecisive, and terrified, but we also *know* that we are powerless to help ourselves. All we can do is endure it.

That New Mexicans respond to zozobra by anthropomorphizing it as a colossal demon and engulfing it in flames points to our inability to get a handle on what it is or how to deal with it in everyday life. Thus, seeing it burned to ashes on Labor Day weekend seems like a good way to free oneself from its tenacious clutches, at least temporarily.

The problem is that, just as blowing up an effigy of Judas can't stop the Crucifixion, the burning of Zozobra doesn't dispel people's sense of dread, gloom, despair, uncertainty, fear, and all those things that define the emotional state it represents. A huge bonfire with a raucous crowd on a warm September evening may get people "out of their heads" long enough to forget their troubles, but once the flames die down it all goes back to the way it was.

∾

Recently, my wife left home early in the morning for her yearly mammogram. She stopped to get some coffee and then headed to her doctor's office. She texted me about dinner, suggesting she would pick something up.

Our lives continued as usual for a couple of days after her appointment—coffee in the morning, dinner plans at noon, dinner in the evening, and so on. Then the results came in. They showed an abnormality, a dense mass in one of her breasts. She was called in for a biopsy. It was cancer. They did other tests and identified the type and its stage. Luckily, they had caught it early enough that she would not need chemo, but she would need surgery, radiation, and almost a decade of Tamoxifen.

In the span of a week, both our lives had been turned upside down. But hers especially. She spoke about her fear of dying, the sense of indeterminacy and uncertainty that now pervaded her waking life. Her morning routines were disrupted now by an unexplainable, invasive, and malignant feeling of dread and unease. Zozobra had set in.

Jorge Portilla described zozobra as being "transfixed by nothingness." It is not simple fear or worry or nervousness about the future, but a feeling of being paralyzed by what's standing right in front of you. To experience zozobra is to be hypnotized by the possibilities of ruin or devastation. The nothingness and uncertainty of a cancer diagnosis would transfix anyone, hold them in suspense as they stare at their own death and wait for the worst that they feel is certain to come.

For months, my wife was transfixed by the nothingness of death, of the future, and of the possible. She felt her world slowly coming apart with every breath she took. Zozobra filled up her hours. And there was no way to treat it, no chance to burn it away. Emilio Uranga says that in zozobra every moment foretells a coming "catastrophe."[1] And for months, this was my wife's holding pattern, a waiting for calamity, unsure if it would come, gripped by every terrifying possibility. These possibilities were imagined, of course (in this sense, they were *nothing*), but they were still fueling her zozobra, her restlessness. Life-affirming thoughts were scarce, and when these made their way into her thinking, they were quickly confronted by their opposite extremes. And so the hope brought about by the news that the cancer was treatable was ultimately cancelled out by the fear that, even if she survived it *this* time, it could recur. Likewise, the comfort she felt at knowing that others had endured worse and survived, quickly dissipated at the devastating realization that, in any confrontation with her own death, she would always be irremediably alone.

Mexican philosophers, sensing a fundamental unease among the Mexican people, have made zozobra a theme of their philosophizing. They recognize that this unease is, of course, existential, or an aspect of our being human, but it is also historical. It is historical because the violence of conquest and colonization lives in the collective memory, as do the various wars for independence and the traumatic Revolution of 1910, not to mention the persistence of political corruption, economic insecurity, geopolitical marginalization, and so on. This history translates into everyday life as an always-just-below-the-surface sense that the worst is yet to come.

When looked at as an existential state, some philosophers, including Luis Villoro, have imagined that zozobra is really just the feeling of having to choose between what is known and what is unknown. What is known, Villoro calls "misery"; what is unknown, he calls "infinity." Both what we know (e.g., the cause of our present misery) and what we don't know (e.g., the infinite future) can be sources of despair.

But, for Villoro, that uncertainty is present always and everywhere, and it can also serve as a source of something unexpected: *hope*.

> [In zozobra] existence remains suspended between two abysses—one of misery, one of infinity—thus keeping itself in suspense about itself. Instability is its permanent condition, uncertainty its natural state. Perpetually oscillating between extremes and unattainable situations, man travels on, unable to steady himself, fearful and trembling. In fear and trembling, yes . . . but, also, in *faith* and *hope*?[2]

What this means is that, if instability is your permanent existential condition, then at the very least you have some certainty in your instability. And if this is the case, then isn't your uncertainty certain enough that it can offer some stability? This is not unlike a popular view shared among recovering addicts who encourage one another with the thought that *once you hit rock bottom, the only way to go is up*. The idea is that once you have run out of options, have exhausted all resources, burned all your bridges, and caused all the damage that can be caused, recognizing your situation for what it is can lead to that moment of clarity when you can see a possible way out, or up. Similarly, the recognition that all of your options are either uncertain or unattainable, horrible or impossible, offers you an opportunity to accept things for what they are and perhaps gives you hope that you can survive it. After all, you've probably survived worse things.

The faith and hope that Villoro finds in *zozobra* require owning up to it as something real, present, and unavoidable—as something that can't be burnt in effigy. It requires acceptance and the peace that comes with that. This sort of acceptance is what Uranga calls "submergence." To accept our zozobra is to "submerge" ourselves in it.[3] The metaphor of "submergence" should remind us of the etymology of zozobra as "sub-supra," under and over. If we think of it in this way, then our submersion requires us to simply let go and accept it, the idea being that if we go under we will eventually *go over*—we will emerge. On this reading, submergence means being willing to face the nothingness that transfixes me, and accepting the despair and uncertainty that may come.

Zozobra is uncertainty, unease, fear, anxiety, and despair all mashed together into one overwhelming mood that makes you feel as if there is no hope for you or for the world. But accepting it, submerging yourself in it, allowing yourself to feel it, grants you the possibility to see that this mood is not yours alone but everyone's, and that together *we* can survive it. Going back to the addict who's hit rock bottom: For a time, this person suffers the punishment that comes with his addiction. He tries to stop but can't. The consequences pile up—he loses his money, health, and family. In a moment of clarity, he accepts that he has a problem and that he is powerless to solve it on his own, surrendering to the uncomfortable thought that he cannot help himself. This motivates him to seek fellow sufferers, those who have likewise surrendered, and by finding them he finds community. It is now that his healing can begin. The *hope* internal to *zozobra* says that we will, in time, converge with others in spaces of empathy or sympathy. The result of this convergence will be community and togetherness, a space of communication and dialogue, a space for the sharing of individual experiences and trauma—a space for recovery and transformation.

I end with the aftermath of my wife's cancer diagnosis.

Once the surgeries were done and the rounds of radiation were behind her, the fear and anxiety over recurrence began to resurface. Zozobra was not done with her.

However, she soon remembered that her *zozobra* was part of her experience, part of her narrative, and not indicative of any determinate future. It is then that a community of survivors emerged. Women equally shaped by this particular type of *zozobra* coming together and sharing their stories and their fears—a community of hope.

Of course, her zozobra is not gone. She often imagines her existential possibilities as those between the possibility of more sickness and death, between misery and infinity—between equally dark extremes. But in accepting these possibilities head-on, in submerging herself in zozobra, she dulls their edges.

Ultimately, zozobra may at some time terrorize us all, but to know this is to be ready for it. This readiness involves knowing that nothing is certain and that our sense of security is an illusion, that everything we imagine as stable and consistent can break down at any moment. For this reason we must recognize that our choices are not clear-cut, that choosing is terrifying, and that whatever we chose may harm us. But we must surrender to this terror, a surrender that can bring with it hope, community, and transformation.

13 | ENGAGE IN A BIT OF *RELAJO*

When we are young, our parents tell us not to associate with So-and-So because, they say, So-and-So is "trouble." By this, they usually mean that So-and-So easily gets into trouble and that the kind of trouble So-and-So gets into is the kind that rubs off, the kind that sticks to you. If you hang out with them, you'll be trouble too. The trouble that my own mother feared I'd become or get into was of the criminal sort.

I tried listening to my mother when she said this, and tried to avoid consorting with kids who were swiping stereos, breaking windows, shoplifting random things from hardware stores. The problem was that my mother's advice didn't extend to those kids who were just loud and obnoxious and who existed in what seemed like a perpetual state of rule-breaking. While breaking some of those rules wasn't as bad as shoplifting, it was serious enough that avoiding those kids was always a good idea.

This is the kind of trouble that my eighth-grade classmate Alex was constantly in. Alex seemed to have an allergy to rules, to procedures, to teachers' authority. He never did what he was "supposed" to do, especially if he was told that he was supposed to do it. Now, Alex didn't fight, or steal, or bully other kids; he simply lacked a working sense of seriousness, which meant that he was always in trouble. Because a lack of seriousness can often appear as playfulness, Alex's lack of it also meant that, when he got into trouble, those around him inevitably got into trouble too. No one can deny that "playing around" is more fun than studying or paying attention. Nevertheless, this wasn't the kind of trouble my mother warned me about; this was another, noncriminal, sort of trouble.

One incident stands out. Mr. Sinclair was a small oval-shaped man with a fat, bald head. As the resident eighth-grade history teacher, he carried himself with a know-it-all air. He wore a suit and tie most of the time, a symbol of his seriousness and training. On "casual Fridays," he'd spice it up a bit with a white dress shirt and a clip-on tie. But on one of these casual Fridays, Mr. Sinclair went rogue: he wore a black T-shirt with the face of the country singer Waylon Jennings emblazoned on the front and "Waylon Jennings" printed in bold, pink cursive across the top. It was odd to see the usually serious Mr. Sinclair in such a loud T-shirt, but it *was* casual Friday!

Casual Friday or not, there was history to be taught, and today it was the Hundred Years' War. Some of us took notes (as we were *supposed* to), others dozed off (they couldn't help it), while still others feigned attention and doodled on their notepads. Now, what everyone understood—nappers and doodlers included—was that we were in school, in a classroom, where a certain classroom discipline was being observed, where certain rules and expectations were in place that everyone was meant to follow. But as we sat there quietly listening to Mr. Sinclair relate the events leading up to a conflict between England and France a long, long time ago,

Alex, seemingly out of nowhere, blurted out, "Hey, Mr. Sinclair, is it true that Waylon Jennings slept with your wife?"

What?! We all turned to Alex, who appeared to be waiting for the answer to his question, then to Mr. Sinclair, who stared back at Alex with a confused look, frozen with rage, his round face filling up with blood like a water balloon. The moment stretched into eternity. Under a weighty tension, some students quietly asked, "Who is Waylon Jennings?"

In a moment, the murmuring began. "Uh-oh, Mr. Sinclair's gonna pop!" one student whispered. "You're gonna take that, right, Mr. Sinclair?" said another loudly. A bloodthirsty chorus egged Mr. Sinclair into a fight. Some had seen enough and tried to divert attention away from the old man and toward the instigator: "I heard Waylon Jennings is *your* dad, Alex!" Laughter erupted. I still had no idea who Waylon Jennings was. History itself, for a moment, was forgotten: the Waylon Jennings Affair was in progress. Some followed up with the joke referencing Alex's mother, his paternity, laughing, screaming, cussing. Most wondered out loud, *Are we laughing about the guy on the T-shirt?* Mr. Sinclair was lost in his rage. Any classroom atmosphere had been suspended, replaced by chaos.

I was annoyed. I wanted to know, *How did the Hundred Years' War end? Who won? Did it really go on for 100 years?* But answers wouldn't come. History had suddenly stopped. The whole class was swept up in an orgy of unseriousness.

Finally, in a thick Missouri accent that was usually barely noticeable, an angry Mr. Sinclair growled, "Alex, out! To the principal's office, git!" Alex calmly got out of his seat and walked out, but not before taking one last shot: "Tell your wife to say hello to Waylon for me!" Trouble having been sent to the office, we could now get back to the drama brewing between the House of Plantagenet and the House of Valois. Or so I thought. That, too, would have to wait. Mr. Sinclair couldn't recover. He ordered us all to read on our own, in silence, for the remainder of the period.

The events of that day stayed with me. I was an English-language learner, and up to that point I'd had a hard time picking up on things. So I tried to focus and learn what I could when I had the chance. This interruption had stolen one of those chances, and this filled me angst. So for a while I resented Alex . . . and Waylon Jennings. In the years since, however, I've come to see the entire episode under a different light, and come to appreciate that what Alex had done was much more complex than simply being disruptive. He had shown me, perhaps for the first time in my young life, a way to free myself from the bonds of rules, expectations, and rituals. In other words, he had shown me the liberating power of unseriousness.

The Mexican philosopher Jorge Portilla has a name for what happened that day in my eighth-grade history class. He calls it *relajo*, a term referring to a kind of action or behavior that is at the same time disruptive, distracting, *and inviting*. *Relajo*, says Portilla, undermines "seriousness," which is doing what you are expected to do in a given situation. As students in a classroom, the expectation was that we sit, listen, take notes, ask questions about the subject matter, and so on. The classroom atmosphere itself demanded seriousness; Alex's comment about Waylon Jennings undermined that seriousness. The comment was certainly disruptive and distracting, but it was also inviting, since it opened the door for others to join in on the disruption. Once others accepted the invitation, our hope for doing as was expected of us (as students in a classroom) was gone. *Relajo* had set in and we just had to wait for it to end.

Portilla defines *relajo* as a reiterated action that "suspends seriousness." Moreover, he says that seriousness is a saying "yes" to the "demands of value." There is a value or set of values attached to education, to the Supreme Court, to the Search for Extraterrestrial Intelligence (SETI), and so on. Seriousness is saying "yes" to what these things demand of you. To say yes to the value represented by the Supreme Court, for instance, is to respect the institution and abide by its rulings. Alternatively, to say no to the value represented by SETI is to mock it, ridicule it, to not take it seriously. *Relajo*, in suspending seriousness, is an attitude or behavior that disrupts, dislocates, displaces, or undermines value. *Relajo* in the Supreme Court might involve interrupting its proceedings via a string of jokes, noises, or other actions that would call attention away from what the Court is tasked with doing. Because of the interruption, its proceedings would be emptied of seriousness or order or expectation, and what remains would be disorder, unseriousness, and chaos–*relajo*. Like the Waylon Jennings Affair.

Or think of a funeral. Imagine if the funeral procession for Queen Elizabeth II was interrupted by a low-flying Garfield blimp. The appearance of the blimp is itself not *relajo*, but what happens next will determine if the occasion devolves into it. If on the appearance of the giant Garfield, mourners begin joking about it, making cat noises, whispering "I hate Mondays" to one another, upsetting the Royals, panicking the horses, quickly turning what is supposed to be a somber event into a chaotic, loud, festival-like joke, then we would say that the seriousness demanded by the funeral had been suspended.

In either case, the funeral procession or my history class, the initial instinct is to denounce the interruption or the interrupter (Alex or the Garfield blimp). I initially did this with Alex; Portilla himself would certainly do so on both occasions. He argues that *relajo* stunts personal and social growth. Regarding my history class, Portilla would say that *relajo* made it impossible for me to learn, and thus grow as a student and as a person. Regarding the funeral procession, he would see *relajo* as devaluing traditions and rituals that have been around for hundreds of years, which cannot be good for communal and social cohesion.

However, just as I eventually realized with Alex, there is a different way to think of *relajo*. This is to think of *relajo* not in a negative sense, as a disruptive suspension that stunts our growth and sociality, but in a positive sense, as an opportunity to get out of our routines, a chance to throw off the yoke, to question our duties, to live freely—even if only for a moment. In history class, one could say that *relajo* made it possible for us to escape, if only briefly, from the rote of classroom learning. During the funeral, it could be argued that *relajo* would have given attendees the opportunity to unburden themselves of their blind obedience to funerary rituals and outdated traditions.

If we think of relajo in this positive sense, then we would want more of it. But *relajo* is not easy to initiate. Conditions need to be right; we also need *relajientos*. *Relajientos*, Portilla says, are people who live to bring about disruption and are always ready to crack the Garfield joke, insult the history teacher, or, generally, initiate the chaos that will turn a somber or serious occasion into *relajo*. Through his actions, a *relajiento* will suspend seriousness, or value, or worth and not think twice about it. We thus say that *relajientos* or *relajientas* (because these could also be women) *personify relajo*.

Relajientos are enemies of seriousness. They will not take anything seriously, but especially social rules, conventions, or expectations. If they come across a serious situation, one regulated by rules or traditions, like a church service, a political protest, a history lesson, or the reading of a will, they will not waste the chance to interrupt it in a way that will challenge it, deny its value, suspend its seriousness, or negate its purpose. *Relajientos* are overly relaxed (the meaning of the Spanish word "relajiento" is literally "the one who is relaxed"), lackadaisical, unoccupied, or, even, like my friend Alex, always looking for a chance to be disruptive. In Spanish, we would say that they are "siempre listos para el desmadre," always ready for hell to break loose. Their speech and behavior suggest that what they value most of all is the freedom to do as they please.

We do fear, however, that *relajientos* will show up at the worst possible time—that is, a time demanding seriousness. Thus, their sudden appearance at an otherwise serious event, such as a book reading, a meeting of the chamber of commerce, or a wedding, might make us nervous. Their arrival forces us to attend to them, to wait for the joke, the noise, the chaos. Although anxious for what may come next, for instance, "a shower of jokes that will dissolve the seriousness of all topics, reducing them literally, to nothing," their very appearance frees us, if only momentarily, of our commitment to what would otherwise hold our attention.

You may be recalling friends and acquaintances who are surely *relajientos* like Alex. They are fun companions. In their company everything is laughter and play, gossip and innuendo. They can always make us forget our immediate concerns, at least for a moment. And in doing so, they involve us in the suspension of values and seriousness, in a little *desmadre*. "The relajiento," Portilla says, "does not bring about preoccupation but rather inoccupation."

Again, Portilla's take on *relajo* and *relajientos* is negative. He believes there is little room in our society for such behavior, and that we must respect values, seriousness, and order or risk not progressing personally or as a society. On this point, however, I don't fully agree with Portilla. Contemporary culture demands that we take almost everything seriously or risk being seen as insensitive, offensive, or even anti-social. But at times such demands can feel oppressive. The social imperative that one must respect values and be serious at all times, for one's own sake and for the sake of the social good, seems like an imposition. And therein lies the virtue of *relajo*. It has the ability to break us out of our routines. In witnessing the suspension of seriousness, we get a glimpse of a kind of freedom from cultural demands and social imperatives to which we may otherwise remain blind. While we may not want to partake in a prolonged *relajo* event—which could turn out to be disappointing, boring, or even frightening—it is nice to take a break from seriousness by letting the chaos sweep us away, if only briefly.

So I think there's nothing wrong with engaging in a bit of *relajo*. In suspending seriousness we play and enjoy life, even if it involves "wasting our time." To think this way is also to think that *relajo* can be an act of resistance. An easy example is *relajo* in the context of institutionalized religion.

You walk into a sixteenth-century baroque cathedral with thick walls and high ceilings, its walls covered with gold-plated images of saints and scenes from Christ's Passion. It's one of the oldest Catholic churches in Puebla, Mexico. The place is heavy with the smell of hundreds of years of incense and burnt candles.

The worshipers take their seats. Almost 2,000 years of rules and rituals seem to thicken the air in the centuries-old building. There is a seriousness about this place that must be respected. There are values internal to it that must be brought to fulfillment through the actions of the supplicants. One must pray quietly, reverently, while focused on nothing else but the unimaginable suffering of Christ on the Cross. We know what is required of us—speaking in hushed tones, sitting or kneeling quietly, and, if attending a mass, following the expected rituals of when to sit and rise, receive communion, and pray. To go off script would be an act of disrespect, an act of contempt against the Church, Christ, oneself, and one's community. One feels the value that holds the entire scene together as one feels the damp air; it is in the atmosphere, dominating the space.

Now imagine an individual for whom these rituals seem frivolous and oppressive. Rather than bow his head in obedience to tradition, again, to values, he loudly proclaims, "Mexico's World Cup chances actually aren't that bad this year. Maybe we should pray for victory!" The priest, who has been reading out loud from the Gospel of Mark, looks up and stops reading. This outburst displaces the attention of the worshipers, but it is not yet *relajo*.

But then someone in the back responds, "Mexico's team won't make it past the second round!" Another adds yells, "Sit down! Neither of you has seen the new squad!" Immediately, a discussion breaks out about Mexican soccer. Some people laugh, others shush, others silently wonder whether Mexico really has a chance against Germany this year. Thinking about Christ on the Cross now seems impossible. *Relajo* has set in. Finally, the priest gives up and retreats. Now, the values that underlie all the usual rituals that are followed in this space have been let go. If only for a moment, the colonial values that have dominated the discourse and behavior in this particular place for almost 500 years have been overcome by a series of negations and displacements.

In this case, we can see how *relajo* can be an act of rebellion against established religious rituals. In Mexico, one could call it an anti-colonial strategy, an instance of free expression in an otherwise oppressive setting. Against Portilla, one could thus argue that *relajo* could play a similar liberatory role in many other oppressive situations. Not to follow the rules seems like a good way to stick it to the system!

The problem is that *relajo* does not destroy seriousness; it merely suspends it. That is, it does not permanently destroy our relation to values. We do not become permanently unserious. Just because the Church service broke out into *relajo* that particular Sunday does not mean any of those people will stay away from Catholicism or its rituals. Just as in our history class, we eventually learned about the Hundred Years' War!

Because a *relajo* event will be temporary—we went back to studying history, the funeral proceeded as planned, people went back to church—it is not a kind of anti-colonial, decolonial, or liberatory strategy that we can employ politically. But we can take advantage of it when it comes. For the sake of social or communal progress, it is best to take things seriously, but we should not do so excessively. We should respect values, while also recognizing that values often contribute to our unfreedom, that seriousness can be oppressive, and that rituals and traditions are artificial constructs against which it would be healthy to rebel once in a while. So let's not avoid *relajo*—let's allow ourselves the opportunity to appreciate those moments when we are free to engage in a bit of *desmadre*.

14 | ARE YOU AN *APRETADO* OR *APRETADA*?

El Tambor is a small hamlet in the western Mexican state of Michoacán. It is officially a part of Acuitzeramo, which is itself barely a town. El Tambor (The Drum) boasts about 100 residents, a number which quadruples during December and January, when sons, daughters, and grandchildren briefly return from their wanderings in El Norte (The North—i.e., the United States), where they've been diligently toiling for their cut of the American Dream.

El Tambor was my home as a very young child. I lived there with my grandparents and my mother in an adobe house built sometime in the nineteenth century, itself built atop another building built sometime in the eighteenth century, and on and on. I remember life being slow-paced, predictable, quiet. Things picked up in December when the "wanderers" arrived. Most moved into homes they'd left behind when they migrated north. They were happy to be back, even if only for a short while. They would make the journey north again in January.

The recently returned strolled through town loud, joyously and carefree, wearing cowboy boots and cowboy hats, bright shirts and new blue jeans, symbols of their prosperity and their success *en el otro lado*—on the other side. And most were generous with their time and their money, wasting no opportunity to splurge on food or drink, inviting anyone around to join them. The whole town would come alive. It seemed that we all benefited from their arrival.

But there were some who were not so generous. They carried themselves with an air of superiority that seemed out of place and was annoying to most of the permanent residents. It seemed as if they didn't want to be there. Even if they had been born and raised in El Tambor, they now treated the town and its people with disdain. Something had changed in the time they'd been gone. They were now "Americanized" and wanted everyone to know that they were, in fact, "del Norte," of the North. In their mannerisms, their dress, and their treatment of others, they proclaimed themselves to be part of an exclusive set: *Americanos*. In every respect they sought to fully embody what it meant to be *Americanos*. Seeing them out and about was to bear witness to an instance of "American culture." Looking back, I can say that they were "full of themselves." As such, they had no need for any of us, since there was nothing we could add to their sense of fulness. And they knew this. They were closed-off, "stuck-up," arrogant. What their superior attitude communicated was that we, the townsfolk, were "below" them. But while they thought of themselves as "Americans," the townspeople didn't call them that. My *abuela* and many others called them *apretados*.

You have known *apretados*. You may know them as snobs because they are full of themselves, take themselves way too seriously, and arrogantly believe that they are, in all things, always right and correct. If you don't believe what they believe, dress as they dress, or act as they act, then you are somehow inferior and not worth their time.

The literal translation of *apretado* is "tight." To *apretar* something is to tighten it. Applied to persons, we say that So-and-So is an *apretado* if he is "tight" with his money, refusing to spend it even when necessary. *Apretados* are not generous. We may also talk about So-and-So being *apretados* if they are "set in their ways," refusing to their worldview, and hold on to what they value "no matter what." Thus, we can say that *apretados* are passionately, enthusiastically, fervently, and fanatically committed to those ways on which they are set.

The popular television show *The Daily Show* has given us a great example of *apretados* as set in their ways. Its correspondent Jordan Klepper has often infiltrated political rallies held for or by former president Donald Trump, where he encounters and interviews Trump supporters, to both the amusement and the horror of his viewers. In one instance, he is confronted with someone who believes Trump is still the president.

"So," asks Klepper, "does he still hold the powers of the presidency?"

"Well," the supporter responds, "he's been flying around the world on Air Force One."

Confused, Klepper says, "I thought Joe Biden's technically on Air Force One." He's met with an adamant "No!"

"So they're faking it?"

"Yeah, it's not even a presidency."

"Who is running the government right now?"

"President Trump."

These supporters are fanatical, set in their ways. Nothing will change their minds. Facts and evidence are not important. "Donald Trump supporters" is *what* and *who* they are. In their dress, their beliefs, and their attitudes about non-supporters, they are steadfast. They believe themselves to be different, members of an exclusive club of believers who know the truth, while those outside the club are simply ignorant or brainwashed by "the mainstream media." Like the Americanized migrants I saw in El Tambor as a kid, these folks too are *apretados*.

Jorge Portilla has thought a lot about this type of person. The *apretado*, he says, is the opposite of the *relajiento*—the troublemaker type we met in the previous chapter. According to Portilla, *apretados* are "*afflicted* with the spirit of seriousness." This "affliction," like all afflictions, means that *apretados* are tormented with the need to be serious. It pains them not to be. In their seriousness, they will zealously commit themselves to certain values (represented by personalities, ideas, belief systems) and always do precisely what such commitment demands of them. The *apretados'* unconditional commitment to their beliefs—to their values—sets them apart.

A different way to say this is that *apretados* identify values with truth or reality; that is, what they value *is* the truth or the real. They come to internalize this identity (my value = the truth) and come to see themselves as identical with their values and thus with the truth or reality. Portilla says that apretados see "no distance . . . between being and value." We thus recognize *apretados* from what they say and how they say it, what they wear, and how they act. Such recognition is possible because, Portilla says, *apretados* "carry their value in the same way that they carry with them their legs or their liver."[1] And so just like they are attached to their legs or their liver, they are attached to their values. Take, for instance, a man who values celibacy above all else. If he's serious about it, there will be no "distance" or no distinction between his personality and his staunch belief that any type of sexual contact is impure, immoral, or unbecoming. Everything about him—his dress, his walk, his speech—will scream "celibate!"

Many of us are familiar with religious *apretados*, who we can also refer to as religious fanatics or extremists. They set their ways to their religion, and their religion is the truth. It orients their lives. They defend it against naysayers and chastise those who don't value it the way they themselves do, or those that have a different understanding of what the value of their religion may be. Religious *apretado*s always have the correct interpretation of religious doctrine. They loudly push their religion as the only true religion, and believe themselves to be in possession of its right and proper definition. They don't tire of promoting it—in person, on social media, on the streets. Some of them also aim for a certain look, depending on their sect. Their faith is all they talk about. An open discussion about popular culture is beneath them, unless the aim is to dissect it critically in accordance with the "truths" of their faith. I imagine that these *apretados* will find this book too secular to read.

In Mexico, the values available to an *apretado*, those that they may uphold or embody, are usually colonial or foreign values. Colonial values have been handed down by history and tradition, while foreign values will have been picked up from someplace else, often from a culture perceived as superior to their own (e.g., the United States, France, or Spain). The *apretados* in El Tambor took "American" (US) values as their guides—in what they wore, how they spoke, and how they treated us and each other.

❧

Apretados take certain values and adopt behavior intended to reflect those values. To set their ways like this is to allow those values to orient their lives. Life is lived in strict adherence to the value's demands. As *apretados* embody these values and never tire of promoting them, we think of them as fanatics. Their fanaticism closes off the possibility that their values will be challenged, altered in light of new experiences, or discarded. Ultimately, fanatics are willing to die for their values, and many do. This is because, as Portilla puts it, for *apretados* "values are not ever-attainable guides for self-constitution, but rather actual ingredients of their own personalities."[2]

Of course, this is not strictly a Mexican phenomenon. In fact, we can all exhibit *apretado*-like tendencies via behaviors bordering on fanaticism for values, for personalities, for activities and so on. So, ask yourself, *Am I an apretado or apretada*?

Check your symptoms.

☐ **Excessiveness**

The first symptom is an excessive enthusiasm for what is valued. *Apretados* are zealots for those things that they think are important. They are excessively committed to upholding those things or promoting their value and will embody what they believe even if this means isolating themselves from family, community, and society. They will fully represent what they value, and others can see it in the way they dress, speak, or act. Once they are committed to what they consider *the* truth or reality, they will go all in, doubling down in the face of contrary evidence. Religious or political fanatics readily come to mind, as do obsessive sports fans.

☐ **Possessiveness**

The second symptom is a belief that the value can be owned or possessed. *Apretados* live as though they have ownership over those things that they consider valuable. But more importantly, they behave as though the values they uphold are properties of their own personality. They will think of themselves as their proprietor, and will defend them just as one would defend one's home from thieves. Because they stake a claim of ownership on those values, moreover, they will consider those who do not value what they themselves value as "dispossessed," less-than, as subhuman. We find an example of this second "symptom" in religious *apretados,* who typically imagine that they actually own their religion. Portilla says that *apretados* "live in calm possession of their properties." Ultimately, as proprietors, *apretados* relate to the world and to others through "a having, a possessing," which means that, as they see it, "the one who possesses is; the one who does not possess is not."[3]

☐ **Exclusiveness**

The third symptom is a cultish attitude about their values. *Apretados* want to be exclusive, to exist apart from those not sharing their own special relation to values, though this desire for exclusivity obviously requires others who lack such possessions or excesses. Their personalities rely on always being better than others and in believing (even if not knowing) that others see them as their superiors based solely on their exclusive relation to the values that identify them. As Portilla puts it, "Exclusivity is the supreme category in the world of the apretado."[4]

☐ **Abstractness**

A final characteristic of the *apretado* is "abstractness," a belief that one can *become* what they value. In this state of self-deception, one thinks of oneself as more than a mere mortal, but as the value itself. This is because *apretados* want to achieve a level of abstractness that signals simultaneity and identity with the abstract values that they own and defend and that characterize them. The process of abstraction begins with exclusivity, with a distancing from others (the have-nots, the *relajientos*). But because they are excessive, *apretados* double down on their commitment to their value; they seek the "exclusivity of exclusivities," that is, to *be* as the object of their affection, to be more abstract than real, and thereby out of reach. I recall decades ago saying something disparaging about the history of the Catholic Church to a Catholic *apretado,* and the person has not spoken to me since. Such people, in their obsession with what they value, may come to identify with it to the point that insulting an institution is the equivalent of insulting them.

So, are you an *apretado*? Is your wardrobe a reflection of your political allegiances? Do you feel like what you value makes you special? Do you get offended when someone offers the slightest criticism of your faith? If so or if you checked any of the boxes above, you should ask yourself about your value commitments. You might consider detaching yourself experimentally from those things or ideas that seem to constitute your identity, if only to consider whether you've become fanatical about them, and perhaps to test whether there's an alternative way to live, one with more leeway to value many different things and points of view. However, if being married to such values is how you access life's meaning, then you will likely continue to tighten your grip on them, becoming more *apretado* and not less. But I wouldn't recommend it.

15 | PRACTICE IRONY, BUT BE SOCRATIC ABOUT IT

I came home from school to find my mother in a conversation about immortality with a yellow-haired woman in a bright-pink coat.

"But you would like to live forever, wouldn't you, *señora*?" asked the woman in Spanish, the kind of Spanish spoken by educated, high-class folks, the Spanish they teach in college. This was not my mother's Spanish. Her Spanish, I was once told once by someone in Mexico City who heard me speaking it, was *Español de rancho*—countryside Spanish, hillbilly Spanish! Although I've gotten used to such microaggressions, this one stung a bit.

My mother smiled at the yellow-haired woman. She had always been generous and welcoming, which, in the past, people had confused for ignorance, or naïveté, or gullibility. "I would love to live forever. Who wouldn't?" she said. The truth is that she didn't want to live forever. She'd often say that life was too hard, and too tiring, and too painful—one life was enough! Even though she was a Catholic, she didn't care to believe in everlasting life. In this, she retained a belief consistent with her Indigenous roots that a desire for everlasting life was the epitome of greed and selfishness— in order for other things to live, everything had to die. Nevertheless, decency demanded that she continue listening and conversing with the woman, so she said, "Imagine all the things you could do with eternal life. All the conversations you could have!" (I knew this was a lie. My mother detested conversations like this one. She said this ironically, and only I knew it.)

"Jehovah is the way. We are promised a paradise without pain or worry or trouble. There is only love and peace and fellowship," said the yellow-haired lady while holding up a picture of a happy couple in this paradise, who, walking past a tiger drinking from a stream next to an antelope, exemplified the promised bliss. "*Señora*, there is no time. You have to come to Jehovah, because the end of the world is near!" I sat next to her because I knew she was running out of patience and wanted it to end. I knew she thought it ridiculous to promise such things. She had always been a fatalist and, I can see now, an existentialist to the bone. For her, there was no afterlife, there was no paradise—and there was no coming Armageddon! She used to say, "El mundo se acaba para todo al le le toque." In other words, we each get our own individual apocalypse–our own personal death.

"So no pain, no death, no worry, eternal life, a world without end?" asks my mom pensively.

"That's right!" said the woman excitedly, perhaps thinking that she'd secured a sale.

"I would love that!" said my mother. "But can I ask you something?" I knew this was coming. We'd arrived at the end of her patience. "Do we get kicked out of paradise if we misbehave?" she asked, implying with her expression that I myself could be in trouble. "Because I can imagine that people would still want to do things that are against the rules in paradise." The woman struggled to answer, evidently wrestling with the question, *Are there rules in heaven*? She began to suspect that my mom was not as naive as she seemed.

"Well, um, you will not misbehave because there is no reason to do that. You misbehave when you want something that you can't have. But in heaven, you will have all you need. You will be blissfully happy. So there is no reason to act badly."

"So I will not *want* anything?" says my mom, still smiling. "Everyone walks around without any desires? That's great. Because, you know," she said in her *español de rancho,* her hillbilly Spanish, "it's those desires that make life difficult. Sounds like people in paradise are satisfied . . . always satisfied. So there's no need to do anything else. But why would we want that forever? It doesn't sound like life at all." She maintained an innocent smile as she said all this.

"No, *señora*, people do think and have thoughts and desires," she said, nervously laughing. "But our desires are for Jehovah. We always desire more of Him." I could see she was struggling to keep her story straight.

"I'm starting to think that paradise is like being drunk. But you'll have to tell me more about this because I'm confused," said my mother. "So if there's no pain or suffering, and just feeling good, how do you know you're in paradise and not someplace else? I mean, how can you appreciate where you are if there's nothing to compare it to? But it does sound much better than *this,*" she said, gesturing with her hand to the old, broken, sofa on which we sat, the worn-down carpet beneath our feet, and main door, that for some reason was held together with tape and wires.

I knew the encounter was over. The woman had noticed the irony. She couldn't answer my mother's questions in a way that satisfied them both. And maybe, just maybe, the yellow-haired woman herself had never thought about these questions be-fore: *How do you know* that it's paradise and not someplace else? Regardless, at this point she realized she had to find a reason to leave. Which she did, promising to come back another day and bring literature.

As she walked out, my mother turned to me and said, "Imagine that! No pain, no wants . . . so just like being dead? *This, mijjo*, is all the paradise we will ever get. You want some wienies with ketchup?"

My mother's irony was Socratic. She always found a way to make everyone believe that she was clueless about a particular subject before delivering them to the truth of their own ignorance. I'm sure she didn't learn the Socratic method in school, having barely completed the second grade. Some (not her, of course) could have made the case that she learned it in a past life, as Socrates himself suggests in the *Meno*, and was thus born with a supernatural ability to see through bullshit.

The beauty of Socratic irony is that it is a great way to reveal falsehood or arrogant posturing for what it is. This is brilliantly illustrated in the Platonic dialogue *Euthyphro*. Socrates, who is on his way to court to defend himself against the charge of "impiety," runs into Euthyphro, who is likewise on his way to court to accuse his own father of the same crime. In a humble, naive way, Socrates begs Euthyphro to remind him of the na-ture of "piety," since Socrates himself has apparently been impious without intending to be. Euthyphro obliges, giving

Socrates one definition after another, after each of which Socrates responds with more questions. The more Euthyphro explains, the less Socrates claims to know, and toward the end, Socrates seems more confused than before. Finally, Euthyphro, tired of explaining his position, is led by Socrates to reveal that he, Euthyphro, really doesn't know what piety is, showing us (readers) that sometimes we know little about things that we claim to be knowledgeable about.

We've come to call Socrates' use of irony in his so-called Platonic dialogues "Socratic irony." And there's a formula to it, which goes something like this: Socrates claims ignorance about X so as to get an interlocutor, one who claims to be an expert on X, to admit or expose his own ignorance about it.

In my mother's case: she claims not to know anything about paradise so as to get the yellow-haired woman, who claims to have knowledge of such things, to ultimately expose her own ignorance about it. Socrates' interlocutors, just like the yellow-haired woman, never truly admit defeat. Like her, Euthyphro finally excuses himself and departs, leaving Socrates without an answer. Nevertheless, Socrates has accomplished what he seemingly set out to do—namely, to unsettle the dogmatic tendencies of someone who claimed to have a hold on knowledge. Those of us listening in and reading the discussion 2,500 years later are thus implicitly invited to take up the challenge—more than likely in an undergraduate philosophy class, where a professor asks students thumbing through their iPhones, *So, guys, what is piety, really?*

࿇

According to Jorge Portilla, Socratic irony is an approach to values and to life that is neither *relajo* nor fanaticism. As Portilla describes it, the Socratic ironist represents a middle way that avoids the extremes of *relajientos* or *apretados*.

In the two previous chapters, we learned from Portilla about these two extreme stances toward value and we saw how they can be a threat to your pursuit of the good life. The first is *relajo* as the suspension of seriousness. *Relajo* is a threat to the good life because in *relajo* you can't take anything seriously, not even life itself. It is possible, through a constant suspension of seriousness, to dismiss the value of everything and live aimlessly and without purpose. In this way, *relajo* would make it so that living itself becomes a waste of time.

The second worry has to do with excessive seriousness. Taking things too seriously can make you unbending or fanatical. Being unbending, like an *apretado*, is a threat to the good life because it anchors people to rigid beliefs or values. Unwilling to change your mind, you will live life imprisoned to one way—your way— of looking at things. Being excessively serious about what you value or what you believe in means that all other values, beliefs, or perspectives will be considered false, while your worldview will be the only one that matters. Such a life is oppressive and unfree.

These two attitudes are opposites of one another. They are both relations that you can form with values or with what is valuable. Portilla thinks that both are harmful. As far as he's concerned, your attitude to value should not be lackadaisical or fanatical, but *ironic*. Put differently, you should not accept things as they are, nor should you reject them wholesale, but should instead constantly challenge them, interrogate them, and make them answer for themselves. You can do this with the use of Socratic irony.

As Portilla understands it, Socratic irony is the middle way between the *relajiento*, who rejects values, and the *apretado*, who embodies them. Socratic irony is motivated by a "will to truth," or by a desire for truth. The will to truth demands a critical attitude toward values, but not one lacking understanding of what those values are or what they mean. Portilla writes, "Irony is a liberation that founds a freedom for value."[1] In my mother's case, Socratic irony was the only way she was able to liberate the value of life (or what it means to be alive) from the religious dogmatism of the lady in the pink coat—even if the lady in the pink coat didn't stay long enough to appreciate their liberation. Portilla would say that my mother had a well-developed "ironic consciousness," a kind of consciousness necessary to overcome both *relajo* and/or fanaticism, since only an ironic consciousness can take a healthy interest in things without rejecting them or authorizing them without question. In the context of Portilla's philosophy, irony is thereby the means whereby people can open themselves to more of what life has to offer.

As we've seen, the most valuable function of Socratic irony is that it allows you to challenge the purported truth of established or popular beliefs, especially when these are noxious or harmful. Now, clearly you can't change the harmful or unfair opinions out there in the world if you ignore or devalue them (like a *relajiento*), nor can you change them when you completely buy into them, embody them, or defend them (as with *apretados*). But, you can bring about change by helping to expose them for what they are.

Consider two examples. The first deals with a popular political movement that has been growing in intensity in the past few decades, fueled by certain conservative ideas that seem medieval in their cruelty and blindness. It is driven by one message: that immigrants are being shuttled into the United States so as to "replace" white, Christian "Americans." It is called the "Great Replacement Theory," and it is broadcast on conservative radio, cable news networks, and social media, promoted by sitting senators, presidential candidates, and so on. Because of this, it has authority.

Now, we could just mock the theory, joke about it, and devalue it whenever we encounter it. In *relajo*, we could simply draw attention away from it whenever it comes up in conversation. Or we could accept it, take it seriously, make it matter more than any other social concern. If we agree with it, we could join a border militia and try to stop the "invasion"; if we disagree with it, we could become anti-Replacement Theory warriors and dedicate our life to protesting it. However, in either case, *relajientos* and *apretados* rarely affect such theories at all; they typically leave things as they are.

Enter Socratic irony. We might use it like this: by feigning ignorance about the theory's origins, its scope, and its purpose when speaking to people who wish to advance it. The proponent, a middle-aged white man, explains Replacement Theory, as best he can, while you, the listener, as enraged or bothered as you may be, simply listen and ask innocent-seeming questions. "Ah," you ask, "so are you saying that each immigrant who comes into the country *replaces* a white person? What happens to the white people who are replaced? Where do they go?"

"Well," he may counter, "they don't go anywhere. What we mean is that the immigrant is taking the white person's job."

"In the fields? In the back of the kitchen? What job is the white person losing?"

"Actually," he responds, seemingly remembering a talking point, "what I mean is that one immigrant replaces either one white person who has died or one white person who was *never born,* which is why keeping our birth rates up is important."

"So when a white person dies, an immigrant replaces him or her? The immigrant becomes the husband to the dead person's wife, or the mother to the dead person's kids? Is that what you mean?" Soon the proponent (like Euthyphro or my mother's visitor) begins to realize that he doesn't know the answers to the questions that his position raises. He may then realize one of two things: either that he doesn't know why he believes in the Theory, or that he doesn't even know what the Theory actually entails.

It could be the case that the proponent is well-versed and so can faithfully explain and account for the totality of the Theory. But by taking a Socratic posture, by motivating the conversation with a "Tell me more," the Theory will be articulated for all to hear. Whatever is true in it should reveal itself, as well as whatever is false. In a theory like this one, however, grounded on fundamental misunderstandings or purposeful distortions about immigration, immigrants, demographic shifts, and so on, its falsity will reveal itself to anyone paying attention. Challenging it in this way will expose it for what it is.

My second example deals with Critical Race Theory, or CRT—commonly, and mistakenly, understood to describe teaching students simple facts about American history, including the history of racism in the United States. This is a similarly hot-button issue among white conservatives. Opponents complain that they want none of it in schools. However, the idea that it is being taught in schools is a fallacy created by the conservative right for shock value; it's actually discussed almost exclusively in law schools. In spite of this misunderstanding, teachers have been pressured into not teaching students about race and racism even in the most basic ways. Some teachers push back. I read of a high-school teacher who, when asked by a parent whether CRT was taught in her school, replied brilliantly, "If you tell me what it is, I'll tell you if we teach it." The parent couldn't tell her what it was, perhaps because he didn't actually know and was merely repeating what he had heard on a conversative news outlet. His ignorance exposed a blind spot in the anti-CRT movement—namely, that most folks who are against it don't know what it is they're against.

The teacher's use of irony in this example is perfectly Socratic. She is a true ironist who, Portilla says, "notices the distance between the possible realization of a value and its supposed realization by someone with a pretense of fulfilling it. It is, so to speak, the adequate response to the 'self-assuming person.'"[2] In this example, the teacher immediately recognized that the parent was "self-assuming," so she confronted him in a way that exposed his ignorance, or what Portilla calls the "distance" between what he knew and what he claimed to know. Now, she may not have convinced him that he didn't really know about CRT, but responding the way he did allows us, and especially those in the audience, to consider the possibility that we can undermine the anti-CRT movement by pushing back on the very questions being asked about it. This should reveal that what lies behind the movement is right-wing news propaganda, or, even worse, a concern that students might actually learn about slavery as a major reality in the history of the United States.

In the case of the Replacement Theory or the anti-CRT movement, a healthy use of irony will help reveal the truth, along with their proponents' more nefarious intentions. Though such an approach may not succeed right away, it may begin a conversation that will continue after the encounter and eventually expose these advocates for what they really are.

Socratic irony is a healthy way to get to the bottom of things. You can cultivate such an attitude in the following way:

(i) By practicing a kind of skepticism both about what you are told and about what you think you know. Like Socrates, you must from the outset not claim to know anything with certainty but instead approach all things with a kind of caution that seems closer to openness than to stupidity.

(ii) Holding your tongue and listening, so as to let others speak. You want to be well informed before you make up your mind about the value, meaning, or truth of things, and this requires listening. This also suggests that you are motivated by a "will to truth." You are ironic because you desire truth.

(iii) And resisting the sometimes overwhelming desire to attack the other person's point of view before they're done telling you what that is. Too abrupt an attack makes it more likely that the person whose point of view you have just exposed will double down on it, burrowing deeper into their position.

Using irony in a healthy way demands that you stay (i) open, (ii) generous, and (iii) patient. This practice will help you achieve the freedom that comes with calling attention to falsity and ignorance. It should be employed without ridicule or sarcasm, but instead with attention and listening. Like the yellow-haired woman all those years ago, ignorant people, if allowed to speak long enough, will reveal their ignorance all on their own.

16 | SET YOURSELF APART

The early history of philosophy in Mexico has its share of singular figures. You're now familiar with Alonso de la Veracruz (1507–1584), who in 1540 taught the very first philosophy course in the Americas in a small convent in Michoacán. There's also Sor Juana Inés de la Cruz (1648–1695), the very first feminist philosopher in the "New World." We may also include the scholar Carlos de Sigüenza y Góngora (1645–1700) on this list. Better known than Veracruz and Sigüenza y Góngora (though not Sor Juana) is Bartolomé de las Casas (1484–1566), who in 1550 fearlessly fought for the rights of the Indigenous peoples of New Spain in the court of the Spanish King, Charles I, something no one had attempted before.

There's indeed something special about these figures. Las Casas and Sor Juana, for instance, appear to embody an admirable degree of purposiveness and unselfishness. Their willingness to stand up to both governments and tradition transcended the material concerns that would keep the rest of us from doing anything of the sort. Las Casas stood up to the Spanish Crown and demanded fair and humane treatment for Indigenous peoples, at a time when it was unpopular and dangerous to do so. Sor Juana, a nun, called out the misogyny and hypocrisy of Church authorities, which eventually led to her persecution by the Bishop of Puebla. Both were singularly dedicated to doing the right thing, and did so at risk to their reputation, life, and liberty.

That "something special" shared by Las Casas and Sor Juana appears only rarely in the history of humanity. We see it in twentieth-century figures such as Martin Luther King, Nelson Mandela, Cesar Chavez, Martin Luther King, Jr., Rigoberta Menchú, and Emiliano Zapata, to name a select few. In each case, their commitment to truth and justice was more than what was required of someone who in any normal sense would be considered honest or just. They seem to have possessed a kind of enthusiasm for justice that most of us can only marvel at. And we marvel at it because such enthusiasm is not something we think we can ever achieve—it seems, in a way, unnatural or superhuman. A look at their biography, at where they were born, who they married, what they read, and so on, doesn't explain why they were the way they were. Their specialness seems *extra*.

We thus hold up these figures to our children (or at least we *should*) as "role models," exemplary people who they should strive to emulate. And we do this because we want our children to model the right behavior (caring, selfless, truthful, sincere, etc.) and to live so bravely and act so righteously that they themselves can one day be seen as role models, ideals to which others can aspire.

Brave, legendary people tend to be admirably unselfish. Unselfishness is a rare quality that seems to be an extra feature of some people, something added to their personalities that cannot be explained when we appeal to a simple inventory of facts about them. Take Sor Juana Inés de la Cruz. She was born to a wealthy Spanish family in Nepantla, Mexico, in 1648, entered the convent at 19, became a Hieronymite nun at 21, lived a life of study and service, and died of the plague in 1695. None of these facts explain or account for her fearless commitment to gender equality—she criticized the established patriarchy in Mexico and in the Catholic Church centuries before such criticism was common. Her fearlessness is certainly *something more, something extra* added to the bare facts of her life; it is something she achieved *in spite of* her circumstance. Samuel Ramos calls this extra something *personalidad*, which we may translate as "true self" or "highest character."

According to Ramos, living things are what he calls *individuals*. Examples include redwood trees, cats, and US senators. Some of these individuals are persons, or "psychological subjects" who are rational and who care for others. Senators, for instance, unlike cats or redwoods, will make commitments to others and (ideally) take responsibility for their actions, and so they qualify as persons. Because persons can be responsible for their actions and for others, they are "moral subjects." As persons, most of us are moral subjects, but an even smaller number of us will have *personalidad*, a "true self" or "highest character." So some moral subjects possess, along with self-awareness and the capacity to take personal responsibility, something extra that makes them stand out as the sort of moral person who others admire and aspire to emulate. "A true self," Ramos says, "is the highest degree reached by some individuals"—a level of being human that is reached only by a very few. History remembers true selves, those who live on past their expiration dates!

Ramos isn't very clear about how one becomes a true self, how one acquires a *personalidad*, but at least three conditions must be met. The first is that one must be a moral subject who is not easily "dragged along" by one's "urges" or overcome by the pressures of embodied existence. So one of the conditions necessary to achieve this status is to master one's impulses—to resist self-serving urges. Selfishness must be replaced with generosity, narcissism with altruism, and neutrality with action. Another condition is that one must "impose oneself" on the world for the sake of truth and justice—in other words, act on the world forcefully and with conviction, but only for the sake of something greater than oneself rather than for domination or profit. A true self, says Ramos, "obeys the norms of truth, morality, and aesthetics" and seeks to live by them.[1]

A last condition is reserved for those who seek to become the sort of true self remembered in history books. Achieving this kind of true self requires not only self-mastery and commitment to truth and justice but a complete surrender to higher values, "even to the point of oblivion or self-abdication"[2]—that is, to ideals that are objective rather than personal or self-serving. In other words, one must live in complete obedience to a higher purpose, even to the point of death.

But there's a catch. Although you will keep your eyes fixed on a higher purpose, you should not be purposely trying to achieve a true self; this should not be your goal. By keeping your eyes fixed on what's greater than yourself, you may perhaps become a true self, but this should not be the reason why you do what you do. Think of Malala Yousafzai's advocacy for girls' education in Pakistan. Believing in the transcendent value of education, Yousafzai has put her life on the line, risking it all to the "point of oblivion" or death. Nevertheless, her surrender to the higher values of justice, truth, and equality was not done for the sake of gaining a true self, fame, or fortune, but was instead done for its own sake. That she has achieved a true self in the process of her sacrifice just means that her surrender was complete and egoless.

Surrendering to the call of higher values, to what is objectively true and objectively good, means surrendering your desire for a true self. You cannot gain a true self by force; you cannot force yourself to be a role model. You must let it reveal itself in what you do, lending to everything you do an "imprint," a "stamp," or a "seal" that announces to others that *a true self was here*.[3] Letting go of your desire for glory and fame is thus as important for gaining a true self as living in accordance with higher values. Your ego becomes the enemy here, since "to aspire consciously to affirm one's own true self is the surest way of losing it."[4] Ramos adds that a "condition" for gaining a true self is, then, to "forget" that that is the goal. All of this means that developing, gaining, or becoming a true self should not be your primary concern. This would be an individualistic tendency, an egotistical desire. In selflessness, obedience, and surrender you should act according to truth and justice, and *only then* will you be a candidate for gaining a true self. A true self is the pinnacle of good and right living, which means being charitable, sacrificial, and a benefit to others.

But this is obviously a tall order, and perhaps you just don't know where to begin. You want to be more than what you are; you want to have character and possess a true self, while also working with what you have, within your capacities and capabilities. But how should you go about this?

Again, the trick here is to pursue higher values for their own sake and not for the sake of being seen as a true self, "better than the rest." So one thing you will not do is blindly imitate those you admire in the hope that, through simple imitation, you will achieve a status similar to theirs. Yes, you want to set those you admire as models, finding motivation in their dedication, their drive, and their actions, but not by losing your identity in theirs. You could model the actions of Las Casas, Sor Juana, Rigoberta Menchú, or Martin Luther King without seeking the kind of fame and glory that they achieved through their deeds. After all, it was hardly the pursuit of fame and glory that motivated them to do what they did! So you set them up as role models only; you put their posters up on your wall but without wanting to be them. In your own pursuit of higher values you will do things differently— namely, in accordance with your own capacities and what you are allowed to do by your circumstance. What remains the same is that if and when you achieve your true self, your *personalidad*, you will do so by doing things your own way, via your own sacrifice and your own inner power.

What if, after all that, you have still not achieved a true self? Well, at least you've activated those behaviors and ways of existing that have made you a better, less narcissistic, more praiseworthy moral subject.

While some true selves are easier to model than others, all true selves can serve as inspiration for us. Consider Emiliano Zapata, arguably Mexico's greatest revolutionary figure. Unlike other leaders of the twentieth century's first revolution (there would be more), Zapata was not ambitious to achieve political power, money, or fame, but rather to serve the interests of his people. Putting the interest of the poorest of the poor at the heart of his fight, he waged war against the Mexican government for land distribution so that the poorest members of society could feed themselves and their families. Assassinated in 1917, he continued to inspire millions not just in Mexico but throughout Latin America for the next one hundred years.

How can we model Zapata? First, by being selfless and other-directed, caring for the least-advantaged members of our society. Second, by surrendering to our destiny, whatever that may be. And third, by living in accordance with an uncompromising sense of truth and willingness to risk one's skin in order to defend that truth.

Ramos tells us:

> The mission of a true self [*personalidad*] is to keep the human spirit from coming to a halt. Socially, he is one who incites revolution [*un fermento revolucionario*], who, by virtue of his distaste for established values, drives culture forward by discovering ever new horizons for human aspiration.[5]

Certainly, Zapata fits the bill, and our modeling of his true self should at least make us accomplices to his mission, to his continuing ability to open new "horizons for human aspiration." Or we could just take inspiration from his sacrifice and determine to be self-sacrificing ourselves.

To summarize: do not consciously pursue being a true self, but rather act in such a way that you are at the very least modeling the actions and behaviors of a great moral exemplar, while remaining careful not to fall into imitation. Imitating a true self is futile, because the singularity of your model, the essence of what he or she is as a person, will not translate to you, or to anyone. Not to mention that such imitation is likely to be self-serving and individualistic making what you do always "I-directed." However, if in the process of modeling their actions or their character you become a true self, the reward will be humanity's and not merely your own.

One of Zapata's most significant contributions to the history books is perhaps the "Plan de Ayala," the declaration of war and manifesto for land reform written in 1911 and signed by a collective including his top generals. If anything reflects Zapata's "true self" as we understand it here, it is this Plan.

The Plan de Ayala contains fifteen points that could serve as the blueprint for a future society, one that privileges the needs of the poorest among us. The Plan states that it is "in favor of the poor, who will [once it is enacted] be able to acquire a piece of land for themselves to cultivate, so as to support their families without the necessity of subjecting themselves to the slavery of Capitalism." The sixth, seventh, and eighth points of the Plan are specifically directed toward the equitable distribution of land. The fifteenth point reminds people that Mexico's current president (in 1911) has broken his promises and must be deposed, and that, in order to end the bloodshed, more bloodshed will have to be spilled.

Its final words are apt to our lesson here. It reads: "We are not personalists! We align ourselves with principles and not with men!"[6] By "personalists" Zapata means simply individuals who are easily seduced by the mere image of a powerful figure, usually a politician who through the use of charisma, fallacious arguments, and theatrics convinces others to be on his side. By "principles," the Plan means those higher values or truths that guide the actions of true selves, like Zapata himself, and that transcend time and place. Zapata thus urges his readers to align themselves with higher values and not with whoever tells them the more convincing story at any particular time—that is, in the terms I've been using here, to model our lives after true selves and not mere individuals.

17 | THE WAY OF DIGNIFIED CYNICISM

On a work trip to Culiacán, Sinaloa, in 2019, as I'm being driven back late at night to my hotel from a party thrown by my university host, my driver is stopped at a police checkpoint. A federal police officer pointing an AR-15 semiautomatic rifle directly at our windshield waves us to the side of the road. He asks to see my driver's registration and license. My driver says he has neither. The policeman says, "Well, I guess you're spending the night in the can." To which my driver calmly responds, "No, I'm not."

As this is happening, I try to figure out where I am relative to my hotel, since it looks like I might have to get back on foot. This is a scary thought—the last thing I want to do is walk miles through a strange city at night, especially *this one*, home to a notoriously violent international drug cartel.

"Oh! And why's that?" asks the officer, noticeably irritated at my driver's response.

"Because," says my driver as he slowly slides 200 pesos into the officer's shirt pocket, "you have other things to do." I think, *This Jedi mind trick cannot possibly work.*

"Add fifty pesos more and maybe I do," says the officer. They stare at one another knowingly. As soon as my driver tucks another few bills into his pocket, the officer waves us through.

I ask my driver how he knew that would work. "It always does. They're not out here protecting anyone; all they're doing is robbing us when they can of whatever they can get. We're used to it. From top to bottom, they're all thieves! That's the reason why they're out there, just to get their cut." Of course, he doesn't exactly say "just to get their cut"; he says "*no'mas para su mordida*," which literally translates to "only for their bite," as in "they're out here only for their bite of your wallet."

Clearly, my driver's cynicism is warranted. This was police corruption in plain view. While ideally police are meant to serve the public good, this was clearly not happening here. In Mexico, as in many other places throughout the world, police and government corruption is an everyday affair. People are cynical about these institutions because they have to deal with corruption as a fact of daily life. And here in Mexico the corruption is so ubiquitous and ordinary that no one even bothers trying to hide it.

To my naive surprise, my driver isn't bothered by what had just happened. He tells me he was prepared for the *mordida*—he is *always* prepared for the *mordida*. "Most people are!" he tells me emphatically. "But," he asks with a grin, "did you see how smoothly I put the money in his pocket? That was to show him that I *knew* he was a crook!" He says this with a tone of satisfaction, even triumph. "He knows I see him. He knows I know the truth," he tells me. I am impressed with his confidence, but above all I am amazed by how paying the bribe actually seems to have empowered him.

The driver was certainly savvy and knew how to handle his circumstances, but was he wise? Is his the sort of wisdom we should emulate? Can such cynicism be adopted—is that healthy? Philosophers from Socrates onward have suggested that it can be, but only if it is the sort of cynicism that ends by throwing into relief—at least for ourselves—the truth of a state of affairs that may empower us. Following Emilio Uranga, we will call the kind of cynicism that empowers "dignified cynicism."[1] While the usual definition of cynicism identifies a general distrust of the (selfish) motives of others, dignified cynicism is the sort of distrust that actually comports with dignity. Defined in this way, we can say that my driver was a dignified cynic whose cynicism helps him live and deal with the truth of his own social-political situation.

Social media is full of cynics. However, the cynicism we often see online can be easily confused with arrogance or resentment, because that cynic is usually jaded, bitter, and resentful. Convinced that "the system" is rigged against him, that he will never get a fair shot, he resorts to tirades on social media, thereby sinking deeper into his own powerlessness and resentment. Whereas in "real life" he may be meek and silent, lacking in will and dignity, online he becomes overconfident and loud, while in fact burdened with negativity.

My driver's cynicism was not like the online cynic's. He wasn't loud or negative, resentful or meek. His type of cynicism is "dignified" because it is not self-indulgent or egotistical but instead other-directed, issue-directed, socially directed, empowered, and rebellious. It is rebellious because it directs its power and purpose to conditions, social and otherwise, that are usually oppressive, demoralizing, or dehumanizing. As such, we can think of dignified cynicism as a kind of cynicism that can serve us as a strategy of resistance in an otherwise corrupt or unjust world.

Another way to say this is that my driver's cynicism was dignified because it aimed at exposing a state of corruption and injustice that continues to be both real and widespread, one that affects not only his own circumstance but that of his community. You may say he was hardly rebelling if he gave the police officer just what he expected and wanted all along. But it was *the way* my driver did it—his *performance*—that was dignified. Watching him slip the money into the cop's pocket in such a flagrant and scandalous way educated his passenger on how things worked in this corruption-afflicted part of the world. There was no resentment in his performance, no hatred. His dignity reflected not a sense of submission to a dominant power (in this case, the State) but instead control over his own world. Implicitly scoffing at the corruption and hypocrisy of the officer—not quite a defender of law and order after all!—represented in fact a revealing display of power!

When faced with trying circumstances against which you must find small, powerful ways to resist, you should try to be more like my driver. Rebel, but in a dignified way. Being a dignified cynic will allow you to survive and navigate your circumstance with control and dignity, not hatred or resentment. This requires knowing your own circumstance and how it tends toward justice or injustice, freedom or oppression. This in turn means—under other circumstances—having the courage to speak up in honest and brutal ways about injustice and oppression without allowing resentment to build up. To live like a dignified cynic, then, requires courage, self-control, knowledge, and a really thick skin.

A dignified cynic will expose the truth of her circumstance even at the cost of likeability, since, as Uranga says, she will appear to many as "cold-blooded" and "brutal."[2]

The dignified cynic is "cold-blooded" when what she says or points out strikes others as insensitive or offensive. An incisive remark to your conservative-leaning friend suggesting that a border wall is merely a political distraction without any actual effects on the flow of immigrants into the country is cold-blooded because it ignores how your friend *feels* or what your friend believes to be true about such things. Incapable of sugarcoating things, or simply unwilling to do so, you will insist that it's better in the long run that your friend hears the truth than to keep on hearing only what he wants to hear. One of my closest friends, Arturo, is cold-blooded in this way: he will tell the truth in spite of hurt feelings. I once heard him assure a new father—who was also our friend—not to worry because all babies are born ugly. "Yours will grow out of it too," he said. Our friend was speechless, especially since he hadn't asked him what he thought of his baby's looks.

The cold-bloodedness of dignified cynics will appear brutal because what cuts through the illusion, or accepted opinion, will often feel like violence. Indeed, offended parties would call out Arturo's cruelty, feeling violated or injured by his cold-bloodedness. This is because those that feel violated by the cold-bloodedness of the dignified cynic may have been at peace with the illusion—that is, they may have known that what they claimed to believe was actually false and they were okay with that. To be told the truth in such a direct and unfiltered way is another way to call out their conformity; indeed, the dignified cynic's brutality and cold-bloodedness will probably often call *you* out!

Dignified cynicism is a weapon against oppressive values, rituals, and institutions. It is especially useful anywhere that is marked by authoritarian power structures, pervasive corruption, and systemic injustice. Unless you enjoy living under immoral and unscrupulous political or social arrangements that consistently deprioritize your social well-being, it is important to voice your skepticism about the ways things stand. That is why, for Uranga, cynicism is liberatory work.

Take corruption. For most of the population in Mexico, Central America, and South America, corruption is a fact of everyday life. According to the Global Corruption Index, three-quarters of all Latin American countries are seriously corrupt (in all varieties of corruption including bribery and abuse of power). As of 2023, Venezuela was identified as the most corrupt country in the region, with a Corruption Index rank of 183. Mexico did somewhat better, with a rank of 118, though only narrowly better than Russia, at 127. (For comparison, Finland's rank was 1, while the United States' was 24.)[3] Mexico also has the highest "bribery victimization rate" in the Americas, meaning that proportionally more people are forced to pay bribes there than anywhere else on the two continents.[4] Knowing that corruption is rampant can be demoralizing and disempowering.

Maintaining constant awareness and reminding others that most of those in power are only out for their own selfish interests is the sort of essential work that society needs. But it is also the sort of work that can empower you, that can make you feel useful and valuable. As a dignified cynic, you cease to see yourself as a passive victim and instead become an actor, someone who acts to "save the circumstance." Uranga thus asks us to be dignified cynics, and not merely cynical in a dismissive, contemptuous, fearful, and resentful way.

Let's return to my experience in Culiacán. A modern-day social-media cynic would have had a hard time at the police checkpoint. Based on this isolated brush with police corruption, our cynic would have condemned all social structures in Mexico as equally corrupt, pessimistically evaluated his own status of powerlessness and inferiority before the mighty powers of the state, and devalued Mexican culture as a whole, maybe as primitive or barbaric.

But my driver, a dignified cynic, instead made a straightforward, cold-blooded assessment of the state of things. Corruption in Mexico is rampant, in spite of what the government says. He held no resentment about this, but neither did he accept the situation as it was. His act of protest was to bribe the police officer almost sarcastically or sardonically, letting the officer know that he understands the officer's game and can also play it. And in doing this he explained the way things worked to me, an outsider, speaking the truth in the midst of this encounter with corruption. Before this, I had been under the illusion that things like bribery and corruption were kept hidden and invisible. I am no longer under that illusion.

The question is: does being a dignified cynic lead to a better, more fulfilling life? Actually, it seems like an exhausting way to live. Constantly calling out corruption, untruths, deception, evil, and wrongness seems tiring. But ignoring such things doesn't make them go away. So we need a healthy dose of cynicism, a dignified dose, in order not to fall for the illusion that everything is perfect. Calling out injustice, inequality, and corruption so as to keep them from becoming normal, everyday affairs makes us responsible for ourselves and others. And it also gives us peace—not peace as renunciation, since ours is an ongoing battle, but the peace that comes from knowing how the game is being played and knowing that one can play it oneself.

18 | DON'T BE A TROLL

Driving my sons to the beach on a hot summer day used to be a chore. Although the beach was only an hour away, they would complain the entire way—about each other, about the heat, about the music, about everything! Their subsequent discovery of TikTok and Instagram and Snapchat and Facebook made this one-hour trip much easier. Now even during a family trip of two or three hours, all you'll hear is an occasional giggle or a muffled "Daaaamn!" Once in a while they'll show their screens to one another, but those moments are rare; the rest of the time they're alone with their content. And a lot can happen in that time. They can get into arguments, they can find love, they can be betrayed, they can bully or be bullied, they can hurt and get hurt.

If I had daughters, they would be more likely than boys to fall into depression, anxiety, and loneliness because of their social-media use.[1] Nevertheless, the truth is that we are *all* negatively impacted by social media in one way or another. This is because, according to a number of studies, social media makes it easier to compare oneself to others, and especially to standards of beauty that are almost impossible to achieve. It is easy to feel inferior to someone who, on social media, appears to be perfect, without physical flaws or body fat. And no matter how badly we want to achieve an ideal standard we will inevitably fail to achieve it, no matter how much we exercise, no matter how much we change ourselves.

This inability to achieve perfection can lead to feelings of inferiority, and such feelings often have dangerous side effects. For some, the reaction may be isolation, body dysmorphia, depression, self-harm, or even suicide. Others may react to their feelings of inferiority by "trolling," deliberately annoying or even harassing other people online, usually anonymously. Some do it for fun, others out of boredom or *just because.* But many do it to hide their own self-doubt, attacking or shaming others, and especially the way they look, which gives the troll a sense of superiority or achievement. Rudeness, bullying, and other abuses persist until the troll achieves his objective: to bury his own feelings of inferiority by asserting a momentary sense of power over his intended target, thereby achieving a certain (fictitious and worthless) victory.

As awful as this behavior is, we can imagine why people sometimes act this way online. From safely behind a screen, it may be tempting to want to disparage someone with more wealth, prestige, power, or perceived beauty in order to avoid dealing with one's own personal failings. And this is purportedly safe to do; after all, they can't see me, and if I really want to hide they will never know who I am.

❦

What, you may be asking, does this have to do with Mexican philosophy? One of Mexican philosophy's most controversial theses has it that Mexicans suffer from a collective inferiority complex, a swirl of emotions similar to those that can motivate online trolls. Inferiority may be expressed both individually, as your persistent neurotic feeling that other individuals around you have it better, and collectively, as the general sense that *we* (Mexican, Latinx, Midwestern, or whoever *we* are) are not as strong, as advanced, as economically well-off, as other groups of people.

In *Profile of Man and Culture in Mexico*, a monumental book in the history of Mexican philosophy originally published in 1934, Samuel Ramos finds the roots of this "complex" in Mexican history:

> At its birth, Mexico found itself in the civilized world in the same way that a child finds itself before his parents. It came into history when there was already a mature civilization. . . . From this disadvantageous situation is born his feeling of inferiority made worse with the conquest, mestizaje, and even by the disproportionate magnitude of nature.[2]

Ramos's observation is basically this: the history of the conquest and its aftermath made Mexico in many ways a "child" of Europe. A child, moreover, that is still immature, unprepared, vulnerable—a child not nearly as strong, settled, or capable as its parents, and still in need of direction, protection, and approbation. While Mexico's independence from Spain in 1820 did reveal a readiness to branch out on its own, its submission to France a few decades later, and its chaotic revolution decades after that, show that it was unprepared for its independence—still immature, inferior, and not ready for adulthood.

Ramos is aware that diagnosing an entire culture as suffering from an inferiority complex may be a sweeping generalization. He is clear, however, that inferiority is just a feeling and not an actual state about the culture itself. The culture is not inferior; the individual people that make up the culture *feel* inferior, and they tend to express this feeling in ways that often seem immature. I recall the first time I caught a fish. I must've been eight years old. My uncle, already in his late 20s, was fishing on the other side of the pond with no luck (we weren't fishing together; he just happened to be fishing at the same time I was). I could see he was frustrated. I suddenly got a bite and pulled out a giant catfish—this thing was as long as my arm! My uncle ran to where I was, and taking a long look at it, said, "These are poisonous. I better take this for my dog." He took my fish and later cooked it and ate it. This became a family scandal. My mother was furious. My grandmother sat me down and gave a reason for my uncle's behavior: he had always been an immature and petty man and had taken my fish simply out of resentment and jealously. It had nothing to do with me. His inferiority complex had gotten the better of him.

None of this should be unfamiliar. When you feel "less than," do you ever feel the need to disparage a thing because you can't have it? Or, maybe you feel like taking it or destroying it for the same reason? Perhaps you act out in less dramatic ways, for instance, by drawing attention away from yourself by pointing to someone else's flaws. Have you ever bought something you can't afford just to give the impression that you can? These are all signs that you may be masking an inferiority complex.

But you are not alone. Inferiority is a complex feeling, and one that has plagued people from the beginning of time. Aesop's fable "The Fox and the Grapes" is a classic illustration. Told over 2,500 years ago, the story is simple: A fox wants to eat grapes from a vine, but the grapes are too high for it to reach. Rather than accept that it is unable to reach the grapes, the fox convinces himself that those particular grapes don't meet his standards of excellence anyway, shrugging off his failure by asserting his superior taste. In Samuel Ramos's account, foxes include people who disparage their neighbor's home, for instance, simply because it is not *their* home. They may have wanted to buy this home themselves at some point. But for any number of reasons, including and most likely financial reasons, their neighbor's home belongs to the neighbor and not to them. The only recourse now is to deny ever wanting to buy the home, to complain about its size, to imagine that it is probably too expensive to maintain, too costly to repair, and so on.

You may know someone like this, someone who behaves like Aesop's fox. They will express their sense of inferiority in various, mundane ways. In an effort to compensate for a lack of power or money, for instance, they may not tire of speaking ill of those who have either or both while proclaiming the many reasons why their own lives are better. That they are merely covering up for their inadequacy and don't actually think that they have it better than the rich and powerful is revealed when they confess that, if they had money or power, they wouldn't live the way they live now.

Others might express their feelings of inferiority in other ways, including always wanting to show off (or "predominate," to use

Ramos's term). Show-offs want everyone to know what they have, how rare it is, and how much it's worth. There is no real existential or social need to do this other than the desire to feel superior to others. If no one pays attention to their display, they may react like online trolls, with frustration, resentment, and malice.[3] Ramos says that such people are engaging in an "exaggerated preoccupation with affirming their personality."[4] The idea is that, if they are constantly flashy and boisterous, others will not see their weakness and powerlessness. Thus, if all I hear from you is an inventory of all the things you have, then I probably won't notice how deep in debt you are.

People struggling with substance abuse are usually advised to avoid resentment at all costs. And this is because resenting others is usually a way to shift the blame for your struggles onto someone else, to convince yourself that another is responsible for your problems. But such blaming never solves anything, it never affects the person being blamed, it is powerless to change the external world. What it does do, however, is that it gives the person struggling a reason to avoid responsibility. If I am not responsible for my struggles, then I am a victim. This gives me an excuse to feel sorry for myself, to feel inferior, and, ultimately, to self-medicate. In this way, resenting another only hurts the person who resents and never the person being resented. So it is said, *resentment is like taking poison and expecting the other person to die*. The same holds true for feelings of inferiority: allowing feelings of inferiority to overwhelm you only hurts you. The challenge is thus to avoid such feelings as much as possible. But how? The key is to be honest with yourself, recognize and accept the reality of your situation, and not flee from it.

Fleeing from your situation will look different for different people. The most common is to overcompensate and project an illusory version of themselves. They will exaggerate their personalities, seeking always to be first and to outdo others. In their behavior and speech they will portray themselves as self-assured, well-ensconced in their professions, and confident in what they have. But always portraying oneself in this way so as to hide one's true condition can be exhausting, and as a result someone who acts this way will eventually reveal their incapacity and their powerlessness. The clearest example of this are people that go into enormous debt in order to project an image of prosperity and wealth. Eventually the bills come due, the image dissolves, and they are revealed in their true state. Resentment and misery soon follow.

Again, the way out of this vicious cycle of misery and resentment is a calm acceptance of your situation informed by autognosis, the sort of knowledge gained by taking a careful and honest look at your capabilities and at what you can afford to do, in terms of both power and resources. Such knowledge can lead to an acceptance of your limitations, which is never a bad thing. Ramos says plainly: "If we adjust our desires to our power, then the feeling of inferiority does not need to exist."[5] Adjusting your wants to your capabilities is equivalent to tempering your expectations to align with your circumstance.

Aligning with your circumstance just means having a sense about your capabilities within the limits of that circumstance. It involves being aware of the resources you have at your disposal and how to use them so as to "live within your means," and thus temper your expectations accordingly. This relates to what was said about resentment: if resentment is like taking poison and expecting another person to die, then avoiding resentment demands having a sense that your expectation about the other's death is not tempered by reality, by how poisoning someone actually works. Or, you're just ignorant to the fact that by taking poison the only death you should expect is your own.

In addition to trolling and expressions of resentment, there are other ways in which the complex of inferiority, as described by Ramos, may rear its ugly head.

Nativists and xenophobes always understand themselves in opposition to nonnatives or immigrants. Nativists join populist political parties in the hope that government action will stop the influx of immigrants, expel those who are "illegally" in the country, or, if all else fails, force the latter to assimilate to the native or home culture. Nativists are driven by the fear that their culture will disappear if nothing is done about the "invaders." However, underlying that fear—grounding it, feeding it—is the fear that their culture may be weak, fragile, and in ways inferior to that of the immigrants. This calls for action: nativists activate other nativists in order to stop the other way of life in its tracks, forcing immigrants to either turn around and "go back to where you came from" or, if this proves impossible, to give up whatever makes their culture distinctive and assimilate to the "American way of life."

The inferiority complex of the nativist is doubly rooted in, on the one hand, a shared, collective feeling of powerlessness in the face of the unstoppable flow of human movement, and on the other, the failure to achieve the ideal "American" society in the present, one that supposedly existed in the past and to which they believe America must return—thus the contemporary longing to "make America great again." When all is said and done, anti-immigrant nativists, like the fox in Aesop's fable, suffer from a disconnect between their dreams of a past America and their reality, in which they regard their idealized vision as true and the reality as false or deceptive.

Would self-knowledge of the type proposed by Ramos be of any help here? What is it that nativists must know? What is the circumstance that they have to recognize? More importantly, what is the expectation that must be tempered? Like the trolls we began with, nativists need to reconnect with their reality, to see it for what it is and not for what they wish it to be. They need, for instance, to accept that immigrants are necessary for the proper functioning of society, and always have been. Moreover, they need to temper the hope of returning to an idealized bygone era by recognizing that such an era never truly existed. After all, Europeans were immigrants to America once upon a time. The only people with a real claim to native status in the United States are the Indigenous peoples of the Americas, but even they are treated today as foreigners in their own land.

Almost a hundred years after Ramos published his analysis, we can see that his observations were not too far off as descriptions of the Mexican situation of the time. However, we also now know that they are not restricted to the Mexican experience. For reasons that are mostly historical, Anglo-Americans today also feel powerless and vulnerable. Unfortunately, this feeling of vulnerability can be powerful enough that it forces them to look for scapegoats to blame. From a sense of inferiority, some white Americans will blame welfare recipients, Muslims, Blacks, Mexicans, and the LGBTQ+ community for the current state of the country. With Internet access making the blaming game much easier, they will seek to troll, demean, and humiliate others online whenever they get the chance, thereby transforming their sense of inferiority, at least temporarily, into false power and illusory superiority.

As a Mexican-American, I find that Samuel Ramos's thesis about the Mexican inferiority complex strikes a nerve. From the time that he first articulated this theory, multiple Mexican thinkers have made it a point to argue against it, showing that as a generalization it is far from conclusive. But to the extent that it remains accurate, his analysis is certainly instructive. The truth is that a profound feeling of inferiority probably affects almost all of us at some point in our lives, just as most of us are capable of occasionally acting like trolls. And at these times, we can indeed act in the ways described by Ramos. Resisting such behavior requires knowledge of ourselves, our circumstances, and our capabilities. So even where Ramos's psychoanalytic reading of Mexican culture falls short or seems unflattering, there is value in his analysis. If nothing else, it reminds us to take stock of where we stand before we get dragged back down by resentment and feelings of inferiority. So when you find that you're comparing yourself to someone else who, unlike you, seems to have it all together, bear in mind that this person is undoubtedly comparing themselves to others just as you do.

19 | TELL YOUR OWN STORY

Contemporary anti-immigrant discourse is full of generalizations about who immigrants are, what they do, and how they live. The historian and activist Aviva Chomsky calls these "myths."[1] One myth says that immigrants take American jobs; another says that immigrants don't pay taxes; and another, voiced by a former US president, suggests that immigrants are violent criminals and "bad hombres."

These are all dangerous myths. But for me, the myth about immigrants being "illegal" is the worst. What is explicitly meant by an immigrant being illegal is that he or she has broken the law in the act of coming to the United States; that they have trespassed and are here without permission. What is implied is worse—not that they've committed an illegal act but rather that *they themselves are illegal*. Now, to be illegal in this way is to exist apart from what is socially permitted, allowed, or legal; it is to exist outside the space of legality. Outside of this space of law, human beings are unprotected by federal constitutions or a country's Bill of Rights and can thus be treated as we treat other illegal things, such as illicit drugs, child pornography, or murder—we can call for their eradication. Ultimately, calling a person "illegal" is both an inaccurate way to describe a person, since persons are not reducible to things, and dangerous, because for those that come to believe that persons can be illegal, eradication is a fairly logical next step.

For immigrants, then, these are more than myths. They constitute a framework of understanding through which immigrants are seen and through which they eventually come to see themselves. My father saw himself as "illegal" not because he was such a thing but because this is the framework that had been presented to him as the right or objective framework—the framework authorized by society, history, and the law.

It is not surprising that such worldviews exist and persist. The anti-immigrant discourse in which "illegality" is key has been named by the sociologist Leo Chavez "the Latino Threat Narrative."[2] According to this "narrative," Latinos are a threat to traditional "American" society because of their refusal to conform to it—an absurd generalization if I ever heard one!—and, more strikingly still, because they are part of an invading army intent on retaking lands that Mexico lost in the Treaty of Guadalupe Hidalgo, a questionable treaty signed in 1848 that transferred the territories of what are today California, Nevada, Utah, and New Mexico, as well as most of Colorado and Arizona, to the United States. Of course, the Latino Threat Narrative conveniently forgets that a great number of Latinos are US-born citizens, many of whom have never been south of the US-Mexican border, know only the US way of life, and have no allegiance to any possible foreign invaders. Nevertheless, the pervasiveness of this narrative in media and popular culture lends weight to a belief that Latinos should be approached with suspicion, that they should be treated as a threat. And more damaging still, that those Latinos who are resistant to assimilation, don't speak English, or look a certain way should be considered as illegal, and thus not as human beings worthy of dignity and protection.

A cursory glance at conservative cable news networks highlights the centrality of the narrative to Anglo identity: the Latino Threat as a rallying point. White-Anglo culture seems to require such a narrative so as to construct an identity around a common anxiety. The reproductive force of this narrative has recently been illustrated by a twisted rhetoric pushing a "Replacement Theory." This narrative warns white, US-born Americans that brown, foreign-born immigrants are here to replace them as part of a broader political conspiracy spearheaded by the political left.

Having returned to Mexico sometime after my birth, my parents traveled back to California in the mid-1980s. My father had taken a job on an agricultural ranch north of San Luis Obispo and just south of the town of San Lucas.

San Lucas is a small town at the end of Rte. 198, a windy corridor that connects Rte. 101 to I-5 to the east. There is a post office in San Lucas, as well as a liquor store, an elementary school, and a couple of hundred residents within the town's limits. We lived a few miles south, on Paris Valley Road, just off the main highway.

We moved into a single-wide trailer parked beneath a tall and voluptuous oak tree in the middle of nowhere. The trailer was decrepit, with thin, fragile walls and holes in the ceiling. It was cold in the winter and hot in the summer. Really hot. If it hadn't been for the oak tree, the sun would have baked us alive.

Cement had been poured around the structure, apparently in an effort to civilize it, to make it look as if it had a yard or a porch. Wooden stairs led inside. It smelled like rotting flesh. Not rotting human flesh (I had smelled rotting human flesh once when a body turned up near the Rio Colorado in Acuitzeramo) but rotting animal flesh, something small like a rat or a possum. It always smelled like this.

The trailer was narrow and long. With all of us in there, it felt and looked like a crowded hallway. There was a small shower near a small kitchen; two tiny "bedrooms," and, near the door, a seating area that also served as my own bedroom. Six of us lived there amidst the smell of death: my sister, mother, father, and me, along with two of my father's cousins, who shared the bedroom in the back.

We lived on a ranch that the school-bus driver called "Los Chiniques." The rancher, a short, fat man I remember only as David the Texan, had hired my father and his cousins to irrigate his crops, moving sprinklers around the ranch; to dig ditches, trenches, and canals; and to skin the occasional deer or wild boar unlucky enough to get shot while grazing on the broccoli sprouts. He had also provided the housing. The deal was that my father would man the irrigation pumps at all hours of the night, turning them on and off at certain intervals. Along with the accommodations, David would pay his workers five dollars per hour.

Sometime toward the end of 1984, David the Texan informed my father that he would be unable to pay him for some time, as the crop had not yielded what he expected and the ranch was in financial straits. He asked my father and his cousins to continue working, making sure that they noted their hours on a ledger. Whenever he passed by my father in the fields, David the Texan would pantomime with his hands "Write your hours!"

While his labor was going into the ledger, we starved. My father and his cousins would leave the trailer at night to drink and hunt. If they hadn't drunk themselves into a stupor, they would bring back rabbits, deer, and quail, which we then ate for breakfast, lunch, and dinner.

My father pleaded with David the Texan to give him his money, since I needed school clothes and food. The Texan showed up a couple of times with a few bags of groceries and shirts that were too big for my sister and too small for me.

Late in 1985, David the Texan had yet to pay my father for an entire year's worth of work. At the end of the year, with his family starving, my father demanded his pay. David told my father that he just could not pay him, as the ranch still wasn't turning a profit. My father got angry and persisted, but David calmly informed him that if he mentioned the matter again he would have him arrested and deported. "Don't forget, Ticho, you're nothing but a *wetback*."

My father dropped it. We would never see a dime.

"Why did he call you a 'wetback'?" I remember asking him.

"That's what I am," he said despondently. "Soy illegal"—I am illegal.

My father's response bothered me then and did so for many years. *What does it mean to be a wetback? How can someone be illegal?*

The fact is that my father was stuck in a narrative created to oppress and dehumanize him. This narrative said that people without official permission to work and live north of the US-Mexican border were *outside the space of law* and therefore wetbacks or "illegals." This narrative was promoted by the government and the media. That people like my father were "wetbacks" and "illegals" was in those days the objective reality.

Above all, the fact that this is how he understood himself meant that my father could not see himself outside this narrative. His identity was tied to it; *as a matter of fact*, he was a wetback, an illegal. He had no recourse against his employer's horrible exploitation—which included starving his family—because this was the status assigned to him. But in a sense even deeper than this, on this self-understanding, what he did and what he thought—his autonomy and identity—were determined by something outside of himself.

I myself took on some of that. Being a child of illegal immigrants made me illegal as well. Because I was only a child, there was no way to assert my citizenship on my own (again, I myself was born in the United States). So when my parents hid or ran, I hid and ran too. They didn't call attention to themselves and I didn't either. I grew up believing myself to be an accomplice to an unknown crime.

Thus believing that my life was determined by forces outside of my control, I conformed to what I was expected to be, or *not* to be, by those stereotyping narratives about immigrants and their children that floated about in the ether of my circumstance. Not until my later teenage years did I realize that I didn't have to do or be what those narratives told me to do or be—that, although I was determined by my circumstance in many ways, I could challenge, with the singularity of my own experience, the narratives that tried to fit me into this or that stereotype. For me, challenging that narrative meant graduating from high school, going to college, and—to the surprise of everyone, including those who knew me and those who only *thought* they knew me—going to graduate school and becoming a professor of philosophy. I did this motivated by memories of the hardship, perseverance, and overcoming that defined the experience of my immigrant identity.

I defied the stereotype attached to being a child of immigrant parents by undermining what it expected of me. In other words, I challenged the purported objectivity of a certain social narrative about me by *being* me. This brings me to a central tendency in Mexican philosophy, observable in most of the philosophers we have encountered thus far: the tendency to promote the subjective over the objective point of view and to reject the dictatorship of objectivity.

The myths propagated by anti-immigrant discourse are sold to people as reflections of the way the world actually is. Those that spread them want you to believe that they are objectively true: that immigrants *do* steal American jobs, that they *are* a drain on our economy, and that their children *do* threaten the national culture. Those who sell these myths desire to institutionalize them, to make them the official story about immigration and immigrants, and ultimately to transform them into law. Current enforcement strategies suggest that the anti-immigrationists are succeeding.

Leopoldo Zea calls the tendency to objectify in this way the "imperial passion."[3] Zea finds this passion in the conquerors and colonizers who sought to make everything and everyone they encountered fit the culture they had brought with them from Europe, a culture they believed to be objective and universally valid. Whatever didn't fit that picture was deemed unnatural, uncivilized, or even demonic.

In contrast to the "imperial passion," the tendency to generalize or objectify, there's the value and force of subjective experience that the Mexican feminist philosopher Rosario Castellanos (1925–1974) referred to as "narcissism." For Castellanos, narcissism is the ability to speak from your own experience about the way the world is, the way you find it in that experience, the way it treats you, and the way you navigate it.[4] Narcissism, in her account, is a strategy against certain forms of domination, meant to disrupt patriarchal, objectifying, and official narratives by inserting one's own experience into them. Rather than meaning "overly self-interested," as it is commonly defined, narcissism can actually be a form of self-love, a form of power.

Against the "objectifying" myths trafficked in the prevalent anti-immigrant discourse, people with stories like mine must speak "narcissistically" about the particular experience of immigration. This means, at least, telling stories of immigrant life, and at most, allowing immigrants to speak about themselves and their struggles. Doing this allows people like my father to reveal themselves not as "illegals" but as real, flesh-and-bone, people with a language and a world who are worthy of dignity and protection. Of course, immigrants speaking on their own behalf will also require the allyship of non-immigrants and advocacy groups, as well as protective laws; but firsthand stories of the realities of immigration, once they have gained wide circulation, will go far in undermining the imperial passion.

◦∿◦

The imperial passion is an obsession with objectivity that forces some to discount the unique experiences of others. It is imperial because it assumes that whatever serves as the official story, whatever is institutionalized as objectively true, whatever determines the prevailing narrative is the authorized and official "passion" or desire of those in power—of the empire! Zea warns us that the imperial passion results in wanting to ignore or forget the influence of one's own realities and circumstances, and thus seeking passionless detachment from one's own experience. Worse, the colonialists or imperialists expect others, especially others they see as inferior or subservient, to do the same—an expectation for obedience that can accurately be described as "imperialist."

An imperialist is someone who is in service to an empire, promoting its interests and its mission. The imperialists that we're talking about here are in service to a Western conception of truth and knowledge that is detached, impersonal, and, ideally, passionless.

But the irony is that the imperial passion is still a *passion*, and passion is subjective. Passion is committed, implicated, and one-sided, and always reflective of our circumstance. Understood in this way, passion is, ironically, anti-imperial or counter-imperialistic. Passion is not objective!

What guidance can you take from all of this? It truly doesn't matter if you're Latinx, share in the immigrant experience, or have never thought about the passion for objectivity that defines the West, the truth is that your singularity is under constant threat by any number of dehumanizing narratives. So the guidance is this: you must endeavor to proclaim your difference whenever possible. You must speak your difference, which is also your truth, against and in spite of the prevailing social myths that may otherwise speak for you. Speaking out is essential. Even if it seems narcissistic, yours will be a kind of narcissism that disrupts imperialist and totalizing claims about you, revealing them as products of certain perspectives that, through force and power, attained enough prominence to *become* "official."

You do this against the insight or "truth," often attributed to Winston Churchill, that "history is written by the victors." That is, the official story is the one that wins out among other stories, and it will win because of power and passion, not because it is objectively true. To realize this is to see the weakness of official narratives, to grasp that, rather than being impersonal and objective, they are grounded in power and motivated by passion.

Stereotyping narratives disempower us and limit our possibilities, just as they disempowered and limited my father decades ago. But we can push back and insert our own experiences into them until they become diluted or until the narrative cracks open, revealing prejudice, bias, and often bad faith. Only then can we drain stereotyping narratives of their power. I like to think that when more people understand that there is no such thing as an "illegal" person, slowly things will begin to change, in the real world as well as in the myths attached to it.

20 | LOVE WITHOUT VIOLENCE

At the age of sixteen, my mother was "taken" by the man who would become my father in a brazen daytime abduction involving a horse, a gun, and a funeral.

The towns of Villa Mendoza and Acuitzeramo lie less than five miles apart on the northern border of the Mexican state of Michoacán. The towns have been bitter rivals for generations, and it has something to do with men from one town "taking" the women from the other, along with broken deals on cattle, fixed horse races, and other forgotten resentments—but mainly the first. Mothers would tell daughters to behave, or else a *viejo* (old man) from Acuitzeramo would snatch them while they slept.

Patricio, the man who would become my father, twenty-one years old at the time, had met Guillermina, the woman who would become my mother, while she walked home from church. He had been going south to Villa Mendoza regularly, mainly on Sundays, and many girls had caught his eye, but this one seemed particularly modest. He liked modest women; he'd been told they made good mothers. (Such things were told and believed by all.) Patricio had seen her once during a Christmas *posada*, and he went back almost daily to try to spot her again. Guillermina caught on to his stalking and started changing her routine, so he kept missing her. But after much observation and patience, Patricio noticed a pattern in her movements. He knew that she visited the church in the evenings right before nightfall and got out late, when darkness had set in.

Patricio waited by the post office. When Guillermina hurried by, he followed her in his car. He stopped beside her and asked for her name. She hesitated. Giving the man her name was an invitation. Patricio asked if he could visit her at her home and talk. Because it would have been considered impolite to refuse a visit without good reason, she reluctantly said yes. The next day Patricio showed up at her home and asked her father if he could speak to her. The father knew the deal—he had eleven daughters older than this one—and he said yes, so long as Patricio stayed outside and Guillermina stayed inside a large wooden gate, which was to remain half open.

On his first visit Patricio and Guillermina met for a couple of hours. There was not much speaking. The rendezvous was full of uncomfortable silences, broken here and there by even more uncomfortable questions from him to her, which she refused to answer, irritating both of them. She tried not to look at him directly. She didn't like his face; it was reddish around the cheeks and chin and white around the forehead. She didn't like where he was from. She also felt she was too young for him. She hoped that refusing to answer his questions would give him a clue, that he would get tired of standing outside and leave.

On the second day, Patricio asked Guillermina to be his girlfriend, to which she said no. They both knew what this meant: that next he would try to "take" her—a common practice in the early 1970s. (Yes, you read that right, the late twentieth century!)

On the third day, Guillermina's mother died. The funeral lasted a few days. Prayers and arrangements had to be made. As one of the only daughters still living at home, it was Guillermina's responsibility to pray and host the rosary. Patricio stopped coming for a week or so.

On the last day of the wake, she saw him circling about on a black horse. The horse bore an ornate saddle with carvings of roosters on the skirt. Patricio wore a cowboy hat and boots and a carried shiny silver gun in a holster on his waist. This peacock-like spectacle, far from impressing her, only annoyed her. Her mother was dead, and she was not in the mood for such a display—not that she had been a fan before losing her mother either. He rode up and down her street for an hour or so and left.

On the day of the burial, while she walked home with her sisters, a car pulled up with three or four men inside—all strangers. They demanded she get into the car. She refused, then turned and ran as fast as she could. Her sisters, walking a block ahead, saw what was happening. Having seen this before, they yelled at her to run even faster. But there was not much they could do, and no one else intervened or protested. Guillermina screamed and fought, but she was no match for the brute force of tradition.

Everyone knew who was behind it; no one needed confirmation. Still, confirmation would come a few days later in the form of an invitation by the man who would become my grandfather to attend *las pases*, "the peace," a ceremony at the man's house that symbolized the end of the courtship.

At Patricio's house, the family waited for the arrival of Guillermina with food and music. The pleasantries and welcomes did not allay her terror. She trembled and cried, while her future mother-in-law attempted to comfort her by promising that all the traditional procedures would be properly followed. The peace ceremony was quickly followed by a civil wedding presided over by a municipal judge.

This was all routine. Courtship and marriage had followed this traumatic blueprint for centuries before Guillermina was taken, and everyone knew the steps. I recall attending more than one of these "peace" meetings as a child. I remember thinking about how none of the women in my family—my grandmothers and my aunts—ever had a real choice as to who they married. It seemed that they were all forced into it. In rural Mexico this remained a common practice well into the 1980s.

Of course, there was a price to pay. Though their marriage has lasted for almost half a century (as of this writing, forty-nine years), my mother still has trouble saying that she loves my father. My siblings and I have always known this. The trauma of her abduction and marriage is still very much alive.

All of this illustrates a simple point: love requires respect, and without respect it is violence. My mother's case involved both basic disrespect and violence. Respect was missing from the start, and it was followed by violence, real and symbolic. The line between love and violence is not as thin as certain songs make it out to be; to go from one to the other requires a conscious decision.

Luis Villoro (1922–2014) makes this point more than once, but most clearly in a brilliant essay from 1949 titled "Solitude and Communion."

There, Villoro makes a seemingly obvious observation about human relationships: specifically, that we cannot force another person to be who we want them to be.[1] The other person will never perfectly fulfill our expectations. This is because they are *radically other* to those expectations and to the space where those expectations are conjured up—namely, in our own minds. More importantly, what we see—what they allow us to see when we interact with them—is only a minute fraction of who and what the person really is. The other person, according to this line of thinking, will always reserve for themselves that mystery that the "I"—me, the knower—will never resolve. And the same holds true the other way around: the other will never resolve *my* mystery. Holding on to the hope that more prodding, more questions, more investigation will reveal who the person really is can even be seen as violence. I can only imagine that my father's attempt to know my mother in the years after they married was motivated by a sense of guilt, perhaps responsibility. But clearly a relationship that began with something as invasive and forcible as an abduction cannot set right with knowledge. With the trauma of that first act, a wall sprang up that will be there for the rest of her life.

Resigning yourself to the idea that you will never fully know the person that you love is truly to love that person. True love lets go. Experience should tell you that the very act of desperately trying to know a person usually makes things worse and pushes people deeper into their mystery. This is because the act of knowing is essentially violent. Think about it: In trying to know the nature of a moth, scientists have to first capture it, then dissect it, then abstract information from it, and then categorize it so as to make it fit with all the moth knowledge that already exists. The act of trying to know a person completely is equally invasive: As with a dissection, one tries to abstract information from a person to get them to reveal what's inside of them. This is knowledge that can be used, in the best of cases, to learn how to coexist with them, and in the worst of cases, to control them.

While my parents' case is extreme, less extreme cases involving such violence are relationships between people based on expectations that one person has for the other. These one-sided relationships are usually defined by control or the lack thereof. There is no reciprocity here either, and as soon as one of the two realizes that the other holds a mystery, something that defines them and has not been shared or is not known, then the violence of control and possession (that is, of knowing) begins. Domestic violence often begins with the frustration of such efforts to control, possess, and know. All of this is to say that, when there is no love between two people, the attempt to know by one can feel like (and at times might actually become) an act of violence to the other.

My father sought to "figure out" my mother by asking her questions about how she felt, what she was thinking, and why she was the way she was. It was an intrusive questioning that never resulted in satisfying his curiosity. Often in my youth, this resulted in actual violence. There is a reason for this: his desire was to know her completely, to know what made her tick, what her inner world was like. But no words could accurately paint that picture. He struggled to accept this; he struggled to accept her mystery.

My father struggled because love is a kind of reciprocity involving mutual respect. To love is to respect an unknown while refusing to possess it. Love is radical refusal. Love, Villoro suggests, exists between two mysterious others who refuse to possess each other or to fully and completely *know* one another. The abduction of my mother was an act not of love but of possession, followed by frustrated attempts to know her. Simply, it was emotional violence.

Real love is not violent. The person that I fall in love with, being "radically other to myself," will take me by surprise.[2] In my case, I would not have been expecting them. But meeting them and falling in love with them doesn't mean I should now seek to possess them. I will remember my beloved's unexpected arrival, how she came as if from nowhere. To possess her, to capture her forcibly, whether violently or not, is to behave as if she only exists in order to be loved by me.

When she does appear to me, her freedom and her impenetrable, mysterious interior life will keep me guessing. Respecting that freedom and that interiority—her solitude, or, perhaps more to the point, her existence as a separate person from me, who will decide how much she wants to share of herself and how much she will hold on to—will mean that I accept the unknown and value it as part of her personality. In conversation I may find out things about her, perhaps by observing quirks in her speech or her movements. But these outward appearances hide her secret truth, her true self—that which, Villoro says, is the "negation of external manifestations."[3] In other words, what I see only hides that interior self she reserves for herself.

My mother certainly hid behind her external manifestations. This meant that my father could only know her in her appearance. The woman he abducted was hiding an entire life under her skin. Later he discovered that he could never truly know her, that behind her face and body lay something that was beyond all knowledge, what Villoro calls her "transcendence." My father should have been reading Villoro when he wrote, "I cannot make the other thoroughly mine, because there is always something about her that escapes me . . . and this is because I know her as freedom, and, as such, I can never determine her, fully predict her actions, capture her entirely in my significations."[4] Villoro's point is simple: one cannot make another person one's own.

Ultimately, my father would not allow my mother to surprise him, nor could he allow her to be free in herself. From the first time he saw her from atop his black horse, there was no recognition of her interiority or her capacity to bestow meaning on the world. Even if, as some might claim, my mother's abduction and marriage is an isolated case, it is instructive even so. There is no spectrum in which the rejection of another's transcendence does not represent the same kind of violence and disrespect.

Is it possible to love without violence? It seems as if any attempt at knowledge will necessarily be violent. But don't we want to know our beloved to some degree? If so, how should we proceed?

First, you should not base your loving relations on knowledge, but rather on loyalty, or what Villoro calls "fidelity" to the loved one. Fidelity translates to a certain kind of respect that is also acceptance of what will not reveal itself—namely, the interiority of the person. Love, he says, will grow not from a "first impression" of the person, from what you see, but from something that does not impress itself upon you, something that you do not perceive. There is an unknowable factor that attracts you to a person, and even though you cannot see it, it is that to which you must be loyal and respectful. That fidelity, care, and respect to what does not initially impress you should be the true foundation of your loving relationship.

Second, you should remember that loving someone is a paradox. In love, you desire to possess the loved one while realizing that the loved one needs to remain who he or she is. To have the first without the other is not love. To have only the former is violence, while to have the latter is respect. Villoro says that "love aims to appropriate the other but, at the same time, it demands that the other remain independent, because if for the moment the other ceases to be irreducible, the loving relationship would disappear; there would not be two alterities facing each other, but one alterity in solitude."[5] The paradox is simply that you desire to know your beloved, but love becomes impossible if you pursue this desire.

Prioritizing fidelity while remembering the paradoxical nature of love together make possible a violence-free, loving relationship. The loving act is respectful of that which you don't know, the mystery that keeps you in suspense, but that is always the other half of their person. Villoro tells us that if you were to know *everything* about the other, then love itself would disappear. The two of you would no longer be "alterities" but instead merely things to be inventoried among the other things you already know. They would be objects for the taking.

I imagine that the possibility for love between my parents ended the moment that my father's desire to know my mother turned into the action of appropriation and possession.

❧

As my parents' story nears an end, things have turned out much better than some might expect given the way it began. They've remained together well into old age. Through fifty years, they've struggled together against society and against history, against one another, against love's supreme paradox. They've shared their misery and, at times, their triumphs. They've come to the point now where they respect one another's solitude, and they've accepted that they can never truly know one another. Neighborhood gossips would say they love one another. But the truth is much more complicated than that.

As for the rest of us, Villoro insists that we should learn how to love without violence. This involves fidelity and respect, as well as a special kind of ignorance, the kind that lets go of an almost instinctual desire to know the loved one inside and out. This is hard, but it is possible.

21 | DON'T BE TOO JUDGY

There are millions of earthlike planets in the Milky Way galaxy. Of those, astrophysicists tell us it is highly probable that some harbor intelligent life. Now, imagine—as countless films, books, and Internet podcasts have done—that intelligent beings from another earthlike planet one day discovered Earth. We would watch as they deboarded technologically superior crafts, engaged with one another in highly sophisticated yet unfamiliar ways, and made sense of their experience through complex systems of understanding.

We can ask how *we* would adjust ourselves in order to understand *them*. But since it was they who found their way here, the more interesting question would be how our non-Earth visitors would understand *us*. Here's a scenario: On encountering us, the non-earthlings would initially try to make sense of what we are. They would try to fit us into a picture of the universe they already have, inserting us into existing inventories of objects they've previously encountered and then comparing us to them. They would notice our physiques— for instance, the bilateral symmetry of our bodies and our opposable thumbs. They would take note of the repetitiveness of our languages, of our frequent use of "the" and "my" and "I." But they might also find some commonalities with us, enough to lead them to believe that we are intelligent beings worthy of being spared from the planet-killing laser they carry on their mothership.

However, aside from some minor similarities, our alien visitors would surely find us and our ways radically and absolutely foreign. The common ground they discovered would probably be very small; the rest of what we are, how we think, and how we live would not make sense to them. The recognition of an unbridgeable chasm between us and them might force their hand; if they decided not to destroy us, they would assimilate us. For our sake, we would be strongly encouraged to become like them. However, assimilation would require that we give up our differences, that we abandon what makes us who and what we are (human) and instead habituate ourselves to their alien way of life.

But assimilation has a limit. There are aspects of being human that we simply would not be able to abandon. These might include our language, our views on love, death, and God, and perhaps also our accomplishments, enshrined in our history, our literature, and our science. They would not be able to fully understand why we hold on to our primitive views or our simple accomplishments, and would ask us to abandon them and embrace their ways. But we would balk at this request.

Eventually, our visitors would run out of patience, tolerance, and empathy. Those things that we would be unwilling to abandon would prove incompatible with their cosmology. Our lives would eventually become *offensive* to everything that they know, believe, and desire. As a final act of good will, they would give us an ultimatum: either deny those things that make us who we are as earthlings or die.

⁓

While my example is of the science-fiction type, it is inspired by historical events. According to Luis Villoro, this is the process of understanding that Europeans went through when they first encountered Native Indigenous peoples of the Americas in the early sixteenth century.

The historical facts are well known: Spaniards landed on the eastern coast of Mexico in 1517 seeking riches and glory. They brought horses, guns, the Gospel, and an arsenal of concepts capable of identifying a wide array of natural things, terrains, and peoples of the world. They could also identify different social phenomena such as tribes and pagan rituals and compare what they saw to forms of humanity they had encountered elsewhere, specifically in Africa and Asia. Such knowledge would prove instrumental in the process of evangelization, conquest, and domination.

On entering the Valley of Mexico (Anáhuac), the Spaniards were astounded by what they saw. Some of it seemed easily recognizable, in that it "fit" with what they already knew. They knew, for instance, that the inhabitants were "people" and not, say, animals (although they would go on to treat them as such). They could recognize, moreover, that the layout of Indigenous cities, the hierarchies of their governments, and the organization of their armies pointed to the existence of advanced culture and politics, philosophy, and religion.

Villoro calls this the "first moment" in the understanding of the other,[1] a moment of objectification, a moment when the new or the strange was translated or transformed into something the Europeans already understood. Through analogies with previous experience, that is, they were able to understand Indigenous life. Villoro explains:

Understanding the other through those categories in which the world is interpreted requires the establishment of analogies between aspects of the alien culture and similar aspects of one's own, eliminating in this way all difference. It is what Europeans did, from Columbus to Cortés. . . . a "cacique" is a king . . . a "Tlatoani" is an emperor in the Roman style, an Aztec temple is a mosque, its idols, Moloch, its cities, new Venices or new Sevilles.[2]

This was the Europeans' initial reaction to Indigenous life. It was all about reducing what they found to something already known, something already familiar, already present in their own consciousness. They had little interest, in these first days of conquest, in understanding these peoples and their cultures on the latter's own terms—as different or unique. Because they were largely projecting what they already knew onto the Indigenous people, the conquerors believed that they had found common ground. The Indigenous culture was just like other primitive cultures they'd encountered elsewhere and could thus be similarly dealt with. Once the native peoples had been understood, or objectified, in this way, the Spaniards could proceed with the colonizing mission.

What I'm describing here is not an uncommon occurrence in everyday life. You meet someone for the first time and, in your sociable eagerness, you tell *them* about *themselves*. You might say something like, "You're from San Francisco? It's nice there, but so expensive, you must have a good job. Don't the tourists and the homelessness drive you crazy!" Such assumptions turn the stranger into someone familiar *to you,* into an known object, the abstract "citizen of San Francisco." Too many times to count, I've been introduced to someone who, before I've had a chance to speak, notices my facial features, my name, my tattoos, or other identifying markers and asks me what part of Mexico I come from. This is objectification, and I tend to find it somewhat insulting, even though in most cases the person doing the objectifying has no idea of what they've done, which is to fit me into a picture of the world that they already possess.

The conquering Spaniards did something similar, on a grand scale. But soon a problem arose. What they understood about the Indigenous people was only what they found familiar—just as people who first meet me understand me only insofar as they understand the abstract "person of Mexican descent." Eventually, for the Spaniards, the unfamiliar became too much to ignore, and they recognized that there were things about the Indigenous culture and people that could not be easily known or predicted. Because both the evangelizing and the colonizing mission depended on knowing their new subjects and predicting their behavior, there was a real threat of failure at this stage.

This brings us to a second moment in the understanding of the other: assimilation. Since the Indigenous peoples refused their objectification by the simple fact of being unlike any previously encountered peoples, the next step involved something like an invitation to assimilate to European ways. Far from a polite invitation, however, this turned out to be more of an ultimatum, one that demanded that they either give up their differences and assume the truths of the European worldview or perish. Though it was phrased as an invitation to equality, this was equality in name only, and more specifically an equality in the eyes of God. This proposal had another agenda: If the Indigenous people were equal to the Europeans in the eyes of God, then they could be baptized, and if they could be baptized, they could be saved. But salvation, it turned out, would have no effect on their daily lives. For the most part, Indigenous people gained no benefits from salvation or assimilation, and remained mere exploitable bodies, resources meant to fill the labor and sexual needs of the colonizers. Ultimately, in gaining "equality" in the process of assimilation (and salvation), the Indigenous people would lose their culture, their cosmology, and their language.

In this scene of the sci-fi episode with which I began, our superior alien visitors would send envoys and intellectuals, scientists, and historians to mingle with us in an effort to learn from us and gauge how we could be incorporated into their galactic mission. They would invite us onto their ships and make us feel as if things were looking up. They would tell us that we could have the same rights and privileges as everyone in the galaxy only if we followed their laws, customs, and rituals and let go of our own. But, they would say, our new rights and privileges would be "galactic" rights and privileges that would have little effect on the leveling processes of alien colonization. Our new galactic rights would grant us mercy in place of barbarity, and we would not be destroyed, but we would no longer grow as a human race. Knowing that this was not real equality, we would hang on to some of our human customs, continuing to write our human poetry and read our sacred human texts in secret.

❧

Returning to my earlier example of meeting someone for the first time: Even before the stranger from San Francisco extends their hand in greeting, you've already objectified them. Because you've read somewhere that San Francisco is one of the most expensive places to live in the United States, because it is recognized as a tourist destination, because of the media's obsession with its homelessness "problem," you're able to identify the stranger as both having a well-paying job and as having an opinion on tourists and homelessness. You've objectified them for your own sake, for your own comfort. You like things to make sense, and people who, at first glance, are unknown to you *don't* make sense. In conversation, you get to know them a bit more and come to find out that yes, they have a well-paying job, but no, they're not annoyed by tourists and think the state should do something about the homeless situation. You share their views on tourists, but not on homelessness. You want to be friends with this person, but know that at this stage any possible relationship between the both of you will be built on your similarities, not on your differences. What you don't know, however, is that you may be ignoring that about which they care the most. You ignore their difference. But differences cannot be suppressed, and soon they themselves return to it, emphasizing their stance on homelessness. Because they cannot fully assimilate or think like you, you come to question your compatibility with them and the future of your relationship. As the evening ends, the possibility of a friendship boils down to whether or not you can accept them for who they are and what they believe, though also to what extent they are willing to change for you—the burden falls on them as well.

In the history of the conquest of Mexico, the Franciscan friar Bernardino de Sahagún (1499–1590) exemplifies the attempt to accept the other as he was. "Sahagún," Villoro tells us, "was the first to attentively listen to the Indian and to systematically give him the word."[3] Sahagún's first instinct was not to objectify Indigenous people; rather, from the beginning he listened attentively to them and tried to find common ground. He wanted to integrate them into his own worldview but without fully assimilating them. After a while, however, he realized that he himself could not tolerate the fact that they did not believe in a Christian God.[4] This difference truly vexed him and kept him from coming to appreciate and accept the Indigenous other's "picture of the world."

With our non-earthling visitors, even though they are willing to listen to us, to accept our technological primitiveness, our love rituals, our obsessions with celebrity and spectacle, there are things about us that they simply won't tolerate. Perhaps our worship of terrestrial gods, perhaps our wastefulness, perhaps our cruelty to one another. Whatever it is, they can't get over it, and they decide that if we are to be part of their galactic empire, we must change: our technology, our religious rituals, our obsessions, our barbarity must all be abandoned. And they will do everything in their power to make this happen, even if that means ridding us of all remnants of our humanity.

The history of the conquest is a painful inheritance for Mexico, but it also provides a helpful metaphor. These are the steps we go through when we seek to understand other people that seem different from us. But if this is the case, then it seems that all of our encounters will involve, as happened with the Spanish, some form of objectification, assimilation, or subjugation. Things may get violent. Violence appears necessary because one of the realities of other worldviews is that they are "other" precisely in contradicting some aspects of our own. But is it actually necessary? The simple answer is no. But in order to avoid this fate, we must be able to respect other worldviews, to accept the notion that there are multiple truths; we must recognize that most truths are not of our own design and are unknown to us—and that most of them are valid.

How can you do this? Villoro recommends that, like Sahagún, you approach the other in generosity. This involves making yourself available to those who are unknown to you, who are strangers or unfamiliar; it means talking and listening to them. But in order to listen to what they say, you must, unlike Sahagún, be willing to sacrifice the centrality of your own worldview. Doing so can only expand the boundaries of your own world, and with that the possibilities of different experiences of joy and fulfillment. These days, when I meet someone for the first time, I try my best to hear them out before saying anything or forming any preconceptions about them, even if they seem to be similar to me in language, dress, ethnicity, and so on. As they tell me about themselves, not only do I get a sense about what makes them stand out as human beings, but I also get to fill out my picture of the world just a little more, since what they tell me will always include some difference that enriches my perspective. If they appear different from me in superficial ways, I anticipate a difference also in their worldview. Sometimes this doesn't happen, and I learn little or nothing from my encounter. So it's important that I let them tell me about themselves, rather than telling them what I think I know about them.

In short, if we want to be more tolerant of one another and less like conquerors and colonizers, then we must begin by believing that there are a million ways to look and think about the world, and no privileged points of view. So we must listen attentively and respectfully to the other that addresses us. Our (very anti-colonial) mantra should be that all perspectives are valid. This does not mean that we have to live with contradictions, but rather only that we accept that someone, somewhere, believes the opposite of what I believe, and resolve to be okay with that. In our contemporary cosmopolitan world, this someone could be my neighbor, my student, or even my partner.

22 | BE LIKE THE RABBIT

Those who know my father would describe him as a quiet man. He's reserved, speaking only when something needs to be said, rarely volunteering information, never gossiping, and always listening.

For five decades he worked in agricultural fields in California's Central Coast, moving irrigation pipes, digging trenches, planting seed. His coworkers and bosses, young and old, called him *tío*, which means "Uncle." They called him *tío* out of respect. He had earned the moniker; to be a *tío*, especially to those who were not related to him, acknowledged his experience, his work ethic, his toughness, but most of all his wisdom. Their respect for my father was not the kind of respect earned from fear. The actual source of the respect he commanded was not obvious, and it was this: after years of working with him or for him, neither his bosses nor his coworkers knew *who he really was*. Quiet and reserved, he had never given himself away. This was obvious to my mother and me—*we* knew who he was. He was transparent at home, just not in public—depending on where he found himself, he was a completely different person.

My mother and I knew that *el tío* was a persona, a mask, created specifically to survive the hardships of being an immigrant farmworker. My father's quiet demeanor, the way he carried himself before others, projected a mystery about him, the kind of unknowability that could perhaps disguise a dangerous psychopath—or a brilliant physicist. His bosses, white ranchers all, approached him with caution, since they couldn't fully know him and thus objectify him. They knew him by his work ethic, but that was it. While he was steady and consistent in his labor, he was ungraspable as a person, and the only way to approach him was with respect (or perhaps caution disguised as respect).

His strategy was generally successful. Although they tried to exploit him, it was difficult because he wouldn't do more than what he was paid to do; and firing him for not doing more was never an option, since he was good at what he did. My father succeeded in not letting anyone capture him or assume that they knew what he was about. Those around him kept their distance, while dealing with him deferentially when they had to.

While brutal anti-immigration policies, anti-Mexican racism, and dangerous working conditions were elements of a circumstance beyond his control, my father could at least manage access to his own interior life. This was a space that would always remain untouched by the shaping power of stereotypes and racism and dehumanizing narratives. And he kept this space untouched by being elusive . . . by always *keeping them guessing*.

My father says that this is just the way he is, that his own father was likewise reserved, off-limits, elusive, and "hard to know." But this being hard to know, this elusiveness, is also a time-honored anti-colonial strategy, one deployed by the Aztecs after the fall of their empire long before my father walked into the fields of Central California.

During the early years of the conquest of Mexico, the conquered indigenous peoples were advised by their elders to resist assimilation, lest they should lose the entirety of their cultural identity. The goal was to avoid the colonizer's totalizing, objectifying, determining gaze. As a strategy of resistance, they were told to "be like the rabbit"—shifty and hard to catch. Though they could not outrun the imperialistic overreach of Christianity or Spanish colonial ambition, they could keep their new landlords guessing about their intelligence, their identity, their beliefs, and their loyalties.

Being like the rabbit, "jumping from one place to another, never staying in one place," writes Diego Durán in his sixteenth-century chronicles of conquest and colonization, was part of a strategy of resistance for the Indigenous people. They could resist colonization by employing this "rabbitness" (*empeño conejeril*).[1] To be like the rabbit in this sense means being shifty, elusive, hard to pin down. It means being unpredictable, surprising, indeterminate, and vague—like my father. It is to remain always somewhat anonymous, lacking a graspable, substantial identity. It is, in this way, akin to being *self-less*—that is, not having a self that can be objectified and then dissected, categorized, and abstracted.

In the sense of being "hard to know," the Aztec association of the rabbit with elusiveness makes sense. For us, today, being like a rabbit means lacking that determinable self that can be easily captured by concepts, categories, or stereotypes. The advice here is to be unpredictable in a way that frees you to be whoever you want to be. If anyone claims to know you, they will know you as someone who hides a deeper mystery, adapts to changing circumstances, is *nepantla*, or not tied down to one particular identity. They will know you as somewhat unknowable. A beer commercial from a few years back introduced us to "the most interesting man in the world." And the reason for this title? This man lived many lives, had many selves, did many things. He was not simple. He was complicated and hard to know.

Rabbits are no strangers to philosophy.

The philosopher Ludwig Wittgenstein, in his *Philosophical Investigations*, employed the now-famous "duck-rabbit" image—in which a figure that the viewer sees as a duck might later, perhaps when seen from another position, be seen as a rabbit—to symbolize the role of perspective and interpretation in perception. The point is that we will see different things depending on our perspective, our standpoint, or our expectations: a rabbit sometimes, a duck at other times—it depends.

Coincidentally, the philosopher W. V. O. Quine employed the rabbit as an example of the indeterminacy of translation, the impossibility of perfectly translating a word from one language into another. Quine imagines a certain people using the word "gavagai" every time a rabbit runs by or is thought to be in the vicinity. Someone trying to understand the language will not know whether "gavagai" actually means "rabbit," as it could also mean "undetached rabbit parts before us" or "stages of rabbitness passing by." Here, the rabbit turns out to be elusive even in translation.

Uranga equates rabbithood to the previously discussed concept of *nepantla*—to being always in the middle. But Uranga's appeal to rabbithood as a symbol of elusiveness is also a recommendation: being like a rabbit, being hard to capture, hard to know, and thus difficult to entrap with concepts, is a strategy of resistance against domination. If you keep yourself hard to know (which can be interpreted as "interesting"), as always jumping and evading capture, then it will prove difficult or impossible to dominate you.

In all cases, the rabbit stands in for indeterminacy and elusiveness, for anything that escapes easy conceptualization or objectification. The downside to rabbithood is that being elusive and hard to know in this way can be interpreted strictly in a negative sense, as pointing to one's lack of stability or dependability. After all, how can you depend on someone who evades your questions or eludes your attempts to get to know them? Here, we would have to make a distinction between letting others know *who you are* and letting them see *what you do*. In my father's case, his strategy was to let his bosses see what he did and judge his dependability through his work, while always keeping his inner self, the interiority that defined him, out of reach.

As a strategy for evading conceptualization or domination, being like the rabbit can be practical in a variety of less familiar situations.

In 1993, 41 percent of young men incarcerated in California were Hispanic (by 2020, this number had increased to 53 percent). By the end of that year I became part of this statistic, having been arrested and booked into Juvenile Hall for (allegedly) taking part in violent confrontation between gangs in my neighborhood. To be clear, I was not part of the gangs involved in the ruckus, but I got swept up into the scrap nonetheless—I am still not sure how that happened. The situation quickly escalated into an all-out neighborhood brawl, and before I knew it I was in the back of a police car. I claimed my innocence all the way to the detention center, telling the officers that I was just "in the wrong place at the wrong time," but they didn't care to listen and off to jail I went.

My incarceration was uneventful, but still painful because of the overwhelming sense of solitude and *zozobra* that occupied every waking moment I spent inside my cell. Although we were offered a series of courses, so that those of us who were in school wouldn't fall too far behind, I tested out of them all. Not that I was smarter than the rest; the authorities simply didn't want to teach us anything remotely challenging. So I would spend my time playing checkers with the guards or watching television while the rest of the detainees were in class. I was released after a weeks or so, much to my father's dismay—he had hoped for a longer stay so that I would "learn my lesson."

On the day of my release, I said my good-byes to my cellmates and whoever else had shown me kindness. A few of the guards wished me well. But as I stepped out of the main door, one of them, who was particularly abrasive, called out to me with a confident smirk on his wide, pale face, "See you soon!"

See you soon!? This took a moment to sink in. *See you soon*?! That's right—he expected me to come back. He was apparently familiar with recidivism statistics for young Hispanic males and had no doubt he would see me again soon.

When I returned to class, my teachers knew where I had been. The principal knew. My friends knew. I was *one of them*—a gangbanger, a criminal, a lost cause. I didn't say much. I left them to their prejudices and vowed I would never see the pale-faced guard again. And while my principal and the police waited for the invisible hand of recidivism to do its work—that is, for my re-entry into the criminal-justice system—I immersed myself in my AP History, English, and my favorite class, Journalism.

By senior year, most of my friends had dropped out of school, having been caught up in gang culture or drugs, or forced to work to help their families eke out a living. I had somehow avoided the pull of the streets and stayed in school. I worked the graveyard shift at a local diner to help my family pay the bills, washing dishes while hoping to make it out of high school in one piece.

But I often felt that objectifying glance, that stare that interrogated me, predicted my next move, suspected my intentions, doubted my intelligence, and degraded my humanity. I felt it from my teachers, from other students in my honors classes, in the street as I drove to my midnight shift in my 1979 Cutlass Supreme. And I felt it especially during graduation as I walked across the stage while my friends cheered from behind a chain-link fence surrounding the football stadium.

I surprised people when I went to college and did well. I surprised them when I graduated. I surprised them when I got into a PhD program. I surprised them when I got my teaching position. And I surprise them still. I wasn't supposed to be here. I wonder if the pale-faced guard gave up waiting for me.

My strategy, like my father's, has always been to not give myself away, to do what is right while ignoring, or trying to ignore, what others think is right for me. Indeed, I have been like the rabbit.

If you are like me, you hate corners, pigeonholes, and stereotypes. If you are like me, the predicting algorithms of contemporary culture annoy and frustrate you. Take the advice the Aztecs gave one another: Be like the rabbit, elusive and hard to catch, and refuse to settle into someone's preconceived definition of yourself. Be like the rabbit and maneuver your way past the objectifying gaze of others. Be like the rabbit—and my father—and always keep them guessing.

23 | IT'S OKAY TO BE CHOOSY ABOUT YOUR INHERITANCE

Let's go back a few chapters to the story of my mother's abduction and marriage to my father.

When I tell that harrowing story, people often react in shock. They can't believe such things happened in the late twentieth century. But they did, and they're part of my own story. As I tell it, though, I always feel the need to justify my father's actions. Needless to say, my attempts at justification always come out sounding weak. I finish with, *That's just the way things were done back then*.

That ordeal continued to set the tone for our life once we migrated to the United States. Without going into details, I'll just say that, in our home, a patriarchal order was maintained through force and violence. It devastated my mother, and I, as the eldest, was an inevitable victim of the whiplash. To the eyes of our American neighbors it would have been a distressing and traumatic drama; but for us it was simply *the way things were*.

I am not trying to tell a story of domestic violence here; I'm trying to make a point. And the point is that "the way things were done back then"—in my parents' childhood, in their parents' childhood, and so on—didn't have to be the way things were done. My father didn't have to perpetrate the violence, yet he did; the patriarchal dominance didn't have to be passed down through the generations, yet it was. Violence, it turns out, is inherited.

It eventually stopped once I became a teenager and refused to fight. When I turned the other cheek, my parents were finally forced to face up to their habitual violence. It stopped because, in looking at their actions, they began questioning their dubious parental heritage for the first time: asking themselves what it meant to be a father, a mother, a man, or a child—what it meant to be these things in the present, not "back then." But it could have stopped much sooner.

In speaking with my parents today, it is clear that they sincerely and earnestly believed that their upbringing rested on a solid, morally valid set of principles. They believed that their native culture wouldn't have led them astray. And for the most part they were right. But not all its principles were morally valid or solid. Those principles and the notions behind them included remnants of structures of oppression that had been built for them and for others who, like them, had been encouraged to perpetuate in various ways the violence they themselves had suffered and witnessed. These principles and those notions constituted a cultural inheritance.

Notions of manhood, femininity, child-rearing, power, courage, and so on: these were part of that inheritance, and were now being offered to me as an option for living. In a way, these were a *gift* of their culture, of their community, and of their family; and now they became their gift to me. As a teenager I had denied portions of that gift—thus, for instance, I refused to accept certain cultural notions of manhood, femininity, and discipline; when I became a father, raising my children would not follow the inherited plan.

Indeed, having looked at my inheritance, I made a set of conscious decisions about what to keep and what to discard.

The Mexican philosopher (and famed detective novelist!) María Elvira Bermúdez (1916–1988) was advising this rejection of tradition in 1955—almost two decades before my mother's abduction and marriage. In her analysis of the Mexican family, *La vida familiar del mexicano* (Mexican Family Life), Bermúdez confronts a problem plaguing the Mexican family and the life of the country itself: the damaging persistence of patriarchy in Mexican culture.

Patriarchy reveals itself in machismo, in male aggression and pride. In Mexico, at some point in history, machismo becomes the ideal of male virility and power. From that point on, to be a man is to be macho, and this means that boys learn to be aggressive and violent—toward everyone, but especially toward women. According to Bermúdez, machismo becomes a survival tactic. And it is taught primarily by the *mother*, who in many homes is in charge of discipline and education. The mother perpetuates machismo because of her own inherited notion of femininity. Bermúdez calls this *hembrismo*. Now, the word *hembrismo*—or, in English, *hembrism*—comes from *hembra*, "female." If you look it up, you may find it defined as "female superiority," or even "contempt for men." But as Bermúdez uses it in 1955, *hembrismo* is the belief that the woman's role is to maintain and legitimate male superiority in the home and in society. According to this view, internalized by women via the very patriarchal system that they will then enforce in the home, woman is inferior to man, and all the abuse and punishment that the man dishes out is normal and acceptable.[1]

The woman's role, although inferior, comes with a lot of responsibility. It includes, importantly, forming future men and women. This is done through punishment. Punishment for boys is always more severe, since the point is to condition them into the ways of machismo early and often. This training involves teaching them how, when, and who to punish. Thus, machismo is learned behavior, and the beliefs that validate it are passed down from one generation to the next as a cultural inheritance.

Bermúdez advises Mexicans to reconsider that inheritance, to be more critical of why they do what they do. A first step is to reconsider the nature of machismo, as well as the concepts that sustain it, such as "valor" or "courage."

Deconstructing machismo requires rethinking discipline and education in the home and the role that parental figures have in the matter. To begin with, Bermúdez says, we must "replace the false notion of bravery [*valentía*] with the concept of authentic courage [*valor*]."[2] This is a hard ask, since Mexican men tend to associate *valentía*—with its strong connotation of "boastfulness" or "braggadocio"—with the very essence of manhood. If one is not *valiente*, then one is weak, vulnerable, and not a "real" man. The problem is that proving one's *valentía*, proving that one is not weak or vulnerable, usually requires violence. Manhood is proven by violence against an aggressor or against anyone who questions or threatens one's own *valentía*. And this "anyone" can be a wife, a son, or a dog.

Trading in *valentía* for actual courage, or *valor*, requires re-defining what men think of vulnerability. And this is the key. Authentic courage, or *valor*, requires vulnerability. It requires a sort of bravery that, although not aggressive, is strong in the face of violence or power. To think of vulnerability not as a weakness but as a strength is thus the first step in replacing *valentía* with *valor*.

Bermúdez also recommends an even more consequential re-placement: *cabalidad* for *machismo*. *Cabalidad* comes from the word *cabal*, which means "just" or "upright." A man, Bermúdez says, should be *cabal*, or upright. An upright man controls his pas-sions and respects women: "He sees a woman for what she really is: a simple human being; does not unnecessarily idealize her as a saint or as a whore."³ The goal is to educate young men into being *hombres cabales*, upright men.

A final, necessary step in the undermining of machismo is the undermining of *hembrismo*, as Bermúdez understands the term. "The legend of female self-sacrifice," she writes, must be replaced "with [femininity] as a longing for dignity." Women, Bermúdez insists, should not simply accept "the legend" but instead must rec-ognize it as such. This will allow them to impose their own subjec-tivity on their situation, assert their agency, and demand or "long for" dignity. Dignity requires being seen and respected in one's humanity. And by learning to see that their role has been imposed by a fabricated mythology, women can demand such respect. The power to demand respect or—what is essentially the same thing—to fabricate her own meaning is the essence of "femininity."⁴

So, at the root of the problem plaguing the family, Bermúdez finds inherited dogmas about roles. These are passed down from generation to generation dressed up as concepts that are meant to construct one's identity. You can be a *valiente* if you're a man, or an *hembra* if you're a woman, and each has a standard set of behaviors attached to it. Questioning this inheritance involves questioning these concepts and replacing them with others that are less aggressive or less dehumanizing.

The belief that one can be a good father or a good mother is grounded on the assumption that there's such a thing as being an objectively good father or an objectively good mother. This notion forces some to aim for perfect correspondence between one's own circumstance and the objective ideal. But no such perfection is possible. As a father, I can only teach my children to be "upright" or "just." My own father, once he had realized the violence of his own inheritance, gave me a valuable piece of advice: *Sé cabal*—Be upright, be just.

Consequently, Bermúdez thinks that true liberation for ourselves, our family, our community, and our culture requires a rethinking of our inheritance and the concepts that communicate it. Such liberation is required for a good life, one that we can all aspire to, including our children and their children. Of course, rejecting inherited dogmas takes *valor*, the sort of courage that seeks justice and goodness without aggression or violence. But that's what one must do: examine one's inheritance; consider one's rearing, cultivation, and history; and courageously reject those things that don't seem right and just.

So ask yourself: what part of your inheritance must you reject?

24 | LOVE WHAT YOU DO

We've heard it said, "Do what you love and you'll never work a day in your life." The suggestion here is that if you choose a career that reflects your interests or even your passions, you will barely notice that you're working and you'll get to enjoy your life while also earning a living. But this refrain assumes something important: it is the sort of advice given to those who are in the privileged position of *choosing* what they will do. If given a choice, you will do what you love; if not given a choice, you may end up doing pretty much anything.

When I decided to make a career in philosophy, more than a few people warned me against wasting a rare opportunity to make money and help my parents—rare because no one before me had gone to or graduated from college. Surprisingly, my parents didn't feel the same. My mother's advice was simple: "As long as you *love what you do*, then we don't care what that is." What my mother was telling me was that she and my father would be happy for me so long as I was not miserable doing what I did. But hidden in that advice was a warning and a promise. The warning: you may not get to do what you love to do. The promise: but if you come to love what you do, it won't matter that you didn't get to do what you wanted in the first place.

What I am highlighting here is that the advice to "do what you love" assumes that you have the luxury, privilege, and resources to choose what you will do in life. It assumes that you are privileged enough to be able to choose how you will spend it. It assumes that if you are *not* doing what you love, then that was also your choice. But not all of us have the luxury of choosing what we will do.

By contrast, my mother's advice to "love what you do" doesn't assume such privilege or luxury. It tells you to love whatever it is that you are already doing, even if it is something that may initially not have inspired love at all. Perhaps you had certain plans for your life, nicely laid out, plans involving doing the kind of work that you love, and these somehow fell apart. At some point you had to settle, to do what was necessary in order to "make ends meet." Perhaps, for example, you began working in sales out of necessity. Being a salesperson was never on your radar and was not what you loved, but the opportunity came along at the right time, when you needed a job, money, security. So here you are. And now that you are doing it—having been "thrown into it," for all intents and purposes—you can think of it in one of two ways: as either a curse or an opportunity. If you think of it as a curse, you may come to hate every single day you have to do it. Such misery is obviously to be avoided. Alternatively, you can think of it as an opportunity. This will require a slight shift of perspective.

Once again, my father can serve as my example. My father loves horses; if you ask him, he was riding them before he could walk. But riding horses, or even taking care of them, was not something that he could make a living at. Coming from a poor family, in a poor community, in a poor country, he found his opportunities severely limited. At seventeen, he was forced to migrate to the United States and look for a *real* job, something that could pay him enough money to survive and also help his family back home in Mexico. The kind of job didn't matter; how he felt about it didn't matter.

Like many of his immigrant friends, he ended up working on agricultural farms in California's Salinas Valley. He would end up doing this for the next fifty years. As an agricultural worker, his opportunities boiled down to doing one of three things, all involving backbreaking labor: planting, harvesting, or irrigation. The hardest type of work was irrigation, which is what he ended up doing. There are several types of irrigation work, and for thirty of his fifty years he worked in something called "furrow irrigation." This is an irrigation method in which water is channeled through large aluminum pipes placed at the head of a large field. The water, pressure-pumped through the pipes, is released through tiny openings at each furrow—hence the name. It is let out in increments, controlled by hand, throughout the day, depending on the crop's water needs. Meanwhile, a human being, like my father, walks up and down the field widening or narrowing the furrows in order to get the water where it needs to go—that is, to the root of the plant—quickly and efficiently and at the required speed.

Now, my father didn't choose to do this; it was the only kind of work an undocumented immigrant laborer could get. He started off moving sprinkler pipes, which is also backbreaking work. You had to be able to lift two twelve-foot, thirty-pound aluminum pipes over your head and move them twelve feet to the side, sometimes against the wind, in rain and in the mud, but often under the scorching sun. And you had to do this all day, in fields the length of football fields. But my father did his job well and never complained. As a reward, he was "promoted" to furrow irrigation. This labor was less strenuous but it required better judgment as well as a more intimate understanding of water, how it moves and how it seeps into the soil.

He learned the technical aspects of the work quickly—the rest was instinctual—and he became an expert in no time. Other ranchers tried to lure him away to their own ranches, but he stayed put out of a sense of loyalty (a loyalty greater than it should have been, given our family's needs at the time). What others recognized was that my father had grown to *love what he did*. And they realized this by the way he talked about it, by how efficient he was at it, and by the fact that his fields always looked bright green even in the peak of summer. He perfected the art of furrow irrigation, even though he really didn't have to. He learned to listen to the earth, to the water, to their relationship; he knew when to shovel dirt into a furrow to slow the water down, when to shovel dirt out of a furrow to speed it up. Eventually, he perceived the beauty of the process and learned to love it. In loving it, he mastered it. My father is a quiet man, but if you ask him about furrow irrigation he'll talk until you stop him.

My father did not need to find beauty in this work in order to do it efficiently. In fact, no one would have expected him to find beauty in such technique-heavy work, which bore most field laborers. Water is pumped and released at a certain pressure into furrows and is then pulled by gravity the length of field at a certain speed, gradually seeping into the soil and saturating the roots. The job requires only this knowledge and the ability to tell time and act according to instructions. But by finding beauty in the process, my father found a way to love the work. He says that he could hear the water and the soil speak to one another. And so he listened to them for decades.

Watching my father work taught me early on that there is more to life than what is measurable, calculable, or rational. The beauty of a flowing stream inching its way through a deep earthen furrow lined on both sides by the oversized, bright-green sails of the cauliflower plant is something that the scientific or rational mind may never find the need to appreciate. *Why would they?*

Twentieth-century Mexican philosophy inaugurates itself by proposing that there is something more meaningful and important than the dry scientific explanation of things. It tracks the intuition that the world is more than a collection of knowable facts related in ways subject to technological manipulation. It insists that there are things about life and the world that science simply can't capture, such as beauty and the sublime ways in which we pursue it. It doesn't force itself to deny that, for example, beyond its chemistry, water speaks.

Late-nineteenth-century educational reforms in Mexico saw the growing influence in all aspects of Mexican life of the scientific philosophy known as positivism. Schools cut back on teaching subjects related to theology, metaphysics, and fields outside the methods of experimental science, the motivating idea being that a rigorous scientific education would purge Mexicans of their superstitions, religion, and sentimentality. Behind it was a larger political and economic purpose: to make Mexico competitive in an increasingly industrial and technological global marketplace.

Resistance to positivist social policies began at the start of the twentieth century, when a group of young Mexican poets, philosophers, and writers calling themselves the Atheneum of Youth (Ateneo de la Juventud) brought attention to the concern that such policies were detrimental to the Mexican soul itself. *How could one live without religion? Or art? Or poetry? Or philosophy?*

José Vasconcelos (1882–1959) stood out among the members of the Atheneum. His anti-positivism would eventually lead him to introduce a philosophical doctrine that he called *aesthetic monism.* The notion of aesthetic monism has it that reality is One, Interconnected, or Whole. Within this Whole, however, there is difference. Not all parts are identical to the Whole. This heterogeneity in the parts means that our senses know the world as fragmented, disjointed, divided. Science, or positivism, on the other hand, assumes that heterogeneity is all there is and focuses on the parts at the expense of the whole.

Reason, for its part, ignores this heterogeneity and imagines a Whole without difference. We see this in acts of abstraction where the *form* of the Whole forgets its parts. This is why Vasconcelos proposes an aesthetic, mystical, or spiritual approach to knowing the world, one that depends on creating value and meaning while appreciating difference within the Whole as well as valuing the Whole itself.

Aesthetic monism is the name for a unified theory of life that involves not only the senses and the intellect but also the emotions. It proposes that reality is one (hence the "monism" part), but that within the one there are dissimilarities. Positivists focus on the differences so as to master them; rationalist philosophers focus on the whole to the detriment of the differences. But the aesthetic monist focuses on, or lends attention to, both the differences and the One. This is a kind of attention that respects both the multiplicity and the Whole, that values them and finds in them the source of meaning or sense. Poets already do this: a poem can capture both contingency and transcendence in one stanza. Vasconcelos suggests that philosophers should be more like the poets.

The underlying assumption of Vasconcelos's aesthetic monism is that there's more to life than what is offered by the senses or by reason, a beauty that the senses and reason ignore when they obsess over either the details of life (as positivism does) or its abstraction (as rationalists do). Vasconcelos thus refers to aesthetic monism as "a system which is that of artists and mystics"[1] —thus, an aesthetic and mystical system. It is an aesthetic system because it appreciates the sublime beauty of the world, its hidden poetry. And it is a mystical system because it appreciates the world in its totality, in its transcendent unity and Oneness. In short, it appreciates everything, but especially the mystery of it all. Consequently, Vasconcelos's aesthetic monism seeks to unify all the ways in which we come to know the world. It seeks harmony among our various knowledge-organs: our senses, our intellect, and our sensibility. A true philosophical system, suggests Vasconcelos, can only work with aesthetic monism at its center. The true philosopher, he says, is a "poet with a system,"[2] a philosopher who can appreciate the beauty of what seems irrational or beyond the scope of the senses.

Vasconcelos's knockout punch to positivism is his insight that the sort of knowledge that positivism values will always be fragmented, specialized, and incomplete so long as it relies strictly on the methods of empirical science. The fact is, he says, that "We know as human beings with all our faculties, not as pure intellects."[3]

Aesthetic monism offers an alternative way to know, love, and interact with the world. My father could easily have gone through the motions of letting the water flow for a certain amount of time, shoveling dirt in certain increments, and so on. He could have relied solely on the science of furrow irrigation and the reliability of his senses. Like a mere positivist or technician, he could have treated every field the same, abstracting from the differences in terrain or the differences in water flow. Like a rationalist, he could have simply reasoned himself into the most effective way to do his job and do it effectively. But he chose to love what he did. He opened himself up to the beauty of the flow of water steadily running down a dry-earth furrow. He enjoyed the thought of roots sucking up the moisture like thirsty elephants. He thought of it all as a gift that he lived with his heart.

Doing the work that he did, he told me once, was as close as he ever got to having a religious experience. While he didn't have the language to articulate it precisely in this way, he would have said that the whole of reality became One on each furrow, synthesized in the sound of the rushing water. No manual of furrow irrigation and no description of it could account for that experience.

Now you know how my father came to love what he did: he came to find beauty in work that technically lacked any beauty. I'm suggesting that he personified an aesthetic monist. But, besides coming to love what you do, why would *you* want to be an aesthetic monist? Perhaps for one simple reason: as an aesthetic monist, you would enjoy the freedom to appreciate everything you find beautiful, perfect, and sublime without needing to explain all of its mysteries. There's so much that we don't know and that we will never know; there's so much more that we can just enjoy as it is, as it gives itself to us. There's much about our work, our everyday activities, and our interactions that we can come to appreciate without having a reason to do so. As an aesthetic monist you can allow yourself moments when you don't have to make sense of everything. More to the point, you may save yourself the stress and anxiety that come when explanations end.

My father would eventually stop working in the fields when such work was replaced by more modern techniques like drip irrigation. A sadness overtook him for a few years afterward. It was the poetic sadness of mourning.

25 | YOU REALLY DON'T HAVE TO JOIN A CULT

One can be easily seduced by exclusivity. The idea of belonging to something to which not everyone can belong is attractive. It can become especially alluring if you believe that what qualifies you to be part of the exclusive set is something not everyone has. Imagine being one of the very few people to take seriously the thought that Bigfoot exists. You are absolutely certain that you caught sight of him on a hike up Mt. Shasta in northern California twenty years ago. Even if that's only a faint memory now, documentaries about his existence, his nature, and his behavior continue to justify your belief. Of course, not everyone takes the idea seriously, and most people actually think it's nonsense. But, then you go to a Bigfoot convention. There you meet others who believe *this particular thing* with the same passion and fervor as you do. Now you belong to an exclusive club. Now you get to learn the lingo of the insiders. Now you are plugged into this club's universe, to that expansive set of beliefs that, however outlandish to an outsider, forms the knowledge and wisdom of the group. What makes you special is recognized, and this lends meaning to your life.

Being part of this exclusive community puts things in perspective. You realize that the community to which you already belonged—the one that includes your family, friends, coworkers, and neighbors—does not appreciate what makes you special. This has led you to tone down your enthusiasm for Bigfoot in their presence so that they won't think you crazy or delusional. But it's also led you to gradually distance yourself from these same people, failing to show up at some family gatherings and work parties. And so you now feel closer to the members of the Bigfoot community, who, like you, may also have made themselves increasingly marginalized elsewhere.

Already we can see the potential danger in such communities. While they may embrace something special that you feel is unappreciated by everyone else, that something special may be the only thing about you that they appreciate. You may have to hide or suppress the rest of yourself. And that's a problem: in trying to satisfy the expectations of the exclusive community, you will have to give up aspects of your identity that don't fit those expectations, and before you know it, your entire identity has become mostly a reflection of that community. Before you know it, that is, you have become *inseparable* from that community; before you know it, you're in a cult.

Avoiding such traps—which are really traps laid for a solitary ego begging for recognition—is key to having a more fulfilling life. But how can you avoid those ego traps when exclusivity can be so alluring?

The real danger of falling into ego traps, of course, is not that you will end up joining the North American Bigfoot Association (if there even is such a thing). The real danger, again, is surrendering

your identity to an exclusive and ultimately ideologically restrictive community—that is, ending up in a *closed community* like a
sect or a cult. Surrendering one's identity to a closed community
adds up to sacrificing one's entire personality for the sake of that
one quality about yourself that you deem special or unique—even
if, paradoxically, it's a uniqueness that is shared by every member
of that community.

Mexican philosophy advises us to keep an eye on how this happens and how to avoid it. According to Jorge Portilla, of the various crises diagnosed by Mexican philosophers midway through
the twentieth century, the most pernicious was what he called "the
state of sub-integration" found in certain sectors of Mexican society. Sub-integration is the state whereby individuals lose their
sense of belonging and suffer from "a species of social malnutri-
tion" in which they no longer feel nourished by existing social or
communal relations.[1] Having concluded that society as it is offers
no place for them—that it has left them behind and no longer
values them, what they value, or what they can contribute—they
become unsociable and prefer to spend their day isolated in their
homes, avoiding the public as much as possible. The state of sub-
integration is a state of anti-sociality.

What motivated Portilla's observation was his perception of
the social situation of Mexico itself. Centuries of war, revolution, and class struggle have left Mexicans with an anemic sense
of community. Having lost faith in their individual communities,
they find it hard to orient their lives around a shared communal
vision. In Portilla's words, "community in Mexico is lived at a dis-
tant and unarticulated horizon that does not offer a precise orientation or consistent support for individual action."[2] While Portilla

was discussing the alienation and social disintegration of modern Mexican life, it is an alienation experienced by people in other major postindustrial capitalist societies around the world to this day, and thus a state with which you may be familiar. It is the experience of isolation, of not feeling part of or integrated into the environment in which you live, of thinking that your individual actions do not matter much in the grand scheme of things. In such a state, you feel separated, disaffected, or abandoned. These days, it is likely that you express your alienation while hiding in certain corners of the Internet, trolling in the comments sections but never really joining anything, making yourself known only through mean or self-deprecating posts. The isolation that comes with sub-integration ultimately seems to authorize your misbehavior, since there's really no reason to behave in accordance with any communal standards or norms for someone who prefers to loiter outside their purview.

Still, we can interpret this constant rebelling against community as a desire to be included in one, even one filled with anti-community rebels.

If you are one of these sub-integrated individuals, you may be on the lookout for those communities that might value your uniqueness, whatever you think makes you special. You may begin searching for factions, sects, or groups that reflect the unique ideological horizon of your own personality. In search of other individuals that reflect your own viewpoint in very specific ways, you may "go all in" on your new communities. Supporters of radical right-wing causes are an obvious example of what may ensue: once they find a group that nourishes personal beliefs that are disdained by the mainstream, they integrate fully into them. In this way, Portilla says, sub-integrated individuals become "super-integrated." Now, if you've reached the stage of feeling super-integrated, it is possible that you're already in a cult.

⌘

With super-integration you lose yourself in the group. While in sub-integration you feel left out, in super-integration you feel locked in. Your entire super-integrated world becomes bounded by the ideological horizons that define the group, often producing a militant sense of community. Ultimately, super-integration leads you to value community not as an inclusive, open, and respectful relation among a broad public but rather as a clique devoted to hyper-specialization and exclusion. Because of this, Portilla says that super-integration is "without a doubt . . . an evil."[3]

Although super-integration feeds on sub-integration, it's important to avoid them both. By separating individuals from one another—into solitude and anti-sociality, on the one hand, or sectarianism and exclusivity, on the other—both contribute to the *dis*integration of community. But can either be avoided—especially if, according to Portilla, what makes them possible is an "extreme" version of "bourgeois" individualism that is itself a product of modern capitalism?

Portilla thinks we can indeed avoid both super- and sub-integration. But for starters, it requires rethinking what is meant by "community." Is community, for you, a mere idea, or is it a concrete social space? In other words, is community merely a vaguely-defined notion about where you happen to live and park your car or a well-demarcated set of relations and relationships maintained by coexistence, play, and learning? For most people it's often the former.

Why do we think of "community" as a mere idea? This has to do with how we relate to it. According to Portilla, most of us relate to community as a person, as an "interpretive horizon," or as an "us." However, *none* of these, he continues, orient us to care for the communities in which we actually live to the degree that we can be sure of ignoring the enticing call of solitude or exclusiveness—both symptoms of contemporary forms of radical "individuality."

When we think of a community as a person, we imagine it as an organism to which one can attribute intentionality and purpose—capable of answering for itself, acting on its own, or forging its own path. On this conception, it is normal for us to say things like "Russia's aggressive rhetoric threatens international security" or "The Vietnamese community in San Francisco seeks more rights." Here, both Russia and the Vietnamese community are imagined as persons or intentional entities. However, according to Portilla, this is not a useful concept of community, as it may actually be damaging to the people in those communities. That is, thinking of communities as persons makes it easy to forget that actual persons make up the community, which could, in turn, make us blind to their individual suffering. When we says that the Comanche are thriving in Oklahoma, we don't take account of the dire conditions in which individual members of Native American tribes currently live.

Community is also sometimes understood as an "interpretive horizon," which is to say, as the space in which personal actions make sense, or, as Portilla says, "in which actions are articulated."[4] On this understanding of community, togetherness is made possible by a shared vision of life or a common perspective shared by all members, which informs their thoughts, actions, and beliefs. It is a vision of life that serves as a wall against which "the meaning of our actions bounces back like an echo."[5] The problem with this view is that if community is itself the filter through which we see the world, then every member of a particular community is believed to see the world in exactly the same way. This is never the case, and if it were, a glitch in the interpretive horizon would affect everyone, again, in the same way. Portilla imagines "a certain evil demon, playing a serious prank" that messes with the interpretive horizon. If this were to happen, suddenly nothing would make sense. "We would suddenly find ourselves," Portilla says, "as if waking from a dream, incapable of understanding . . . where we stand, incapable of understanding any of the actions taking place in it." The evil demon's prank would make everyone feel crazy and unhinged; the radical unfamiliarity of the world would have everyone question the "state of [their] mental faculties."[6]

The reason why Portilla thinks that this sense of community as interpretive horizon is not useful is that we never exist in only one community-as-horizon. Rather, he says, "we . . . live in a multiplicity of communal horizons that mix and weave with one another and that always remain potential or actual, depending on whether our action reveals or conceals them."[7] If one of these horizons collapses, others are sure to remain. So if an evil demon were to play a trick on one of my interpretive horizons, he would have to play a trick on them all. And this seems like too much for an evil demon to do.

The final way in which we think of community merely as an idea is when we think of community as an "us" (*nosotros*). This is an abstract "us" made up, for the most part, of strangers who through the "us" connect with one another. I often hear sports fans refer to fans of the same team in this way. There's a "Laker Nation" and a "Raider Nation" and so on, and they speak in terms of "we" and a "ours" when talking about their community. They say things like: "We'll get them next year!" or "We won!" Portilla would say that they are tied together by "a common transcendence"[8]—that is, a common idea that is greater than the sum of its parts. For Laker fans, the common idea is, of course, the very idea of the Los Angeles Lakers. The "us" of Laker fans, like the "us" of Northern California or the "us" of Texas, however, is abstract and imperceptible, based solely on a mysterious relation between individuals who truly don't know of each other's existence. In other words, the "us" is anonymous and incapable of asking anything of its members or holding anyone accountable. If I say "us," who can I point to?

If a community is not a person, a horizon, or an "us," then what is it? According to Portilla, "true community" is only possible as an "us both" (*nosotros dos*). Said differently, a true community is one where its members are face to face with one another or can be face to face with one another. It is formed, moreover, by relations of proximity and familiarity. Portilla says, "True community is not

given except in . . . a "you and I" for whom the relation is immediate."[9] In other words, in a true community, we interact with one
another.

Only the "us both" relation gives us the "interlacing of personal
relations" that can provide the basis for authentic community, because "a society without a face or warmth makes us cold with distrust."[10] A "society with a face," or, better yet, a community with
many faces, is one where we are never alone, it is a moral, interactive, community of familiar speakers and colorfully-dressed
bodies.

But can thinking of community as an "us both" save you from
falling into the traps of your own ego-desires? Can it keep you
from joining a cult? Or getting out of one?

If you think of your relationship with your community as an
active, voluntary, and dialogical (or conversational) relation with
another person, and ultimately *other persons*, then you are less likely
to seek those exclusive communities that prioritize your specialness, or you are more likely to leave them. I recall an aunt who,
years before I was born, had joined a religious cult. At some point
in my early teens, she started coming around our house. She'd sit
for hours with my mom gossiping or cooking. She eventually left
the cult and lived out her days surrounded by family and friends.
We like to think that it was the dialogical, interactive, communion
between her and us that made this happen.

The problem that Portilla addresses is social and political in nature. In his diagnosis, if community is merely a theoretical ideal
to you, you may see no reason to take part in *making* community,
and thus you may retreat into your solitude, into the margins of
your communities, into sub-integration. Or you may find enclaves,

sects, or cults that give you the sense of togetherness and partici-
pation that you feel you need, thereby achieving super-integration.

Today we are no strangers to either sub- or super-integration. The
prevalence of social media has made both of these real options for
living. You can feel isolated, abandoned, and outcast one minute
and part of a Facebook group of similarly isolated individuals the
next. One moment you're alone behind a screen, the next you're
participating in what is essentially a cult. But there is a safeguard.
And it involves taking ownership of your existing community by
engaging with others in its active construction through acts of listening, acceptance, and care.

   Naturally, you can enjoy your own company—enjoy being by
yourself—without abandoning your relationship with the community, and this is healthy and advisable. But you must stay vigilant to keep sub-integration at bay, so that this being-with-yourself
doesn't turn into alienation or resentment toward others. Similarly,
you could join the North American Bigfoot Association or any
other community of like-minded people. But, here again, you
must watch yourself, making sure to maintain perspective on your
difference, because the allure of exclusivity can catch any one of us
off guard. Too much integration and, before you know it, you're
wearing white canvas sneakers while waiting for the end-times.

PART IV

DICHOS

26 | MY *ABUELO'S* FAVORITE *DICHO*

I remember the day my cousin Rubén came to our house wearing the most exquisite blue dress. He looked so happy wearing it, modeling it for my mom and dad, while confessing that this was part of a bigger secret.

Rubén was the second youngest of fifteen brothers—yes, *fifteen*! My father was his mother's brother, so Rubén felt comfortable with us and came over often. On this day, he'd come to announce that he would be revealing his big secret to the rest of the brothers at the next family gathering, a baptism that was to take place the following week.

He was noticeably nervous, fearing his brothers would not take the revelation well. My mother agreed: the brothers would not accept this—they would react violently. My father angrily interjected, saying something in Spanish to the tune of "It's none of their effing business what he wears or what he does with himself!" My father was not known for standing up for causes; this was one of the rare occasions when I saw him do so. He assured Rubén, "If they mess with you, they mess with me, and they don't want to do that."

"Pos sí," my mom concurred, "el respeto al derecho ajeno es la paz."

What my mom had uttered was a Golden Rule in our community: *Respect for the rights of others is peace.* The insinuation was that the Family Peace would be maintained only if Rubén's right to be the version of himself that he chose to be was fully respected—even if not *welcomed*—by everyone.

At the baptism, the brothers reacted as my mother had predicted. They threw him out of the house, telling him that he was no longer welcome to any family function and that they would immediately inform their mother (who lived in Mexico) that he was a disgrace, a "puto."

My father rushed to Rubén's side, got him out the house safely, then stormed back in. He angrily screamed at his nephews, telling them that none of them were "half the man" Rubén had always been. He asked them to reconsider their blind and ridiculous prejudices for the sake of Rubén and the family.

"What do you want us to do, *tío*—he's a *maricón*!"

With emphasis on each word, my dad said, "*El respeto al derecho ajeno es la pinche paz!* Let him be—respect whatever he decides to do with his life! Just like I respect your rights to do as you please, even if I don't like it. Just like you respect mine, even if you don't like it. And just like we've always respected each other's bullshit!"

"It's not the same," one of the brothers said. "He needs to be a man!"

"He doesn't *need* to be what you want him to be—it's not your business! Besides, how does his lifestyle hurt *you*? Let him be!"

There was silence. The brothers were angry. My father was angry. We left the party.

It would take the brothers two decades to understand what my father was saying to them. And for twenty years Rubén struggled alone, occasionally coming over to my parents' house to get their affirmation, their love, and, for what it was worth, their respect.

This is not a unique story, of course. It seems as if we are never *not* talking about respect. Respecting a woman's right to choose; respecting transgender rights; respecting the right of all to marriage; respecting a universal human right to be in charge of one's own life. The reason we always seem to be talking about respect is that there seems to be an abundance of narratives intent on disrespecting these rights.

The lack of peace brought about by disrespect points to the significance of the idea, expressed by both my mother and my father, that respect for the rights of others *is* peace. If only the brothers had respected Rubén's right to his own life, his own flourishing, there would've have been peace. This idea is simple enough.

As expressed by my father as a short, quippy refrain, this simple idea is a "*dicho.*" *Dichos* are nuggets of wisdom passed down orally from one generation to the next. They are mechanisms of instruction, reminders, and guides, dispensed when needed—which is why, I suppose, one doesn't forget them. Their moral value is learned in the thick of things.

And the particular *dicho* that my parents spoke on these occasions holds a central place in the hearts of Mexicans, capturing an inescapable moral truth and commandment, a Golden Rule:

> *El respeto al derecho ajeno es la paz.*
> *Respect for the rights of others is peace.*

It was made popular by Mexico's first Indigenous president, Benito Juárez (1806–1872), and its gist is that, for there to be peace, there must be respect. Juárez's popularity and fame, like those of Lincoln, transcend politics. He is firmly cemented in Mexican history and culture as a representative of the Mexican spirit. Not surprisingly, this philosophical dictum (spoken to the nation on July 15, 1868) found its way into the far reaches of the Republic, into hamlets and hidden mountain villages, into the *pueblos mágicos* that line the postcolonial landscape—and into the heart of my father's moral compass.

Juárez's full statement was "Entre los individuos, como entre las naciones, el respeto al derecho ajeno es la paz": Between individuals, as between nations, respect for the rights of others is peace. Included in a speech delivered after Mexico had won its independence *for the second time* in the 1860s—the first time (in 1820) from Spain, the second time from France—it was intended to call attention to the obligations of other nations to respect Mexican sovereignty, which, to Juárez, was the only way that world peace would ever be achieved. However, what tradition has preserved of Juárez's statement has little to do with international geopolitics. The way it is read and understood today is that each one of us is sovereign over his or her own person, and to disrespect another person's rights is to disrespect that sovereignty, an act that, as with nations, usually leads to conflict.

But this *dicho* is understood to be about more than not disrespecting others—more than what in political philosophy is called "negative freedom," or the freedom not to be bothered. It is also about something more active: namely, respecting the personhood of others by protecting their rights, their sovereignty, and their lives. It is about the "positive freedom" to interfere for the sake of another's well-being. This is how my father understood it. As you can see, there's a lot going on in this *dicho*. It tells us not simply to observe another person's right to self-governance and self-determination but, when necessary, to positively and actively protect that right.

Now, Juárez didn't conjure up this principle out of thin air (although I'm of the opinion that he could easily have done so); it actually comes from Immanuel Kant, in the essay "Perpetual Peace," written in 1795.[1] Nonetheless, in a dramatic turn that would please Kantians worldwide, Juárez in his paraphrase was capable of teaching that basic Kantian insight to the entire Mexican people, a lesson that would burrow deeply into the Mexican spirit and that still remains there.

My grandfather, having learned this basic tenet of the Kantian theory of morality in his youth (without ever knowing who Kant was), would practice the principle often. I remember hearing it from him before hearing it from my parents. He would say it moments of grandfatherly instruction as he pointed out that peace amongst us (in the family, the community, or the broader society) was always possible so long as we respected one another's property, privacy, and liberty. But he also lived this principle: he was known as a peaceful man, with a quiet self-confidence, and would only get riled up when this "regla" (rule) was violated. Toward the end of his life, as he gradually lost his battle with Alzheimer's, he would mutter Juárez's dictum to himself as if it were a prayer.

One particular memory of how my grandfather practiced the principle stands out. As a child, he would take me on horseback into the wild hills of Michoacán. More than once, we came across a wandering calf or cow. He would dismount and carefully—because he was already in his late seventies—herd the calf or cow back into its enclosure, then take great care in repairing the enclosure's stone fence so that the animal wouldn't wander off again. After doing such deeds, he would murmur Juárez's dictum, just loud enough for me to hear, and we'd ride on. No one knew that he took such great care for other people's property except me, and maybe my father and my grandmother. One day I asked him about it: "How is putting the cow back over the wall respecting other people's rights, especially since they don't know you're doing it? And how is that 'peace'?" I would ask as an annoying eight-year-old boy. "Because to respect someone," he would say in a low, shy voice, "is to help them live their life without worry. If I put the cow back before they know it's missing, then they won't worry, and they can keep living their life in peace. Even though I don't know them, I respect their wanting to live their life in peace. I want that for myself, too."

I suppose he was right. If I value the right to exist of the person in front of me, I will show this by not needlessly complicating his or her life. This will represent respect, and if I do it right, it might also be grounds for a lasting peace between us—or, at the very least, peace *within myself* in knowing that my actions have been right and true.

When the Alzheimer's had advanced, my grandfather would lose himself in a jumble of memories. On good days he'd confuse me for my father; but on most days he didn't know me at all. Still, he remembered the *dicho*. The last time I saw him, as I bid him good-bye, he once again gave me some of his sage advice: *Muchacho, don't forget this: respect for the rights of others is peace.* He said this as if it was the only gift he could give a stranger. Although he had given me the same gift many times before, I said "Thank you" before we disappeared forever from each other's lives.

These days, I think about this *dicho* often. I mutter it to myself, just like he did. When I do, I think about my grandfather, the Alzheimer's, my cousin Rubén, and my parents' failed peace efforts on his behalf.

The power of proverbs, or *dichos*, is that they enter the bloodstream without much effort. They are instruments of moral and cultural instruction, meant to help you survive the necessary hardships of your accidental existence. I am convinced that if Juárez's *dicho* entered the bloodstream of contemporary culture, perhaps we would at least see less brutality all around us, and we all might possibly become more vigilant for each other's well-being.

Of course, whether you encounter this *dicho* in Kant or Juárez or get it from your grandfather, it is one of those universal principles that transcends space and time. Wherever you live, you are a better person when you allow others to be who they are, but especially when you do what it takes to help them achieve themselves. This is especially true if, as Mexican philosophy claims, there is nothing necessary about your existence: if you're an accident, if your circumstance is imperfect, and if you find yourself always struggling against history and life. Respect in this case is a way to make things easier, to lend stability to a condition of existence that can otherwise be uncertain and at times violent. Like a grazing cow, you sometimes need to be left alone but may sometimes need help getting back into your enclosure. Respect demands that I know the difference . . . for the sake of peace.

27 | MY *ABUELA*'S FAVORITE *DICHO*

It was quite a thing. My son turned thirteen and suddenly, as if by magic, he *knew more than I did* about most things under the sun. Or at least that is what he insisted on and apparently firmly believed.

"Just because they say they're better than you doesn't mean that they are," I tell him, in my most fatherly tone. I'm trying to make him understand that some kids oversell their social and economic standing for the sake of popularity or to make themselves feel better—or, in the worst cases, by trying to rewrite their own story in order to survive or to bury the violence or abuse in their own homes. We're talking about one particular kid.

"I don't think so," he says like a confident thirty-year-old man. "He doesn't just say he has money. He flaunts it and wears all the expensive stuff. And his mom drives a Mercedes!" he says excitedly. "I know what I'm talking about—people can't just fake that!"

"I'm telling you," I insist, "don't trust everything you see. There's always something you don't know."

"I'll believe my own eyes, pops," he says triumphantly and walks out of the kitchen. In his heart, he knows more than me, my experience, and all the David Humes of the world.

Of course, *I know* that he doesn't really know it all, that most of the time he just pretends to know, for reasons which I myself have forgotten. Because, you see, I was exactly the same. I thought I knew more than most people, but especially my mother. She was wrong about what foods caused indigestion, about how my high-school friends wouldn't be my friends forever, and about how alcoholism "runs in your blood."

As it turned out, I had it all wrong. Eventually I learned that my mother was right and I was wrong about the strength of my stomach lining, my high-school friends, and a certain family inheritance. The way I learned all this, however, was painful and, in a few cases, almost catastrophic. I often think that if only I had valued her wisdom just a little bit more, my trauma would have been less traumatic. It pains me to know that my son too will learn by bitter experience. Because it will hurt. But learn he will, eventually.

A few years ago, I confessed to my mother that as a teenager I thought she didn't know anything. I told her that I didn't think she knew what she was talking about most of the time. However, I proudly proclaimed, *now* I knew that she had, in fact, known a lot, and that my life would've been easier had I listened and done as she said.

"Well, just because I never went to school doesn't mean I don't know things, *mijo*. Remember *el dicho* your grandmother used to say," she began. "*Más sabe el diablo por viejo, que por diablo*": The old devil knows more from being old than from being the devil.

I did remember it. She would repeat this *dicho* all the time. (Again, a *dicho* is a common saying communicating a piece of folk wisdom in a way that is both penetrating and easy to remember.) Because my mother had acted the same way with her own mother as I had with mine, and as my son is now acting with me, my grandmother's oft-repeated refrain seemed to communicate what my mother had been trying to tell me for years: *I'm not asking you to believe me because I'm your mother. I'm asking you to believe me because I've lived longer than you.* In other words, against my naive claims to knowledge, my mother was reminding me that experience is the best teacher.

As we've seen, Mexican philosophy privileges experience over reason, in the sense that it sees solutions to fundamental problems as rooted in history and circumstance rather than in some disembodied (logical or transcendental) rules that at one point were authorized by the (Western) philosophical tradition. Indeed, this *dicho* itself captures the Mexican privileging of history and circumstance.

In a literal sense, the meaning of my grandmother's favorite *dicho* is simple: while the devil may know quite a bit—by virtue of being a fallen angel, God's strongest opponent, and ruler of Hell—his wisdom comes not simply from those attributes but from all the years of being those things. The idea that this *dicho* communicates is likewise straightforward: Experience is a resource that we often disparage, often for the sake of our own ego. Pride is an influential vice, and it forces us to lean on what is most proximal, on what is most visible and solid, which is usually what is immediately before us. We thus often put all our faith in our intelligence, in our ability to figure out the present problem now, using only the most available, ready-to-hand resources, while forgetting that others around us have lived longer, that history exists, and that, even though the world drastically changes, many human questions, challenges, and their solutions have already been thought about, implemented, and shown to work.

And that is perhaps the biggest takeaway from this particular *dicho*: namely, that in the end, whatever wisdom we end up possessing or claiming to possess will have come from what we've been through and not from what we've figured out by using our computational faculties. Our wisdom will come from life and not just reason.

This exhortation about experience is based on one that the American philosopher Ralph Waldo Emerson made famous in the early decades of the nineteenth century. My grandmother's *dicho* contains the heart of Emerson's poetic description when he writes:

> So much only of life as I know by experience, so much of the wilderness have I vanquished and planted, or so far have I extended my being, my dominion. . . . Drudgery, calamity, exasperation, want, are instructors in eloquence and wisdom. [Experience] is the raw material out of which the intellect molds her splendid products.[1]

For my grandmother too, as for the Mexican philosophers we've considered in this book, experience is the "raw material" of the intellect. To Emerson's calamity and exasperation they add struggle, adaptation, marginalization, overcoming, regression, resurrection, carnage, ruin, and death. In the Mexican experience, as in the early American experience, there are lessons to be learned, lessons to share, lessons that can offer wisdom to me and everyone else.

Emilio Uranga, for example, thinks that much can be learned from the ruins and "permanent crises" characterizing Mexican history, something "never before experienced." Insisting that "our normality is our crisis," Uranga goes on to suggest that "we have a lesson to teach" and that this lesson has to do with how to cope with crisis and "catastrophism."[2]

Lessons from previous catastrophes will always be more useful than whatever strategy occurs to you at the moment of crisis. And the longer you live, the more experienced the person you listen to, and the older your country and your culture are, the more catastrophes there will have been to learn from! All of these may prove to be sources of valuable insight.

"The old devil knows more for being old than he does for being the devil."

There are at least two ways you can read this *dicho*. One has to do with using experience as a resource, and the other with respecting your elders.

About the first: I've lived long enough to have stories to tell—stories of success and stories of failure. These stories, archived in my memory, often help me navigate present difficulties. As a father, my hope is that my children will ask about these stories unprompted; this never happens. My hope has to do, I think, with wishing that they not repeat mistakes that I've already made. So, since they don't ask, I offer the stories as an available resource, as something we have together, collectively, something they can harvest for the betterment of their own life when they choose.

About the second: Clearly, my son has no intention of respecting my fatherly wisdom in the way that I respected my grandmother's. Blame it on the changing times. Blame it on social media, consumer capitalism, a decline in moral education, the fall of patriarchy, or whatever you like—he's just not going to do it. This is not to say he doesn't respect his elders; he does, and he'll respect their wisdom. It's just me; I'm the problem—I'm his *pops.* There's something about my status as his father that keeps him from mining my experience for his well-being—call it pride. But if those other elders that he does respect are held up as living resources, as people who have survived ruin and catastrophe, then listening to them will help him navigate both his present and his future.

Recovering alcoholics are constantly reminded that doing the same thing over and over again while expecting different results is the definition of "insanity." Drinking yourself into a stupor every time you go out while expecting the night to go well, when such nights have never gone well, and doing this over and over, means that you have lost control of yourself and that you need help. Insanity is here made worse by not learning from experience, which says that, for you, such a formula simply does not work.

A more recent instance of listening to the devil for being the devil comes from the anti-vaccine movement during the Covid-19 pandemic. While anti-vaccine activists had been around before the pandemic, an anti-vaccine movement gained traction as the US government sought to curb the spread of the coronavirus by mandating immunization. Forgetting centuries of evidence that vaccination was the best defense against an aggressive and hitherto unknown virus, "anti-vaxxers" sought to convince the world that the vaccine was an evil worse than the virus itself, that deaths were being miscounted and wrongly attributed to the virus, and that the virus would gradually disappear by itself.

But experience said otherwise. From the drinking of snake venom by Buddhist monks to immunize themselves against snakebites in the seventeenth century, to the almost complete eradication of smallpox and polio via vaccine in the twentieth century, mass immunization has proved effective against viruses and diseases of all kinds. So why the skepticism? In the case of Covid, skepticism began growing once immunization efforts became politicized, to the extent that being pro- or anti-vaccine came to suggest that you supported one political agenda or another. New claims highlighted the dangers of vaccines, convincing many that they were being used in nefarious government experiments. Of course, some communities had legitimate cause for concern, as the government had experimented on people before (the memory of the notorious Tuskegee experiments, in which unsuspecting Black men were used as test subjects in a long-term syphilis experiment beginning in 1932, is still very much alive for many in the Black community). However, in the case of Covid-19 immunization, abundant and readily accessible evidence should have outweighed any rumors about a government cover-up. Nevertheless, new sources presented conspiracy theories as evidence. In late 2021, online sites were warning that those who'd been vaccinated could be dead by the following spring, some would be growing animal tails, and some would be implanted with a Bill Gates-designed

GPS microchip. Scenarios fabricated by cynics with their own agendas and platforms succeeded in fostering widespread confusion, panic, and fear. Large swaths of society relied on these new "authorities" and went unvaccinated. Many died.

This was a case of listening to the devil because of who he was rather than what he'd been through. So far, many of us who listened to the old devil because of what he'd been through have been rewarded with less fear and uncertainty about the future and about each other. Though the coronavirus may not disappear completely, and more people—even some vaccinated against it—will die before it is eradicated, life has largely returned to normal. Listening to experience can have this stabilizing effect.

My grandmother wielded her famous *dicho* about the devil effectively. She knew when to utter it, and those around her had no choice but to listen and then do as she instructed. Bent over her adobe stove making tortillas, she would remind those around her that her wisdom was a result of age and experience, of struggle, defeat, and victory over adversity—the wisdom of a long life. But it was also her way of proclaiming *why* she deserved respect. So we listened.

My grandmother possessed and embodied the collective history of her family, and for this she was indispensable. She knew this, and after hearing her parables, stories, and admonitions, everyone else knew it, too. As I write these words and think of how she wielded her experience for the sake of familial power, I feel compelled to call my ageing parents and ask them questions about their lives. They *know* things, and throughout my life I've often forgotten this. But as I myself get older and my offspring remind me that I really don't know much, my grandmother's *dicho* means more and more to me. It reminds me that our elders deserve respect and reverence if only because they are repositories of experience and knowledge.

PART V

MORE ON MEXICAN PHILOSOPHY

28 | BLOOMING IN THE RUINS

MEXICAN PHILOSOPHY AS YOUR GUIDE TO LIFE

We've come to the end. My hope is that I've succeeded in showing you that Mexican philosophy offers you resources for seeing both yourself and the world you inhabit in a new light. Its rich and unique concepts and approaches can illuminate the path that you're currently on, as well as, if you look back, the path that you've just traveled. In other words, what Mexican philosophy says about *nepantla*, history, objectification, marginalization, death, *relajo*, respect, and so on, can guide you to more meaningful perspectives on your own life—its past, present, and future. Your individuality matters, your circumstance matters, your trauma matters! Mexican philosophy allows you to count them all as core elements in any articulation of your individual survival story. But it also assures you that you're not alone in doing this. You are always tied to others to whom these things matter, but especially to those with similar experiences, who through a "thousand accidents of history have been framed by the catastrophic."[1]

But is that all there is to it? Is Mexican philosophy merely a guide for making sense of your experience in a way that ties you to others similarly "framed by the catastrophic"? Of course not. Mexican philosophers—the ones we've discussed here as well as countless others who have unfortunately had to be left out of our account—think there's more to philosophy than "making sense." It is not just about retelling your life story philosophically; it is also about contributing philosophically to life. It is about leaving a legacy for others yet to come, a legacy that will transcend space and time.

A contemporary Mexican philosopher, Guillermo Hurtado (b. 1962), has provided a "road map" that could help you to make contributions of a meaningful—or better, *philosophical*—kind. This map was intended as a guide for Mexican philosophers to follow as they seek to make and leave their mark. However, I believe that you too can follow the map even if you are not a philosopher. And your status as non-Mexican does not preclude you from benefiting from its lessons, either—I would not have written this book if I had thought otherwise. After all, we are not all ancient Greeks, and yet we find it very ordinary to take up the ideas of ancient Greek philosophers and seek to live by them!

So what is this road map?

In Hurtado's view, for ideas or pronouncements to be meaningful in a deep, philosophical sense, they must be *originary*, *ampliative*, and *solid*.[2]

By *originary*, Hurtado means that ideas must be *original*. Not original in the sense of not having been thought before, but rather, as we've said before, original in the sense of *having an origin*. Thus, "originarity" refers to this "having an origin," and the origin that your ideas or thoughts must have is *you*—that is, your own situated, lived experience.

Insistence that "original" thoughts need to be novel or new is an ideological bias of the West. Against this bias, we have seen that in being "originary" your thoughts or pronouncements show themselves to be embodied and rooted in your reality. This is an obvious rejection of the traditional idea that, to be meaningful or philosophical, an idea must be "abstract" or "universal," disconnected from particular persons or places. An originary thought, in this sense, cannot emerge out of a "view from nowhere."

Here's an originary thought regarding the contemporary self. In my view, what defines the contemporary self is unsettledness, or what Mexican philosophers call "zozobra." This unsettledness is not necessarily due to fear or anxiety about possibilities, death, or what's to come (the future). Instead, the essential unsettledness, or *zozobra*, that defines the contemporary self is related to an insecurity about material bankruptcy—losing our possessions, our property, our means. Now, this thought is not original in the sense of novelty. I'm sure it has been thought by others before me—even if it was dismissed as nonsensical. However, I think the thought has sense and is originary (in Hurtado's sense) in that it is rooted in my own experience of anxiety and zozobra, it is rooted in my time, and in my circumstance. I think this thought from my own life.

According to Hurtado, for a thought to be philosophical it must also be *ampliative*. In other words, the thought must *amplify*, or magnify or expand, the knowledge that already exists. It is not enough for a thought to be originary. It must also contribute to the conversation, whatever the conversation may be. You could easily have an originary thought that adds nothing to what people already know. A thought about the contemporary self may be originary in the sense of being rooted in my own experience; but if it simply repeats what has already been pointed out, or if it adds nothing of value to the conversation about the immigrant experience, then, while interesting, it is not ampliative.

On the other hand, perhaps my thought regarding the contemporary self points to something that others have ignored—it has been overlooked, we might say, that our zozobra is rooted not on our being human (as Uranga or maybe even Martin Heidegger would say) but, simply, on our actual material conditions. If this has, indeed, been ignored, then the thought adds value to the discussion and, in this case, is both originary and ampliative. By being "ampliative," thoughts qualify to take part in a more profound and incisive conversation. There is care and consideration that go into thinking about the contemporary self in this ampliative sense. I want to think about it not just for its own sake but to add value both to the idea and to what people think about it.

Finally, Hurtado tells us that, for a thought to be philosophical, it must be not only originary and ampliative but also *solid*. Solidity has to do with the manner in which the thought is ampliative. If it is ampliative in a *weak* sense, then it is not solid; if it is ampliative in a *strong* sense, then it is. To be solid, or ampliative in a strong sense, the thought must open up doors to discussion, lead to new considerations, and insist on other vocabularies, other discourses, or other forms of understanding. Think of solidity as the weight of a thought. You've probably said to yourself, on listening to something profound, or potentially life changing, "That's heavy!" What you mean when saying this is that the thought poses a challenge to your current understanding, that the web of beliefs that make up what you know or think you know may not be able to withstand the weight of *this* thought, that the thought will break-through the web, causing havoc among your beliefs and thereby changing your life or altering your perspective.

My thought about the contemporary self can be deemed not only originary and ampliative but also solid if it forces a new type of discussion about it. Perhaps the discussion has stalled with the idea that whatever can be said about the contemporary condition has already been said. A solid thought about this topic, however, makes us rethink our opinions and forces us to wonder whether and to what extent our current sense of humanity is tied to what we own, to what we can afford, to our debts, and to our bank accounts.

What about the ideas contained in this book—are they originary, ampliative, and solid? I'd like to think so. Consider the idea of death as a presence rather than as a future event. It is originary because it is born from the Mexican experience and tied to Mexican history. It is ampliative because it should add something to your understanding of death. And finally, it is solid because it unsettles the way you have understood death until now (i.e., as something that will happen to you in the future).

What about your own ideas—are they originary, ampliative, or solid? Taking the lessons of Mexican philosophy to heart requires you to concede that there is always room to learn, adapt, and change, depending on the circumstances in which you find yourself. But it also means that you will not avoid thinking profoundly and carefully about those things that worry or fascinate you. So you decide to speak about your own experience. You carefully look within yourself, as if with a stethoscope, and take yourself and your experience seriously (this will stamp your action or your idea as originary). You accept your experience as meaningful, and hope that articulating it can only add to the collective knowledge about the human condition (this will stamp your action or your words as ampliative). Finally, by speaking your truth, a truth which is original in the sense of "origin," you will break existing dogmas and prejudices, perhaps about yourself, perhaps about others, or perhaps about the sort of experience you describe (this will stamp your action as solid).

Hurtado's road map was intended principally for those who want to make their mark and leave a legacy. In truth, you yourself don't have to spend your days worrying whether your thoughts are originary, ampliative, or solid. Perhaps you just want what you say and think to be meaningful, and maybe uplifting and clarifying for others who've had life experiences similar to your own. If this is the case, you can do what I've done here: tell stories that reveal a deeper philosophical meaning. You've undoubtedly noticed that I've couched most of the philosophical notions in this book in terms of my own biography. In this, I'm simply following the Mexican philosophers who insist that philosophy is always grounded on your own life, in your own circumstance.

In the end, my secret hope is that this book will encourage you to think that you too can *live* big ideas. To believe that you can live big ideas is to believe that truth and meaning are not "out there" in some World of Forms, as Plato suggested, but here, with you. This is what Luis Villoro means when he says "I believe that philosophical reflection is always grounded on personal, lived experiences. . . . I don't believe in reason separated from these."[3] With this sentiment, I encourage you to believe the following: *Your life is philosophical.*

If you believe that your life is philosophical, then there's nothing stopping you from calling yourself a philosopher. I often encounter folks who believe in their hearts that they can never be philosophers, or who say "I just can't think like that," presumably referring to having profound and original thoughts. They are over-awed by the Western (or academic) portrayal of philosophers as having some privileged access to life's mysteries. But there really is no privileged access. If you *live* big ideas, if your life is philosophical, then you are as close to the truth of things, to the mysteries, as anyone else: *You are a philosopher.*

In closing, let me reiterate that Mexican philosophy, as I've presented it here, offers you a way to participate in the philosophical discussion without the burden of obligatory novelty that is just one more colonial imposition. That is, you have been conditioned to think—by your parents, your teachers, and the history of your institutions—that only the "new" and never-before-uttered can be meaningful in a profound, philosophical way, that there's no value in repetition, that copies are always bad, and that only original products can enter the marketplace of ideas. But this ignores the age-old wisdom that experience is the best teacher. If experience has shaped the way you think about the world, then it is a meaningful, valuable, and profound action to articulate your thinking, even if it's couched in words already uttered or ideas already expressed. Mexican philosophy tells you that it's okay to do this, so long as you don't lose touch of where you come from or where you are. It tells you that you can triumph, that you can bloom, even if your past is littered with ruins. And for this reason alone, Mexican philosophy is worth reading and thinking about.

NOTES

PREFACE: HOW CAN MEXICAN PHILOSOPHY GUIDE MY LIFE?

1. Emilio Uranga, *Emilio Uranga's Analysis of Mexican Being: A Translation and Critical Introduction*. Translated and introduced by Carlos Alberto Sánchez (London: Bloomsbury, 2021), 184.

CHAPTER 1

1. Bernabé Navarro Barajas, "Panorama de la filosofía colonial," in *Lecturas Históricas Mexicanas*, ed. Ernesto de la Torre Villar (Mexico City: Universidad Nacional Autónoma de Mexico, 2015), 494–510.

2. Mauricio Beuchot, "Perfil del pensamiento filosófico del fray Alonso de la Vera Cruz," *Nova Tellus* 29, no. 2 (2011), 201–214. For this purpose, Veracruz learned the native language (Purepecha) and taught native people logic and physics. The importance of proving that they were rational was to show that they could be baptized and saved (the evangelizing mission), rather than dehumanized, enslaved, or killed (the colonizing mission).

3. José Vasconcelos, "Gabino Barreda y las ideas contemporáneas," in *Conferencias del Ateneo de la Juventud*, ed. Antonio Caso (Mexico City: Universidad Nacional Autónoma de Mexico, 2000), 106. Translation mine.

4. Antonio Caso, "Existence as Economy and Charity: An Essay on the Essence of Christianity," trans. Alexander V. Stehn and Jose G. Rodriguez. In *Mexican Philosophy in the 20th Century: Essential Readings*, Carlos Alberto Sánchez and Robert Eli Sanchez, eds. (New York: Oxford University Press, 2017), 41.

CHAPTER 2

1. Leopoldo Zea, *En torno a una filosofía americana* (Mexico City: Colegio de México, 1945), 63. Translation mine.

2. Zea, 73.

3. Zea, *La filosofía como compromiso y otros ensayos* (Mexico City: Tezontle, 1952), 137. Translation mine.

4. Emilio Uranga, *Emilio Uranga's Analysis of Mexican Being: A Translation and Critical Introduction*. Translated and introduced by Carlos Alberto Sánchez (London: Bloomsbury, 2021), 109.

5. Uranga, 94.
6. Uranga, 94.

CHAPTER 3

1. Quoted in Emilio Uranga, *Emilio Uranga's Analysis of Mexican Being: A Translation and Critical Introduction* by Carlos Alberto Sánchez (New York: Bloomsbury Academic, 2021), 92.
2. Quoted in Ramón Troncoso Pérez, "Nepantla, una aproximación a un término," in *Tierras prometidas: De la colonia a la independencia*, ed. Bernat Castany, Bernat Hernández, Guillermo Serés Guillén, and Mercedes Serna Arnáiz (Barcelona: Centro para la Edición de los Clásicos Españoles—UAB, 2011), 379. Translation mine.
3. Quoted in Uranga, 92.
4. Frost, Elsa Cecilia. "Acerca de Nepantla." Discurso del ingreso a la Academia Mexicana de la Lengua, 11 November 2004. https://academia.org.mx/prensa/notic ias-seccion/item/acerca-de-nepantla-por-elsa-cecilia-frost-2. Translation mine.
5. Quoted in Pérez, 379.

CHAPTER 4

1. José Ortega y Gasset, *Meditations on Quixote*, trans. Evelyn Rugg and Diego Marín (Chicago: University of Illinois Press, 2000), 45.
2. Leopoldo Zea, *En torno a una filosofía americana* (Mexico City: Colegio de México, 1945), 26.
3. Ortega y Gasset, 45.
4. Ortega y Gasset, 45.

CHAPTER 5

1. Emilio Uranga, *Emilio Uranga's Analysis of Mexican Being: A Translation and Critical Introduction* by Carlos Alberto Sánchez (New York: Bloomsbury Academic, 2021), 103.
2. Uranga, 119.
3. Uranga, 181.
4. Uranga, 156.

CHAPTER 6

1. Leopoldo Zea, *En torno a una filosofía americana* (Mexico City: Colegio de México, 1945), 74. Translation mine.
2. In conversation with Robert Eli Sanchez (b. 1981).

CHAPTER 7

1. Carlos Alberto Sánchez, "Philosophy and the Post-Immigrant Fear," *Philosophy in the Contemporary World*, vol. 18, no. 1 (2013): 31–42.
2. Emilio Uranga, *Emilio Uranga's Analysis of Mexican Being: A Translation and Critical Introduction* by Carlos Alberto Sánchez (New York: Bloomsbury Academic, 2021), 122.
3. Abelardo Villegas, *Autognosis: El pensamiento mexicano en el siglo XX* (Mexico City: Instituto Panamericano de Geografía e Historia, 1985), 7. Translation mine.
4. Uranga, 122.

CHAPTER 8

1. Antonio Caso, "Existence as Economy, Disinterest, and Charity," in *Latin American Philosophy in the 20th Century: Man, Values, and the Search for Philosophical Identity*, Jorge J.E. Gracia (Buffalo, NY: Prometheus Books, 1986), 49.
2. Caso, 49.
3. Caso, 51.
4. Caso, 50.
5. Antonio Caso, "Existence and Economy and Charity," trans. Alexander V. Stehn and Jose G. Rodriguez, Jr. *Mexican Philosophy in the 20th Century: Essential Readings*, Carlos Alberto Sánchez and Robert Eli Sanchez, eds. (New York: Oxford University Press, 2017), 27–45, 44.
6. Caso, 45.

CHAPTER 9

1. Jorge Portilla, "The Phenomenology of Relajo." Translated by Carlos Alberto Sánchez and Eleanor Marsh. In *The Suspension of Seriousness: On the Phenomenology of Jorge Portilla*, by Carlos Alberto Sánchez (Albany, NY: SUNY Press, 2012), 141.
2. Portilla, 141.
3. Portilla, 141–142.
4. Portilla, 142.

CHAPTER 10

1. Octavio Paz, *The Labyrinth of Solitude and Other Writings*, trans. Lysander Kemp, Yara Milos, and Rachel Phillips Belash (New York: Grove Press, 1985), 57.
2. Paz, 51.
3. Emilio Uranga, "La idea mexicana de la Muerte," in *Análisis del ser del mexicano y otros escritos sobre la filosofía de lo mexicano (1949–1952)*, ed. Guillermo Hurtado (Mexico City: Bonilla Artigas, 2013), 193.
4. Paz, 59.

5. Uranga, 193.
6. Uranga, 195.
7. Paz, 54.

CHAPTER 11

1. Leopoldo Zea, "The Actual Function of Philosophy in Latin America," trans. Iván Jaksic, in *Latin American Philosophy in the Twentieth Century: Man, Values, and the Search for Philosophical Identity*, ed. Jorge J. E. Garcia and Elizabeth Millán-Zaibert (Buffalo, NY: Prometheus Books, 1986), 230.

2. Zea, "El sentido de la responsabilidad en en mexicano," in *La filosofía como compromiso y otros ensayos* (Mexico City: Tezontle, 1952), 183. Translation mine.

3. Zea, "La filosofía como compromiso," in *La filosofía como compromiso y otros ensayos* (Mexico City: Tezontle, 1952), 32. Translation mine.

CHAPTER 12

1. Emilio Uranga, "Notas para un estudio del mexicano," *Cuadernos Americanos*, No. 3 (1951), 173. Translation mine.

2. Luis Villoro, "Solitude and Communion," trans. Minerva Ahumada, in *Mexican Philosophy in the 20th Century: Essential Readings,* ed. Carlos Alberto Sánchez and Robert Eli Sanchez, Jr. (Oxford, UK: Oxford University Press, 2017), 155.

3. Emilio Uranga, *Emilio Uranga's Analysis of Mexican Being*, Translation and Critical Introduction by Carlos Alberto Sánchez (New York: Bloomsbury Academic, 2021), 172–173.

CHAPTER 14

1. Jorge Portilla, "Phenomenology of Relajo," Translated by Carlos Alberto Sánchez and Eleanor Marsh. In Carlos Alberto Sánchez, *The Suspension of Seriousness: On the Phenomenology of Jorge Portilla* (Albany, NY: State University of New York Press, 2012), 191.

2. Portilla, 191.

3. Portilla, 192.

4. Portilla, 194.

CHAPTER 15

1. Jorge Portilla, "Phenomenology of Relajo," Translated by Carlos Alberto Sánchez and Eleanor Marsh. In Carlos Alberto Sánchez, *The Suspension of Seriousness: On the Phenomenology of Jorge Portilla* (Albany, NY: State University of New York Press, 2012), 176.

2. Jorge Portilla, 171.

CHAPTER 16

1. Samuel Ramos, "Persona y Personalidad," in *Hacia un nuevo humanismo* (Mexico City: Fondo de Cultura Económica, 1940), 86. Translation mine.
2. Ramos, 94.
3. Ramos, 87.
4. Ramos, 94.
5. Ramos, 93.
6. Emiliano Zapata and Otilio Montaño, "El Plan de Ayala" [Nov. 28, 1911] (Mexico City: Editorial Ruta, 1911). Translation mine.

CHAPTER 17

1. Emilio Uranga, *Emilio Uranga's Analysis of Mexican Being: Translation and Critical Introduction* by Carlos Alberto Sánchez (New York: Bloomsbury Academic, 2021), 146.
2. Uranga, 147–148.
3. Transparency International, "Corruption Perception Index: Mexico," https://www.transparency.org/en/cpi/2023/index/mex.
4. Statista, "Bribery Victimization Rate: Mexico," https://www.statista.com/statistics/1067135/bribery-victimization-rate-latin-america-country/.

CHAPTER 18

1. Ben Lovejoy, "Teen Girls' Mental Health Has Proven Link to Social Media Usage," 9to5Mac.com, February 23, 2023. https://9to5mac.com/2023/02/23/teen-girls-mental-health.
2. Samuel Ramos, *El perfil del hombre y cultura en México* (Mexico City: Imprenta Mundial, 1962), 51. Translation mine.
3. Ramos, 113.
4. Ramos, 51.
5. Ramos, 113.

CHAPTER 19

1. Aviva Chomsky, *"They Take Our Jobs!" and 20 Other Myths about Immigration.* Boston: Beacon Press, 2007.
2. Leo R. Chavez, *The Latino Threat: Constructing Immigrants, Citizens, and the Nation* (Stanford: Stanford University Press, 2013).
3. David R. Maciel, "An Interview with Leopoldo Zea," *Hispanic American Historical Review* 65, no. 1 (1985), 12.
4. Rosario Castellanos, "On Feminine Culture," trans. Carlos Alberto Sánchez, in *Mexican Philosophy in the 20th Century: Essential Readings*, ed. Carlos Alberto

Sánchez and Robert Eli Sanchez, Jr. (Oxford, UK: Oxford University Press, 2017): 206–215.

CHAPTER 20

1. Luis Villoro, "Solitude and Communion," trans. Minerva Ahumada, in *Mexican Philosophy in the 20th Century: Essential Readings,* ed. Carlos Alberto Sánchez and Robert Eli Sanchez, Jr. (Oxford, UK: Oxford University Press, 2017).
2. Villoro, 152.
3. Villoro, 151.
4. Villoro, 153.
5. Villoro, 154.

CHAPTER 21

1. Luis Villoro, "Sahagún, or the Limits of the Discovery of the Other" (Working Papers no. 2), Department of Spanish and Portuguese (College Park: University of Maryland, 1989), 16.
2. Villoro, 16.
3. Villoro, 16.
4. Villoro, 22.

CHAPTER 22

1. Emilio Uranga, "Optimismo y pesimismo del mexicano," in *Análisis del ser del mexicano y otros escritos sobre la filosofía de lo mexicano (1949–1952),* ed. Guillermo Hurtado (Mexico City: Bonilla Artigas, 2013), 149. Translation mine.

CHAPTER 23

1. María Elvira Bermúdez, *La vida familiar del mexicano* (Mexico City: Antigua Libreria Robredo, 1955), 93. Translation mine.
2. Bermúdez, 123.
3. Bermúdez, 131.
4. Bermúdez, 123.

CHAPTER 24

1. John H. Haddox, *Vasconcelos of Mexico: Philosopher and Prophet* (Austin: University of Texas Press, 1967), 14.
2. Haddox, 15.
3. Haddox, 16.

CHAPTER 25

1. Portilla, "Community, Greatness, and Misery in Mexican Life." Translated by Carlos Alberto Sánchez. *Mexican Philosophy in the 20th Century: Essential Readings*, edited by Carlos Alberto Sánchez and Robert Eli Sanchez (New York: Oxford University Press), 189.
2. Portilla, 190.
3. Portilla, 189.
4. Portilla, 183.
5. Portilla, 184.
6. Portilla, 183.
7. Portilla, 183.
8. Portilla, 190.
9. Portilla, 192.
10. Portilla, 194–195.

CHAPTER 26

1. See, Immanuel Kant, *To Perpetual Peace: A Philosophical Sketch*, trans. Ted Humphrey (London: Hackett Publishing, 2003).

CHAPTER 27

1. Ralph Waldo Emerson, *The American Scholar* (New York: Laurentian Press, 1901), p. 26.
2. Emilio Uranga, *Emilio Uranga's Analysis of Mexican Being*, trans. Carlos Alberto Sánchez (London: Bloomsbury, 2020), 185.

CHAPTER 28

1. Emilio Uranga, *Emilio Uranga's Analysis of Mexican Being*, trans. Carlos Alberto Sánchez (London: Bloomsbury, 2021), 185.
2. Guillermo Hurtado, "Filosofía en México y filosofía mexicana," in *El búho y la serpiente* (Mexico City: Universidad Nacional Autónoma de México, 2007), 41–52. Translation mine.
3. Carlos Oliva Mendoza, "La vivencia personal, raíz de la reflexión filosófica: Diálogo con Luis Villoro," *El Metate* 1, no. 8 (May 2006), 5.

BIBLIOGRAPHY AND
FURTHER READING

Now, you may not believe a word that I've written in this book. Perhaps my understanding of the concepts I have highlighted here have struck you as overly simple, or overly complicated, or simply wrong. Whatever your final judgment may be, my hope is that I've succeeded in doing is to make you curious enough that now you yourself want to read the works that I have cited.

Books and articles on Mexican philosophy exist in English and Spanish. The primary sources are in Spanish (of course), and some have been translated into English, but not all. Most of the works of Mexican philosophy that have been translated into English have been cited in the preceding chapters. Books on Mexican philosophy in Spanish, however, are too numerous to count, so in this Bibliography I'll only list those that I think are worth dying for—or, if that's too dramatic, those that would make learning how to read Spanish worth the trouble.

My first list consists of works available in English written by Mexican philosophers, most of which I have mentioned or cited in the foregoing text:

Caso, Antonio. "Existence as Economy, Disinterest, and Charity." Translated by Willima Cooper. In *Latin American Philosophy in the Twentieth Century: Man, Values, and the Search for Philosophical Identity*, edited by Jorge J. E. Gracia, 48–52. Buffalo, NY: Prometheus Books, 1986.

Caso, Antonio. "Existence as Economy and as Charity: An Essay on the Essence of Christianity." Translated by Alexander V. Stehn. In *Mexican Philosophy in the 20th Century: Essential Readings,* edited by Carlos Alberto Sánchez and Robert Eli Sanchez, Jr., 27–45. Oxford, UK: Oxford University Press, 2017.

Castellanos, Rosario. "On Feminine Culture." Translated by Carlos Alberto Sánchez. In *Mexican Philosophy in the 20th Century: Essential Readings*, edited by Carlos Alberto Sánchez and Robert Eli Sanchez, Jr., 206–215. Oxford, UK: Oxford University Press, 2017.

Cruz, Sor Juana Inés de la. *Poems, Protest, and a Dream: Selected Writings*. Translated by Margaret Sayers Peden. New York: Penguin Classics, 1997.

Durán, Fray Diego. *History of the Indies of New Spain*. Translated by Doris Heyden. Norman: University of Oklahoma Press, 1994.

O'Gorman, Edmundo. *The Invention of America: An Inquiry into the Historical Nature of the New World and the Meaning of Its History*. Bloomington: Indiana University Press, 1961.

O'Gorman, Edmundo. "America." Translated by A. Robert Caponigri. In *Major Trends in Mexican Philosophy,* edited by Mario de la Cueva, 58–91. South Bend, IN: University of Notre Dame Press, 1966.

Ortega y Gasset, José. *Meditations on Quixote*. Translated by Evelyn Rugg and Diego Marín. Chicago: University of Illinois Press, 2000.[1]

Paz, Octavio. *The Labyrinth of Solitude and Other Writings*. Translated by Lysander Kemp, Yara Milos, and Rachel Phillips Belash. New York: Grove Press, 1985.

Portilla, Jorge. "The Phenomenology of Relajo." Translated by Carlos Alberto Sánchez and Elenor Marsh. In *The Suspension of Seriousness: On the Phenomenology of Jorge Portilla*, by Carlos Alberto Sánchez, 123–200. Albany, NY: SUNY Press, 2012.

Ramos, Samuel. *Profile of Man and Culture in Mexico*. Translated by Peter G. Earle. Austin: University of Texas Press, 1962.

1. Though Ortega y Gasset was not Mexican, the significance of this text to Latin American philosophy cannot be overstated. It is here that Ortega introduces the circumstantialist principle "I am myself and my circumstances." With this principle in hand, Mexican philosophers found justification for their situated philosophizing and their motivation to construct "la filosofía de lo mexicano."

Sánchez, Carlos Alberto, and Francisco Gallegos. *The Disintegration of Community: On Jorge Portilla's Social and Political Philosophy*. Albany, NY: SUNY Press, 2019.

Sánchez, Carlos Alberto, and Robert Eli Sanchez, Jr., eds. *Mexican Philosophy in the 20th Century: Essential Readings*. New York: Oxford University Press, 2017.

Uranga, Emilio. "The Philosophy of Mexicanness." Translated by Carlos Alberto Sánchez and Robert Eli Sanchez, Jr. *Aeon*, 2019. https://aeon.co/classics/to-be-accidental-is-to-be-human-on-the-philosophy-of-mexicanness.

Uranga, Emilio. *Emilio Uranga's Analysis of Mexican Being: A Translation and Critical Introduction*. Translated and introduced by Carlos Alberto Sánchez. London: Bloomsbury, 2021.

Vasconcelos, José. *The Cosmic Race / La raza cósmica*. Translated by Didier T. Jaén. Baltimore, MD: Johns Hopkins University Press, 1997.

Veracruz, Alonso de la. *The Writings of Alonso de la Vera Cruz*. Five vols. Translated and edited by Ernest J. Burrus. St. Louis, MO: Jesuit Historical Institute, 1968–1976.

Villoro, Luis. "Sahagún or the Limits of the Discovery of the Other." Working Papers No. 2. College Park: Department of Spanish and Portuguese, University of Maryland, 1989.

Villoro, Luis. *Belief, Personal, and Propositional Knowledge*. Translated by E. David Sosa and Douglas McDermid. Amsterdam: Brill Rodopi, 1998.

Villoro, Luis. "Solitude and Communion." Translated by Minerva Ahumada. In *Mexican Philosophy in the 20th Century: Essential Readings*, edited by Carlos Alberto Sánchez and Robert Eli Sanchez, Jr., 141–155. Oxford, UK: Oxford University Press, 2017.

Zea, Leopoldo. "The Actual Function of Philosophy in Latin America." Translated by Iván Jaksic. In *Latin American Philosophy in the Twentieth Century: Man, Values, and the Search for Philosophical Identity*, edited by Jorge J. E. Gracia and Elizabeth Millán-Zaibert, 357–368. Buffalo, NY: Prometheus Books, 1986.

Zea, Leopoldo. *The Role of the Americas in History*. Translated by Sonja Karsen. Savage, MD: Rowman and Littlefield, 1992.

Zea, Leopoldo. *Positivism in Mexico*. Translated by Josephine H. Schulte. Austin: University of Texas Press, 2004.

Zea, Leopoldo. "Philosophy as Commitment." Translated by Amy A. Oliver. In *Mexican Philosophy in the 20th Century: Essential Readings*, edited by Carlos Alberto Sánchez and Robert Eli Sanchez, Jr., 125–140. Oxford, UK: Oxford University Press, 2017.

Zea, Leopoldo. "Is a Latin American Philosophy Possible?" Translated by Pavel Reichl. *British Journal for the History of Philosophy* 30, no. 5 (2022): 874–896.

The archive of readings about Mexican philosophy in English is also growing. Included are my own books, which I cite above because they contain original translations. Interested readers are invited to skim the pages of all volumes of the *Journal of Mexican Philosophy* (journalofmexicanphilosophy.org), where they will find new and original research on this tradition. In addition, the following books and articles should fill in gaps:

Gallegos, Francisco T. "Seriousness, Irony, and Cultural Politics: A Defense of Jorge Portilla." *APA Newsletter on Hispanic/Latino Issues in Philosophy* 13, no. 1 (2013): 11–18.

Haddox, John H. *Vasconcelos of Mexico: Philosopher and Prophet*. Austin: University of Texas Press, 1967.

Haddox, John H. *Antonio Caso: Philosopher of Mexico*. Austin: University of Texas Press, 1971.

Hurtado, Guillermo. "Two Models of Latin American Philosophy." *Journal of Speculative Philosophy* 20, no. 3 (2006): 204–213.

Hurtado, Guillermo, and Robert E. Sanchez, Jr. "Philosophy in Mexico." *Stanford Encyclopedia of Philosophy*. Edited by Edward N. Zalta. Winter 2020. https://plato.stanford.edu/archives/win2020/entries/philosophy-mexico/.

Maciel, David R. "An Interview with Leopoldo Zea." *Hispanic American Historical Review* 65, no. 1 (1985): 1–20.

Pereda, Carlos. "Latin American Philosophy: Some Vices." *Journal of Speculative Philosophy* 20, no. 3 (2006): 192–203.

Portilla, Jorge. "The Spiritual Crisis of the United States." Translated by Carlos Alberto Sánchez and Francisco Gallegos. In *The Disintegration of Community: On Jorge Portilla's Social and Political Philosophy,* edited by Carlos Alberto Sánchez and Francisco Gallegos, 175–190. Albany, NY: SUNY Press, 2019.

Romanell, Patrick. *Making of the Mexican Mind.* Lincoln: University of Nebraska Press, 1952.

Sahagún, Bernardino de. *General History of the Things of New Spain*: *Florentine Codex.* Twelve volumes. Translated by Arthur J. O. Anderson and Charles E. Dibble. Santa Fe, NM: School of American Research, 1950–1982. Reprinted: Salt Lake City: University of Utah Press, 2002.

Sánchez, Carlos Alberto. "Heidegger in Mexico: On Emilio Uranga's Ontological Hermeneutics." *Continental Philosophy Review* 41, no. 4 (2008): 441–461.

Sánchez, Carlos Alberto. "Philosophy and the Post-Immigrant Fear," *Journal of Philosophy in the Contemporary World* 18, no. 1 (2011): 31–42.

Sánchez, Carlos Alberto. *Contingency and Commitment: Mexican Existentialism and the Place of Philosophy.* Albany, NY: SUNY Press, 2016.

Sánchez, Carlos Alberto. "The Gift of Mexican Historicism." *Continental Philosophical Review* 51, no. 3 (2018): 439–457.

Sierra, Justo. *The Political Evolution of the Mexican People.* Translated by Charles Ramsdell. Austin: University of Texas Press, 1969.

Vargas, Manuel. "The Philosophy of Accidentality." *Journal of the American Philosophical Association* 6, no. 4 (2019): 391–409.

Finally, it would be worth learning how to read Spanish in order to read the following works. Many are referenced in the chapters above.

Barajas, Bernabé Navarro. "Panorama de la filosofía colonial." In *Lecturas Históricas Mexicanas*, edited by Ernesto de la Torre Villar, 494–510. Mexico City: Universidad Autónoma de México, 2015.

Barreda, Gabino. "Oración cívica." speech at Guanajuato, 16 September 1867. Printed in Barreda 1941: 69–100.

Bermúdez, María Elvira. *La vida familiar del mexicano*. Mexico City: Antigua Librería Robredo, 1955.

Beuchot, Mauricio. "Perfil del pensamiento filosófico del fray Alonso de la Vera Cruz." *Nova Tellus* 29, no. 2 (2011): 201–214.

Carrion, Jorge. *Mito y magia del mexicano*. Mexico City: Porrúa y Obregón, 1952.

Caso, Antonio. *La existencia como economía, como desinterés y como caridad*. Mexico City: Ediciones México Moderno, 1919.

Castellanos, Rosario. *Sobre cultura femenina*. Mexico City: América, Revista Antológica, 1950.

Cruz, Sor Juana Inés de la. *Obras completas*. Mexico City: Fondo de Cultura Económica, 1976.

Cuéllar Moreno, José Manuel. *La revolución inconclusa: La filosofía de Emilio Uranga, artífice oculto del PRI*. Mexico City: Ariel, 2018.

Frost, Elsa Cecilia. *Las categorías de la cultura mexicana*. Mexico City: Universidad Nacional Autónoma de México, 1972.

Frost, Elsa Cecilia. "Acerca de Nepantla." Discurso del ingreso a la Academia Mexicana de la Lengua, 11 November 2004. https://academia.org.mx/prensa/noticias-seccion/item/acerca-de-nepantla-por-elsa-cecilia-frost-2.

Gaos, José. 1999. "Epistolario y Papeles Privados." In *Obras Completas XIX*, edited by Alfonso Rangel Guerra. Mexico City: Universidad Nacional Autónoma de México, 1999.[2]

---

2. Like Ortega y Gasset, Gaos was not Mexican. However, his work is indispensable for anyone interested in mid-twentieth-century Mexican philosophy. Through his lectures and translations, Gaos motivated Mexican existentialism and the philosophy of Mexicanness. In these "personal papers" we are invited to directly witness his involvement in the life and times of Mexican philosophy. His influence on Uranga and his impact on Mexican philosophy are clarified in journal entries and letters to friends and others.

Gómez Alonso, Paula. "La cultura femenina." Unpublished master's thesis. Universidad Nacional Autónoma de México, 1933.

Gómez Robledo, Antonio. *Ensayo sobre las virtudes intelectuales*. Mexico City: Fondo de Cultura Económica, 1957.

González, Juliana. *Ética y Libertad*. Mexico City: Universidad Nacional Autónoma de México, 1989.

Gortari, Eli de. *La ciencia de la lógica*. Morelia, Mexico: Ediciones de la Universidad Michoacana, 1950.

Hierro, Graciela. *Ética y feminismo*. Mexico City: Universidad Nacional Autónoma de México, 1990.

Hurtado, Guillermo, ed. *El Hiperión*. Mexico City: Universidad Nacional Autónoma de México, 2006.

Hurtado, Guillermo. *El búho y la serpiente: Ensayos sobre la filosofía en Mexico en el siglo XX*. Mexico City: Universidad Nacional Autónoma de México, 2007.

Krauze de Kolteniuk, Rosa. *La filosofía de Antonio Caso*. Mexico City: Universidad Nacional Autónoma de México, 1961.

Larroyo, Francisco. *La filosofía de los valores*. Mexico City: Logos, 1936.

Lenkersdorf, Carlos. *Filosofar en clave tojolabal*. Mexico City: Miguel Ángel Porrúa, 2002.

León-Portilla, Miguel. *La filosofía náhuatl*. Mexico City: Universidad Nacional Autónoma de México, 1955.

O'Gorman, Edmundo. *La invención de América*. Mexico City: Fondo de Cultura Económica, 1958.

Pereda, Carlos. *La filosofía en México en el siglo XX: Apuntes de un participante*. Mexico City: Dirección General de Publicaciones, 2013.

Pérez, Ramón Troncoso. "Nepantla, una aproximación al término." In *Tierras prometidas: De la colonia a la independencia,* edited by Bernat Castany, Bernat Hernández, Guillermo Serés Guillén, and Mercedes Serna Arnáiz, 375–398. Barcelona: Centro para la Edición de los Clásicos Españoles-UAB, 2011.

Portilla, Jorge. *Fenomenología del relajo y otros ensayos*. Mexico City: Ediciones Era, 1966.

Ramos, Samuel. "Persona y personalidad." In *Hacia un nuevo humanismo*. Mexico City: Fondo de Cultura Económica, 1940: 84–96.

Ramos, Samuel. *El perfil del hombre y la cultura en México*. Mexico City: Imprenta Mundial, 1962.

Reyes, Alfonso. *El deslinde; Prolegómenos a la teoría literaria*. Mexico City: Colegio de México, 1944.

Uranga, Emilio. "Dos teorias de la muerte: Sartre y Heidegger." *Filosofía y Letras* 17, no. 33 (1949): 55–71.

Uranga, Emilio. "Notas para un estudio del mexicano." *Cuadernos Americanos* 10, no. 3 (1951): 114–128.

Uranga, Emilio. "Optimismo y pesimismo del mexicano." In *Análisis del ser del mexicano y otros escritos sobre la filosofía de lo mexicano (1949–1952)*, edited by Guillermo Hurtado, 147–161. Mexico City: Bonilla Artigas, 2013.

Uranga, Emilio. "El sentimiento de rivalidad en el mexicano: Comentarios a una conferencia de Juan José Arreola." In *Análisis del ser del mexicano y otros escritos sobre la filosofía de lo mexicano (1949–1952)*, edited by Guillermo Hurtado, 212–215. Mexico City: Bonilla Artigas, 2013.

Uranga, Emilio. "La idea mexicana de la Muerte." In *Análisis del ser del mexicano y otros escritos sobre la filosofía de lo mexicano (1949–1952)*, edited by Guillermo Hurtado, 193–195. Mexico City: Bonilla Artigas, 2013.

Uranga, Emilio. "Sobre el ser del mexicano: Carta a José Moreno Villa." In *Análisis del ser del mexicano y otros escritos sobre la filosofía de lo mexicano (1949–1952)*, edited by Guillermo Hurtado, 241–250. Mexico City: Bonilla Artigas, 2013.

Vasconcelos, José. "Gabino Barreda y las ideas contemporáneas." In *Conferencias del Ateneo de la Juventud*, edited by Antonio Caso, 95–110. Mexico City: Universidad Nacional Autónoma de México, 2000.

Veracruz, Alonso de la. *Recognitio summularum*. Mexico City, 1554.

Villegas, Abelardo. *La filosofía de lo mexicano*. Mexico City: Universidad Nacional Autónoma de México, 1979.

Villegas, Abelardo. *Autognosis: El pensamiento mexicano en el siglo XX*. Mexico City: Instituto Panamericano de Geografía e Historia, 1985.

Villoro, Luis. *Los grandes momentos del indigenismo en México*. Mexico City: Colegio de México, 1950.

Villoro, Luis. "Emilio Uranga: La accidentalidad como fundamento de la cultura Mexicana." In *Análisis del ser mexicano*, edited by Emilio Uranga, 9–23. Guanajuato, Mexico: Gobierno del Estado de Guanajuato, 1990.

Zapata, Emiliano, and Otilio Montaño. "El Plan de Ayala" (Nov. 28, 1911). Mexico City: Editorial Ruta, 1911.

Zea, Leopoldo. *El positivismo en México: Nacimiento, apogeo y decadencia*. Mexico City: Colegio de México, 1943.

Zea, Leopoldo. *En torno a una filosofía americana*. Mexico City: Colegio de México, 1945.

Zea, Leopoldo. *La filosofía como compromiso y otros ensayos*. Mexico City: Tezontle, 1952.

Zea, Leopoldo. *La filosofía americana como filosofía sin más*. Mexico City: Siglo XXI, 1969.

Zirión Quijano, Antonio. *Historia de la fenomenología en México*. Morelia, Mexico: Jitanjáfora, 2003.

INDEX

For the benefit of digital users, indexed terms that span two pages (e.g., 52–53) may, on occasion, appear on only one of those pages.

accidentality, 13–14, 16–17, 21–22, 31, 54–64, 78, 80–81, 82–83
alienation, 86, 91, 242–43, 249
anxiety, 77, 92–93, 111, 113, 120, 121, 125–26, 131, 177–78, 188, 238–39, 273
Apretados, 140–47, 152, 153, 154–55
and symptoms, 144–47
Aristotle, 3, 7, 117–18
aesthetic monism, 236–37, 238
Ateneo de la Juventud (Atheneum of Youth), 236
auscultation, 76–83
Autognosis, 79, 82–83, 183

bad faith, 57–58, 196
Bermúdez, María Elvira, 227–30
Barreda, Gabino, 9

capitalism, 93, 167–68, 244, 265
Caso, Antonio, 11, 13–14, 24, 85–91
Castellanos, Rosario, 43, 194
catastrophe, 39, 56–57, 123, 265
catastrophism, 264
Catholicism, 4, 33–34, 35–36, 137

charity, existence as, 87, 88–91, 94
Christianity, 35–36, 219
colonial, ambition, 20–21
elite, 8–9
history, 59, 113
idea of philosophy, 23
indoctrination, 8–9
rule, 20–21, 52–53
values, 136–37, 143–44, 216, 219, 277–78
colonialism, 45–46, 93
community, 23–24, 30, 31, 50–51, 53–54, 85, 97, 125–26, 127, 136, 144–45, 172, 185–86, 226–27, 230, 233, 240–42, 243, 244–49, 257, 266–67
farmworker, 50–51
human, 5–6, 12
Indigenous, 31
Mexican, 96–97, 242–43
Comte, Auguste, 21–22
consciousness, 10, 42, 62, 210
corrido, 115–16
corruption, 123–24, 174–76
Cortés, Hernán, 35–36, 52–54

culture, 11, 20–21, 28, 36–37, 42,
    61, 68–69, 91, 94–95, 113, 135,
    143–44, 166, 181, 184, 189,
    193–94, 209, 211–12, 223, 224,
    226–27, 230, 256, 259, 264
  alien, 210
  American, 140
  Indigenous, 20–21, 31, 210, 211
  Mexican, 6, 46, 175, 186, 227
  Mexican-American, 36–37, 50–51
  narcoculture, 115–16
  Nepantla, Mexico, 36–37
  Western, 3
cynicism, 170–72, 174, 175–
    76, 266–67
  dignified, 172, 173, 174–76

de las Casas, Bartolomé, 160–61, 165
de la Cruz, Sor Juana, 160–61, 165
death, 20–21, 35–36, 54, 84, 99,
    100, 101, 102–10, 123, 183–
    84, 273
detail-oriented thinking, 15–16
dignity, 170–72, 188–89, 194, 229
Durán, Diego, 29–39, 219

economy, existence as, 85, 86
education, 15–16, 96–97, 98, 132,
    163–64, 227–28
egoism, 77–78, 86, 88
Emerson, Ralph Waldo, 263
environment, 40–41, 48–49, 50, 66–
    67, 242–43
essence, 18–19, 65–67, 68–69, 70–71,
    88, 93–94, 116, 117, 228, 229

Eurocentric, 19, 23
evangelizing mission, 6–7, 29, 35–36, 211
excess, 84, 85, 86–91, 154

faith, 11, 31, 32, 35–36, 124–25, 143,
    146–47, 242–43, 262–63
  and hope, 125
fanaticism, 142–43, 144, 145–46, 153
fear, 69, 77–78, 105, 109–10, 120,
    121–22, 124, 125–26, 134, 184,
    217, 266–67, 273
  post-immigrant, 77, 81–82
femininity, 226–28, 229
Fernández, Vicente, 52, 53–54
freedom, 5–6, 21, 71, 100–1, 134, 135,
    159, 172, 203–4, 238–39, 256–57
Freud, Sigmund, 104–5, 108
Frost, Elsa Cecilia, 24, 34–37

Gaos, José, 42–43, 76–77, 79
generosity, 55, 98, 99, 100, 163, 215
ghosts, 104, 105–6
God, 31, 32, 35–36, 59, 61, 88–89,
    208, 211–12, 213–14

Heidegger, Martin, 104–5
hembrismo, 227–28, 229
Hurtado, Guillermo, 43, 272–76

identity, 30, 40–41, 42–43, 80–82,
    93–94, 96, 100, 112–13, 142–43,
    145–47, 165, 183, 192, 219,
    229–30, 241–42
  Anglo, 189
  cultural, 16, 219

historical, 20–21
human, 20–21
immigrant, 192–93, 273–74
national, 23
political, 80–81
substantial, 219
ideology of domination, 38–39, 93, 95
immigration, 27, 77, 156, 193, 194, 218
imperial passion, 193–94, 195
imposter syndrome , 112, 113, 116
Indigenous, 4–5, 16, 19, 21, 22, 29–30,
    32, 38–39, 52–53, 148–49, 209,
    210, 256
  community, 31, 245
  culture, 20–21, 31, 33–34
  ideas, 17
  people, 7, 9, 15–16, 20–22, 33–34,
    37, 38–39, 54, 59–60, 165, 209,
    210–14, 219
inferiority, 21, 22, 59–60, 175, 178–86
  complex of, 179, 180–81
irony, 42–43, 148–59, 195

Juárez, Benito, 256, 257–58, 259
justice, 48–49, 161, 163–64, 172,
    223, 230

Kant, Immanuel, 99, 100, 257, 259

"Latino Threat Narrative," 188–89
liberation, 230
Lincoln, Abraham, 256
lo mexicano, 23, 76

machismo, 15–16, 227–29

Marx, Karl, 16
mestizaje, 16–17, 54, 179
mysticism, 88–89, 236, 237

nepantla, 27–39, 161–62, 220–21, 271
nothingness, 122–23, 125

objectification, 15–16, 209, 210–12,
    214–15, 221, 271
Ortega y Gasset, José, 32, 40–43, 46, 50
  Meditations on Quixote, 40–41

patriarchy, 161–62, 227–28, 265
Paz, Octavio, 106–9
  Labyrinth of Solitude, The, 106–7, 109
personalidad, 161–66
"Plan de Ayala," 167–68
Plato, 15, 17–18, 151–52, 277
poetry, 21–22, 78, 114, 212, 236, 237
Portilla, Jorge, 24, 43, 94–95, 96–97,
    98, 99, 122–23, 131–32, 133–34,
    135, 137, 142–43, 144, 145–46,
    153–54, 157–58, 242–43, 244–49
positivism, 6, 9–10, 15–16, 21–22,
    235–36, 237–38
powerlessness, 171, 175, 181–82,
    183, 184–85
pragmatism, 16
punctuality, 93–101

Quine, W.V.O., 220

Ramos, Samuel, 43, 161–62, 163, 164,
    166, 179, 180, 181–82, 183–
    84, 185–86

Ramos, Samuel (*cont.*)
  *Profile of Man and Culture in
    Mexico*, 179–80
relajo, 15–16, 128–38, 153, 155, 271
resentment, 80–82, 171, 172, 175,
    181–84, 186, 197, 249

sacrifice, 48–49, 88–90, 97, 115–16,
    163–64, 165, 166, 215, 229
Sahagún, Bernardino de, 213–14, 215
science, 9, 235, 238
  empirical, 237–38
  experimental, 235–36
  fiction, 209
  and Positivism, 238
scientific thinking, 9–10, 235–36
Sepúlveda, Juan Ginés de, 7
Socrates, 3, 40
substantial creatures, 18–19
  identity, 219
substantiality, 56–57, 60–61, 62, 63
substantialize yourself, meaning, 61–62

technology, 9–10, 21–22, 39, 75–76,
    207, 214, 235, 236
Tiripetío, 3, 4
tradition, 4, 6, 11, 12–13, 30, 35–37,
    42, 66–67, 68–69, 84, 120,
    136–37, 146, 160–61, 199, 208,
    227, 256
  philosophical, 15, 44–45, 262
  spiritual, 35–36
  Western, 66–67
transcendence, 168, 203–4, 237, 247
trauma, 52, 58, 77–78, 81–83, 113,
    200, 201, 261, 271

Treaty of Guadalupe Hidalgo, 188–89
truth, 5–6, 19–20, 43–45, 50, 55, 57–
    58, 81–83, 113, 142–43, 144–61,
    163–64, 168, 170–71, 173, 175,
    177–78, 186, 195, 196, 203, 206,
    255, 275–76, 277

United States, 12, 16, 33–34, 38–39,
    93, 115–16, 139, 143–44, 155,
    157–58, 174, 187–89, 192,
    225, 232–33
Uranga, Emilio, 18–19, 22, 23–24, 43,
    54–61, 76–77, 78, 79, 80, 81–82,
    108, 109, 123, 125, 170–71, 173,
    174–75, 220–21, 264
  Analysis of Mexican Being (*Análisis
    del ser del mexicano*), 54

Vasconcelos, José, 5–6, 10, 11, 13–
    14, 236–37
Veracruz, Alonso de la, 3, 4, 7, 9, 160
Villoro, Luis, 15–16, 24, 124, 125,
    200–1, 202–5, 206, 209, 213–14,
    215, 277
Virgin of Guadalupe, 35–36

Zapata, Emiliano, 161, 165–66, 168
Zea, Leopoldo, 15–16, 17–19, 43, 44 –
    –46, 50–51, 67, 68–44, 79, 114–
    15, 116–18, 119, 193–94, 195
zozobra, 120–21, 122–24, 125, 126–
    27, 222, 273
  and anxiety, 77, 121, 125–26
  burning of, 120–22
  and hope, 124, 125–26
  and nothingness, 122–23